FROM AN OAK TREE

FROM AN OAK TREE

Frank J. Jasinski

Library of Congress Control Number:		2010904893
ISBN:	Hardcover	978-1-4500-7671-5
	Softcover	978-1-4500-7670-8
	Ebook	978-1-4500-7672-2

This book was printed in the United States of America.

To order additional copies of this book, contact:
Xlibris Corporation
1-888-795-4274
www.Xlibris.com
Orders@Xlibris.com
79370

ACKNOWLEDGEMENT

The credit for this inspirational book of my life and my family's life and struggles was inspired by our family and a friend, Mrs. Geraldine (Jeri) Wittbrod. Jeri not only inspired me to write my story, but she also was continuously nagging me to write and write some more, so she could transcribe it into the typewritten manuscript. I have grown because of Jeri's influence and the entire credit is due to Jeri. God bless Jeri, our friend. Some credits are due to my cousins Anna Bereznicki, Nikolai Bereznicki and her brother for writing this episode. Also credit is due to my dear and loving wife Dorothy (Dot) as well as my children Diane (Nina), Debbie and son Floyd. I also give thanks to Bob Phillippi for editing, cropping and inserting pictures and to his wife, Joan for her many hours of typing and editing and re-editing. Finally to all my friends whom I have known for a long time, who have been asking me to write this as well.

FROM AN OAK TREE

From humble beginnings . . . . this picture represents the purchase of my parents' first home which was vacant farm land. After moving to this land without any structures, they had to live in this old oak tree for about six months, while building a one room house (shown to the right in the background). I believe I was conceived in this tree, so I named this story as such, "From an Oak Tree".

A Polish boy in WWII Poland, came to America, via Russian Siberia, Persia (Iran), Iraq, Trans Jordan, Palestine, Egypt and England . . . . a travel which took a lifetime.

The journey from my birth in Poland to my retirement in America is long, treacherous and tedious. It is filled with joys, deep sadness and unbelievable good fortune. To arrive at the present day took fortitude, deep faith and trust in God. It is embodied in two families, the Polish and the one which came to America. The way was difficult, the road often hard, obstacles which seemed insurmountable but with endurance were overcome. This is the story of my life from Poland to America. Although it will end some day, as it must for all of us, this is written so the story of one Polish man among millions of his countrymen who struggled and died for their country can be told to those unaware of these personal tragedies. It is told to honor the living and the dead. Their story must not be forgotten.

CHAPTER 1

My story begins in a suburb of Kalusz, Poland. Kalusz is a European town located southeast of Lwow in today's Ukraine. It is situated on rolling hills and surrounded by the Carpathian Mountains. The capital city of this region is Stanislawow, today called Ivanov-Franko. This name was changed during the Soviet occupation. Basically a farming community, it was also known for its potassium, coal, and salt mines. All in all the prewar (World War II) economy was thriving, unemployment was minimal. Roads in the larger towns were paved and generally well maintained. Secondary roads throughout the region were unpaved. The market place or town square was centrally located, with various shops and other buildings around it. This was the region's gathering place. The entire square was set in cobblestones, which to this day have been preserved to commemorate this historic place. It was here that the farmers brought their produce for sale each week. The square was also a place for celebrations such as May Day.

The climate consists of four seasons with each one as beautiful as the other. Springtime the entire area would turn green with new growth, the air filled with many wonderful fragrances of the various flowering fruit trees, foretelling of the delicious fruits to come. Spring gave birth to the wild flowers growing along the roadways, especially by the creek and in the small valleys. Gardens begin to glow in the colors of the many varieties of plants and flowers so lovingly cared for. Work begins in earnest preparing the soil for vegetable gardens. Farm orchards and vegetable gardens often provided a family with all their needs and the excess was carefully canned or put into cellars to be preserved for use during the winter. Summer was warm, children played outdoors and in the small local river. In autumn the leaves change colors and sounds from farmers in the fields tell us of harvesting their wheat and other grains. Winter is very severe, with freezing weather and heavy snows. Roads would become virtually impassable. The air was clear, the land dressed in white, covered with snow, crispy to walk on. All in all life was simple yet providing all the needs for a good life. People were industrious, hard working and family oriented. Many of the families lived in the area for generations. Therefore, the community contained many extended families consisting of aunts, uncles and cousins. It was common for them to look after and care for each other. There were many joyful family gatherings throughout the year. All holidays, especially Easter and Christmas called for big celebrations.

Polish was the official language, but because of the bordering countries of Germany to the west, Ukraine to the east, Russia to the east and Czechoslovakia to the south, it was common for the people to speak many languages, including those of some minority groups. Children were required to attend school through 8th grade. German and Latin were taught beginning with the 6th grade. Students were encouraged to attend secondary school, but instead often were required to work on their parent's farm or work in other industries to help support their family.

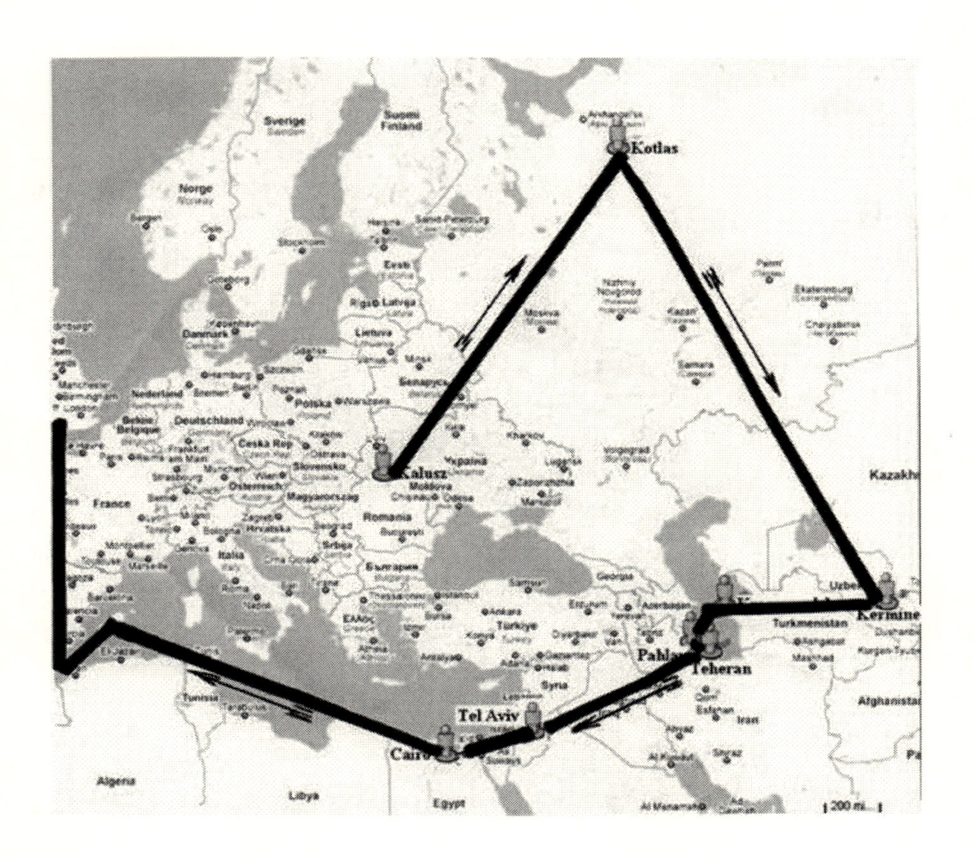

Here is where Frank's story begins:

The Bereznicka and Jasinski families lived in this farming community for about 200 or 400 years. Frank's father and family lived in Bereznicka Szlachecka for many generations and mother Maria's family in Bereznicka.

In the 17th century, the Polish King Jagelo stopped by to water the horses, after which it became a "noble" place. The Jasinski/Bereznicki families were honored by the kind people, and the village name was changed from Szlachecka to Bereznicka Szlachecka after the Bereznicki clan. This was a large village of 5,000 to 6,000 people.

Language came easily to my father. Living in a country with borders with Ukraine, Russia, Czechoslovakia (now the Czech Republic) and Germany, he not only spoke Polish but also Russian, Czech, Ukraine and German.

Maria had two brothers, Pawel and Andrzej and two sisters Olesia and Antonina. John had a brother Michal and a sister Klara. At this time and as common in many countries in the world, marriages were arranged by the parents. So when it was time, marriages were arranged between John and Maria and Pawel and Klara.

When John and Maria married, both of their families gave them some land and they stayed in Bereznica for about 5 years. I (Franek), the third child born to Maria Bereznicka and John Jasinski, who were living in a suburb of Kalusz, was born May 19, 1928. I was born into a family consisting of my mother Maria, father John, brother Joseph 5 ½ years old, Stefania 3 years old and Bronek, who was born in 1930 and died in 1932 at 2 years of age. In 1934 Stanislawa "Stasia" was born. (Twin girls were born in 1922 but died shortly after birth).

When the Bereznica area became very congested, my family decided to move to a place where they could have more land. Studzianka village was an old, established village, and it was occupied mostly by Ukranians. Kolonia Studzianka was being newly developed, thus it was called Kolonia meaning "colony" to designate it as a new development. They learned that a land magnate was dividing his land into parcels for sale in Place Studzianka about 8 kilometers (1 ½ miles) from Bereznica and they purchased their land in 1927. Maria's brother Andrzej was the Polish Government Farm Advisor as well as soil expert, so he advised John and Maria to purchase this particular plot of land because years ago a brewery was erected on this plot. It was dismantled long ago for unknown reasons, but left fermented barley and hops in the soil. This made the soil very productive. "My parents lucked out," as I was told.

My father's land was approximately 40 acres, which was considered large at that time. The purchase document shows that on March 7, 1927, John and Maria paid $760.08 in American currency for the land. Because Poland was going through turbulent times, all major purchases had to be transacted in American dollars. My parents built their first house in 1927. This house was only one room and it was a temporary house. It was better to spend the time being in the house where there was a roof overhead than outside under the awning of the oak tree.

Many of the aunts and uncles also purchased parcels of land. While they were building habitable buildings on their respective property, all families had lean-tos around a massive tree. Living conditions at first were very primitive for all families. Since all were interrelated, most all were welcome to share lean-tos, especially our neighbors such as Bereznicka, Leszynski and others. Here all lived as in a commune, sharing all the activities of family life such as cooking over a common campfire-type fire.

My parents were lucky, they had a small stream right by the big oak tree where they lived, so for them there was no problem washing dishes, clothing or bedding. It provided a continual source of fresh water for all purposes. When it froze in wintertime, a hole was cut into the ice to get the water. Others were not so fortunate. First they had to dig water wells as well as build some sort of temporary lodgings. This was a very old oak tree and at some point it had been on fire. One side of the tree at the bottom had been burned out, so it was hollowed out. The core of the oak tree was quite slim, so it left the interior hollow, which was quite sizeable. So with some kind of an awning it would provide protection from the elements. But we children played about the tree and it took about eight of us kids holding hands to surround the tree. The interior was big enough for our family to stay inside.

My parents built a one room house on their property. My mother's first cousin Mikolaj Leszczynski, husband of Paulina who was my Godmother, had experience in carpentry and thus he was able to help my parents procure proper lumber and items like window panes, as well as helps them build the house. Most of the lumber came from part of the forest. It was cut and brought in to be graded, then cut into boards and other needed materials. (I was told by my parents that it wasn't any too soon that this one room house was almost completed when I was born). All homes in the community lacked electricity and running water.

My father was an excellent farmer and my mother was a remarkable manager. John began building a new, larger home in 1934. Through their combined talents of farming and managing, by the time it was finished in 1938 it was paid in full. A simple but full life was enjoyed. These were happy times for families and the new community. The land also contained a forest which provided wood for the family's needs. There was a cooking stove in the kitchen and a bread oven built into the wall. The oven was constructed entirely of brick, 4 to 5 feet long, about 3 feet wide and about 30" above the floor level; the oven floor was brick. Wood would be burned until hot coals were formed. These would be moved aside, and mother would place the pans of bread in the oven and take them out using a paddle on a long stick similar to today's pizza restaurants. Baking day was a favorite day when the home smelled of the freshly baked bread. Mother would bake every 10 days or so, often up to 30 loaves of bread at a time. She had dough "starter" from her great grandmother. She claimed hers was the best bread in the region and we all agreed!

There was room on the sides and top of the oven which was always warm on baking days. On cold winter days the children liked to sit in the nooks on the sides of the oven to do their homework. Our next door neighbor was our cousin Joseph and his wife Petrunela. They had 5 children: Mikolaj, Anna, Frank, Broneck and Karol. While still a little boy at the age of 8 months or so, Karol drowned in a bucket of water while all were out of the house for just a minute. It was a major disaster in our neighborhood, but we had to overcome such a tragedy. His older brother, Broneck, was something else! He was very strong and hardy at the age of two years. He would run to our house in the middle of winter in the snow which was about 3 feet deep and frost all over. He would knock on the front door to enter, then climb on the baking oven and play with my little sister Stasia. Afterwards, one of my parents would bundle him up and carry him to his house. This was quite a comedy which recurred frequently.

There was also a wood stove in the kitchen. One of the chores of the older children was to carry buckets of water from the stream to the house where it was kept in buckets for drinking, cooking and bathing. For bathing, a washtub was placed in front of the stove and filled with hot water. Family members took turns taking a bath with hot water being added as needed. The first bathers got the cleanest water. Toilet facilities consisted of an outdoor "one seater". Father wisely stacked the woodpile near the outhouse. Anyone using the facilities was required to carry wood to the house on the return trip. The ladies often were discreet and used the expression "I'm going to fetch some wood." But everyone knew it was a dual purpose trip.

In addition to grains, father also raised pigs and cows; the pigs provided meat and the cow's milk. Each farm butchered its own pigs. After butchering a pig, some part was used as a delicacy and each piece of meat sorted for various uses. For example, certain parts were used to make sausage: the port fat was rendered to make lard, other fat portions were salted and placed in wood barrels to preserve them for later use and so on. We had to preserve all of the butchered pieces for later use: by pickling, nothing would spoil and would last a long time until needed for eating.

The milk was kept in one liter jars, some glass and some made of clay. The jars were covered with cheesecloth. When the cream rose to the top, it was used to make butter; the remaining "butter" milk was everybody's favorite drink. When milk soured, mother would place this sour curdled milk in cloth sacks to make her own cheese.

We children walked one mile to school along a dirt road and when the weather was rainy, it was muddy and difficult walking. In summer we would go to school barefoot, jumping in the small river on the way to school and swim across. It was a fun time going and coming to school as it was in the classrooms. The teacher, Miss Ann, was a beautiful slender lady with dark auburn tinted hair, with the kind of smile that made you like her. Besides, she was the smartest of all the people. It was quite easy to be involved in school projects. We had very good teachers and very innovative with few materials. The smaller children would mimic their older siblings. When we got home, all of us had chores to do before doing our homework. We had to look after geese, the horses or other animals, then do our homework. The girls helped with household chores and were taught needlework.

It was a big game to see who could bring home the best report card at the end of each school period. Once I brought home the best report card and of course my parents were very proud. Other cousins' parents were scolding their children, saying, "See that Jasinski is pretty smart. He will some day be somebody. He is very resourceful." Games like these were very common.

Our picture, or what is called a portrait, was taken around August, 1938. from left to right: My picture, because I was a Mama's boy, My Mother, Top Center is brother Joseph (Jozek), center bottom is Stasia, My Father Jan (John), and my sister Stefania.

In the freezing, snowy winter, children were bundled up in heavy clothes, boots, gloves, scarf tied over their faces with only eyes showing. Each breath was a puff of steam. Trudging through the snow and ice during the short, winter days, made the journey seem longer. But the boys had many snowball fights which helped keep them warm.

The school was divided into four classes of 1st and 2nd, 3rd and 4th, then 5th and 6th and finally 7th and 8th grade. My brother Joseph and cousin Karl Leszczynski attended high school which was located in Kalusz.

I started school in Studzianka. During recess one of the games played was "Buttons". Indentations were made in the ground; each student had a collection of buttons which were placed a prescribed distance from the indentations. The buttons were flipped using thumb and index finger into the holes; whoever got the button in the hole won all the buttons in the hole at that time. When I visited the school in 1996, there were no traces of this game to be found.

I was a good student but mischievous. One incident depicting the outlets for my energy involved a girl with long braids who had the misfortune to be seated in the desk in front of me. I decided to use my inkwell, which was in each desktop, to improve the color of her hair by dipping the end of the blonde braid into the permanent black ink. The only way to correct the newly colored hairs was by cutting it off. Fortunately, only the end received my dye job. No big issue was made over such playful incidents. However; being generally mischievous, I recalled that "My mother would swat me with a wet dish rag many times a day".

Four cousins also lived in Studzianka. Frank Leszczynski (a cousin on mother's side), Paulina Leszczynski, mother of Frank and Father Joe; Paulina is also my godmother. Frank Bereznicki also lived in Studzianka and is related to Maria since they are both from Bereznicki lineage. Father Joe is a secular priest rather than belonging to an "order" like Franciscans, Capuchins, etc. he jokes that he belongs to the Order of Malchisidek.

As I was growing, my curiosity led to me exploring the farm with some neighbor friends and cousins. Russian military troops had passed through the area during World War I. There were many trenches on the land where the boys found many rounds of ammunition. They would gather sticks of wood to make a small fire, throw the ammunition into the fire and dive into a trench. The boys considered this "fun". It could well have resulted in death or a crippling event. As it happened, I was hit with a stray bullet in the left brow, which is still scarred to this day. "It was a stupid stunt, but we were young boys and didn't realize the danger. Many kids did die this way."

My father and mother were excellent farmers. Mother was an especially excellent manager. As the farm became more and more prosperous, workers were hired for the harvest. Most were Ukranian women who were not the primary wage earners in their families but worked to earn extra money for their own use. The workers would be paid at the end of the day. The wages were small but workers wanted to work for my mother who was very good to them and the result of their labor was sold to wholesalers. The "contracts" were handshakes between my parents and the wholesalers who took care of the family's needs on a continuous basis.

The family grew wheat, fruits and vegetables such as strawberries, cucumbers, onions, carrots, cabbage, etc. in what would be called a "truck farm" in Midwestern USA at that time. An incident recalled by me: "When I was about 8 or 9 years old, I noticed a commotion among the workers in the field, who were cutting wheat with scythes. They called my mother who went into the center of the commotion. About one half hour later she came out with a baby in her arms. One of the ladies had a baby, rested a bit, and then continued working the rest of the day."

It was common for the prosperous farmers to hire young, local girls to live with the family and assist with household chores. My mother hired Kasia (Katherine).

After 2 or 3 years, she left our household to get married. My mother bought a complete set of brown dishes to give as a wedding gift. I distinctly remember the color of the dishes. These girls were usually not well educated. After being partitioned 123 years earlier, Poland had regained its freedom only in 1918 after the First World War Treaty was signed at Versailles, France. American President Woodrow Wilson made certain the Treaty gave Poland independence from Russia, Austria and Germany. At the time of this story, Poland was struggling to become the independent country it had been. For that reason, it was a very poor country and did not have a broad educational system.

This picture was taken around September of 1939. My cousin Tekla Jasinski donated one room to serve our community as a Kindergarten. She is on the far right standing. My little sister, Stasia is in the front left corner. The person standing in the right corner is Joe Leszczynski, my cousin, who has been a Catholic Priest for over 50 years. (His mother Paulina was my Godmother). The rest of the children were our close and distant cousins.

The worst off were the minorities, such as Ukranians, gypsies and others. Some children could not keep pace with the system, some parents didn't believe in education because they had none themselves, some children and their parents didn't speak Polish. It was quite a big problem for the Polish Government Education Board to assist the populace in not only educating these youngsters but to teach them Polish, which was, of course, now the primary language in the country, For this reason, many young children were missing the importance of education. Ignorance played a role in it. In some cases children in poorer families had to work outside in order to help the family exist.

Father had a battery radio which was used sparingly, only for special events. The battery only lasted 2-3 weeks. When it ran down, my brother Joseph and I had to carry the 12 lb. battery about a mile to Kalusz for recharging. Recharging took 2-3 hours and when it was ready, we had to carry it back home.

This peaceful, happy way of life was to be completely shattered. On September 1, 1939, Germany invaded Poland. In approximately 6-8 weeks, Poland's cavalry army, which was no match for Germany's motorized vehicles and was quickly overrun. Remember Poland had just gained independence in 1918.

One day while helping my father harvest potatoes in our fields, I heard a loud noise in the sky and about 50-60 planes were flying from West to East. Four to five weeks later, for about a week, Russian soldiers on foot and in every type of heavy equipment moved into the area. The population was confused and afraid as they didn't know what to do. This invasion, on or about the first of October, was something which was totally unknown to the locals, having lived peaceably for so many years and worked hard for their livelihood.

The local government and its law enforcement were abolished. Stores were pillaged and forced to close and our former life was turned into chaos. There was no law enforcement which could compete with the Russian takeover as they took over everything. Studzianka was in this state for approximately 5 months until early 1940. During this period, life went on with as much normalcy as possible although those items which were usually purchased from the stores became more and more scarce. But children still attended school. Christmas was observed although not as cheerfully as in past years and with very few gifts. As is still the custom in many European countries, gifts were exchanged on St. Nicholas' Day, December 6th.

I remember that the winter of 1939-40 was extremely cold and as was common, we had a chained watchdog. The only people who could go near him to feed him or care for him were mother and father. One early morning about 3:00 a.m. the dog began to bark incessantly. There was pounding on the front door. It sounded like a burglar was trying to break down the door to get into the house. Father rose, went to the door, opened it only to see six burly Russian soldiers with carbines and rifles. They ordered, in Russian, "Wake up your family. We need this property. We are taking over the house for our use. Take nothing with you, no food, no clothing. We will take care of you and feed you." Mother had just finished the weekly washing that day. It was in the attic where it dried from the heat of the chimney. She quickly gathered up two bundles of blankets, bed linens, and some clothes including some of her best dresses and Father picked up an axe. The four children were all crying so Mother calmed them down. Then she and father, with Joseph, Stefania, Stasia and Frank left the house as ordered.

Since the earth was covered with heavy snow, the Russians herded us into a large horse driven Russian sleds. We were taken to the railroad station in town, about 1 1/2-2 miles from our home. As we were being driven to the station we saw hundreds of people being unloaded from the sleds into the station yards. Many of them did not have the wits to bring extra clothing and warm blankets, even with their warmest clothes, they were shivering cold in the sub-freezing temperature.

Cattle cars of various sizes were waiting on the tracks. They held from 20 to 60 or more people. The townspeople were herded into the cars. There was much panic as parents tried to keep their families together. All the openings which served as windows were boarded up. As each car was filled, the door was closed and locked shut.

Inside the cars were narrow, wooden platforms attached to the sides of the car at different levels. There were far too few for everyone to rest so the people arranged to take turns. There was a wood stove in the car to provide a little heat. There were no sanitation facilities. The men had hidden some farm tools and my Dad brought an axe to cut a hole in the floor of the car to be used as a toilet. Someone found a sheet to hang from the roof of the car around the hole to provide a minimum of privacy. My mother was one of the few who had anything to eat, having hidden a loaf of bread in her bundles.

Our transport to Siberia

The train departed Kalusz in the late afternoon traveling east towards Russia. Being a "cattle train" it moved slowly, often forced to wait on a siding for a passenger or troop train to pass. It took an entire day to travel 82 km (about 48 miles) for the train to arrive in Lwow.

The City of Lwow was a major railroad switching center. In Lwow many other cars such as ours were coupled together. This coupling took some six to eight hours. Departing the City of Lwow the train traveled due east towards Russia. We traveled for a few hours or so it seemed. The train stopped and suddenly the doors to our cattle car were opened. All of us were instructed to dress the small children and bundle all of our belongings because we had to change trains, after which we would continue our journey east. After much questioning we were told that the change of trains was necessary because Russian tracks could only accommodate Russian trains because the space between the rails was about 10 cm closer together. It turned out we moved from one condition into the same. Their cattle cars were equipped the same as the Polish trains. Even the potbellied stove was in the same position. Changing trains took about 8-10 hours. While we were transferring, guards gave us some soup and bread to eat. They told us to prepare ourselves for a long journey because it'd be some time before we'd get our next meal. Eventually the train continued on its journey east.

While we were moving east in the closed quarters of railroad freight cars, day after day, I spent a lot of time with my brother Joseph. We talked about our situation and what the future would hold. Since he was 5 years older than me, in his mind he was very smart and could assess the situation better than I could. I asked him, "Where do you think we are all going and why?" He replied, "I can tell you that we are inside Russia and traveling northeast. It looks to me like we are heading for Siberia. What will happen to us God only knows." He also added that the Russian government was very young at this time.

After the Revolution in the 1920's, it was controlled by the Communists under Lenin. In his view, Russia resembled the United States of America except the ideologies were different. At one point, I asked him, "What is Communism" Joseph turned to me and said I was stupid and I started to cry and he was confused. He didn't realize that we will never go back home and our lives back in Poland. Joseph then held me in his arms, for the first time, ever in my memory, and I was happy to have such a nice brother that cared for me. After this incident, my mother told Joe not to talk to me about such political things for I was too young to understand. As we traveled due northeast, I wondered if my relationship would continue with my brother Joe.

I have always loved my little sister Stasia, but when we left our house in Poland, she was six years old and never remembered much of what was happening around her. While we were in this condition on the train, she stopped talking and was very withdrawn. Her black eyes were never happy and she talked very little. How sad it was for my mother and father to try to keep us in a good family environment. Looking back now as a grown man, I wondered how my sister Stefania and my mother kept up with their hygiene and personal situation. Living in those conditions was devoid of pleasure; they were animal conditions, at best.

We would look for some food because all of us were always hungry. The doors were opened every other day when the Russian soldiers would come with buckets of soup and bread to be distributed to the people. There was never enough to satisfy our hunger. Many healthy people lost considerable weight. By the time we arrived at our destination a lot of people were thrown out of the cars because of death of some kind or another. (Nobody questioned the cause of death.) When the weak died en route, they were simply dumped off the train into the ditches. Fields and fields of snow was all that could be seen through the cracks between the boards of the train as it continued its deplorable journey.

We discovered that the train was uncoupled at different stations en route and occupants of some train cars were unloaded in various camps. We never knew how many cars were in our original train caravan which was originally about a mile long. It took a total of 23 days to reach the railroad station of Piniuk. When we arrived it was obvious to us that more than half the original train was gone.

Here the survivors were ordered to leave the train. The Russians said, "There's a camp for all of you. We'll take care of you, but now you need to walk." It was a three hour walk to Kamionka. The address of the camp was Camp Kamionka, Station Piniuk, Region Archangelsk, USSR. This was located west and north of the Ural Mountains, south of Kotlas. It was a heavily forested, isolated region, far from any civilization. There was no reason for guards because there was nowhere to go either in summer or winter. "You either freeze to death or would be eaten by animals. No way out!"

It was already dark and the ground was covered with 4-8 feet of snow. We could see silhouettes of a camp with five large barracks for 2,000 or more people. Families gathered together as the Russian soldiers herded them into the barracks. Each barrack contained a pot-bellied, wood burning stove and wood bunks. This "Camp Kamionka" was an old camp. The barracks were badly deteriorated and in need of major repairs. Talking with some natives we learned that this particular "Kamionka" was used to hold political prisoners during the Russian Revolution, during the time of Lenin and Trotsky.

As the story unfolded, we were told that many of the former Russian Intelligence, such as doctors, elites or teachers and the most prominent people, were placed in this camp. We further were told that all the imprisoned people either died from one cause or another, such as starvation or execution. No native people of the area were allowed to enter the compound.

The camp lacked sanitary facilities so upon arrival the able bodied men erected a small building about 20x20 feet with a large hole in the middle; over this hole they built seating arrangements with places for six people to use at the same time. This, of course, was insufficient for the large group, so other lavatories of the same type had to be built.

For cooking facilities, the people also built a small building in the center of which they place rock; on top of this they placed railroad rails. This served as a large cooking surface on which the pots and pans were placed. Water was carried by the ladies and children in buckets from a nearby stream.

To wash clothing women first boiled the dirty clothing in a large pan of water on top of the stoves to sanitize them. Then they brought water from the nearby stream and washed the clothes in tubs. Life in the camp was not easy and there were many serious hardships. The imprisoned were afraid to utter words which might be offensive to Russian beliefs.

The camp was controlled by a Commandant named Bocozskoy and the Chief of Police or NKVD (KGB) named Sacharov. They were the main "gods" of the camp. Mr. Sacharov had the right to interrogate anyone at any time . . . . and could punish anyone as he willed. On the other hand, the Camp Commander could do anything he willed, and he was not bashful to withdraw the meager bread rations without even giving an explanation why.

The morning after our arrival, Commandant Bocozskoy announced, "you were taken for your safety. You would stir up problems where you were. You are free to work at assigned jobs for which you will be paid. If you work, you eat; no work, no food," and he lived up to his word.

The camp was surrounded by forest. Since the snow was so deep, the people were directed to cut the trees at the three or six foot level, making sure the logs were cut to a uniform one meter (39") in length. As the seasons progressed and the snow melted, they'd be directed to return to cut the rest of the trees in the same manner as before. The trees were decored and loaded into railroad box cars and shipped to paper factories. The Polish people, mother, father, Joseph and Stefania from my family and others worked from early morning until night earning 1-2 Rubles per day. One Ruble would buy 2.5 kilo (approximately 6 lbs) of bread. Few other staples were available. The people in the camp were allowed to go two miles into town to buy food. My mother was able to trade her best dresses for potatoes and bread. One dress would give the family food for several months. It was very fortunate for us that my mother had brought some of her dresses with her.

Because of my age, I was sent to Russian school in the camp to be indoctrinated into the politics of Stalin. This 'school' consisted of one classroom where all young kids attended. Not only Polish-Catholic people who had been deported, but others such as Polish Jews, Polish Protestants, etc. all arrived after our group. So there was a mixture of children attending the so-called 'school'. The Russian female teacher was quite young and was all engaged in indoctrination. We kids didn't believe she was too bright. She made the children learn the alphabet in Russian and tried to indoctrinate them in Communism, stating there is no God, but Stalin will take care of everything, etc. The children attempted to persuade her that "God indeed is here and without Him we would perish, and because of Him we will be free some day!" Because of some troubles, this school lasted only about six months and again no one asked questions.

On one particular day, the storekeeper named Kapusein, knowing that my uncle Mikolai Leszynski had some carpentry skills, asked him to build a coffin and possibly a cross for his little son who had passed away; he and his wife wanted to give him a Christian burial. My uncle was very proud that this Russian had asked him to do this deed for him.

Mr. Kapusein became friendly with the Polish people. He was sympathetic to us, realizing that we were victims of Stalin's power and for that reason we wound up in Siberia as a punishment for some unknown reason. Mr. (Grazdanin) Kapusein would tell some ladies to go to some villages about 10 kilometers (about six miles) from this camp to exchange some belongings for food which we desperately needed. The whole community of Kamionca Camp learned about this and was very excited because this provided a light in the tunnel for survival. Not long after this news my mother asked me if I was willing to go with her to trade some of her dresses and other belongings for some potatoes or other food to supplement the meager food provided for those in the camp. We were very grateful that mother had the foresight to quickly gather up these things in our hasty departure from Studzianka because now we were able to exchange them for much needed food for the family.

Keeping in mind that Russia was a Communist (atheistic) state and church activity was prohibited, when we visited houses to trade clothing for food, my mother and I observed that in some of them, religious icons were displayed. Returning to Kamionca Camp from our expeditions, we had plenty of time to talk. At one point I asked my mother, "Mama, how come in this communist country religious icons are still displayed in the houses?" Her comments were very simple, "people will always believe what they believe." Returning to Kamionca after about seven hours of walking in deep snow, my father and siblings were very happy to have us all back together again.

Life was very routine from day to day without much change. Soon after the first snow started falling and cold weather started gripping the countryside, my father started getting weaker and could no longer work as a tree cutter. After questioning by KGB officials, they determined he was too sick to work in the forest as a cutter. So after a week of rest, they assigned him new duties. There was need for a bathhouse keeper and also steam room attendant, so he was transferred to his new position. In addition, they were kind enough to assign my mother to help him with his new duties. So life for my parents became somewhat easier to bear in this camp and late in the evening, the whole family could enjoy late baths in private with no KGB officers disturbing us.

As time went on and hunger was getting worse we learned from unknown sources that the reason for the shortages of food was the war between Russia and Germany. In that period of time, Germany had the upper hand over Russian forces and the German army had occupied part of western Russia, including Leningrad. This news was very welcome to the Polish occupants of this concentration camp. Soon after winter was over, which was about late May, we were ordered to gather in the middle of the campground. After waiting for hours for God knows what, and in anticipation of what was going to happen to us, Grand Commander Bocowskoy and KGB Sacharov finally arrived to speak to us.

One of them started with apologetic statements saying the war with the German forces was going nowhere and because of shortages of food and because . . . . and because . . . . without further explanation, they stated that Mr. Joseph Stalin and his government granted ALL Polish people presently held in camps throughout the Soviet Union freedom to leave their camps and to be allowed to travel the same as any other citizen of Russia. And henceforth we no longer were retained by any force and this meant we were granted amnesty or forgiveness. The Commandant told us all the guards would be removed from the campgrounds.

In our disbelief, we were overjoyed and stunned by this event. We are free to go anywhere. The question is, "Where do we go?" Our dear country, Poland, is occupied by Germany. Then there is this battle front between Poland and Russia. How do we cross these battle grounds? The elders of our camp were trying to make some kind of sense of this pronouncement. Most recommended that we discuss our options since we could go to the town of Piniuk, purchase a newspaper, and learn for ourselves what kind of political situation we were experience. Then we could make a proper decision.

Living conditions changed considerably for we were truly free to come and go as we pleased. People still went to work to make some money to sustain themselves, but there were no guards to make them work. Our elders were mapping our next move according to the political situation in the world.

At one point, the "brains of our camp" spotted a blurb in one of the newspapers indicating that Father Joseph Stalin, through his Government, had granted permission to Polish General Wadyslaw Sikorski to form the Polish Army on Russian soil, and when such army was formed it was free to leave Russia and go to combat the German Army with the Allies. All dependent family members of the Polish army personnel would be allowed to exit Russia provided there would be no cost to the Russian Government. The dilemma for our leaders was how to organize a chain of events to leave Kamionca (our camp of enslavement).

There were several alternatives open to us, but the ultimate goal was to have all our people leave Kamionka together, just as we all arrived together. Since almost all of the people who worked in the forest were paid for their work, some saved some money, some saved little and some nothing. The question was how to get everyone out of Kamionka. The leaders agreed to send a so-called scout to learn from the railroad personnel how to transport such a huge group of people out of Piniuk station to the south of Russia, to a place such as Uzbekistan. Because we were free people by Stalin's decree, the railroad people were very cooperative especially since we would pay them for such transportation, thus this plan was formulated by rail personnel. Get all the people from Kamionka to the Piniuk station, then go by tram to the capital city of Kotlas (there was no direct short connection to southern Russia from Piniuk).

We had to go to Kotlas, which was north of Piniuk, but then we could travel south all the way to Alma Ata, the capital of Uzbekistan. The cost was prohibitive for second and third class accommodations; however, there was an alternative. We could leave Piniuk station the same way we arrived, that is by cattle cars. Although it would take two months to get to our destination, the cost would be at a minimum because such trains would travel empty when there were no goods to transport. Our "think tank" of leaders called a meeting of all of the camp occupants.

When all had gathered together, they presented the options of our exodus from Camp Kamionka to freedom. There was a long deliberation with many questions and answers. Of course, some were very scared to take this long trip to possible freedom. It was quite a persuasive meeting. Some believed they could exit the camp under their own effort, others were scared that the journey south was unknown; and others were scared that the Russian Government would derail our hopes and send us to some unknown camps elsewhere. After much debate, we all agreed to go south in cattle cars. The slogan was "We came here in cattle cars . . . . we leave here in the same style". All those gathered agreed that all the money from all the people in Kamionka was to be pooled so all the people could leave together regardless of religious or ethnic background. Another slogan was sounded off, "one for all and all for one". The harmony of the camp was at its very highest spirit. So it was decided by all inhabitants of Kamionka that we would go for a "freedom ride".

CHAPTER II

To transport all of our people out of Kamionka would require some effort. To begin with, our "think tank" found out from the railroad officials that it would cost about fifty Rubles per person to travel from Peniuk to the main switching station in Kotlas and would take about two days' travel. It would cost an additional fifty Rubles to travel from Kotlas to Alma Ata, all-in-all about 3,000 miles and would take about three months. This train would not be traveling on a scheduled timetable. It would be coupled to trains having enough room for coupling. Things would not be working out as planned. It turned out that all the money pledged in Kamionka was not enough. It created ill feelings in that some people claimed the journey south would be unable to sustain them, so self preservation took priority.

The fact that people were thinking of their own survival created other questions. How do you elect who is to go and who is to stay behind? The resolution was simple, the ablest of the able would go first, the rest would be placed in Soviet Union care. The thing was that the Soviets had displaced all Polish citizens to their labor camps. Since some people had lost their health and ability to help themselves, now it was their time to help preserve the lives of these poor people.

There were no other options. After a lot of arguments, it was decided to have our delegation go to the railroad officials and book places on trains as needed. The officials informed our delegation that they would arrange such transportation and in addition they would supply horses and wagons so weak people and children would be transported to the station from our camp. The officials told our group to make preparation to depart and that it would probably take seven to ten days to arrange actual departure time. Even as bad as the conditions existed, it was scary to move on to the unknown. Many started to panic and question the validity of our departure.

However, our leaders persuaded these people that departure was necessary to our lives and possibly saving our poor Poland.

My family happened to save some money. However, my father gathered the whole family together and informed us what was in the works for liberation. He said that his and my mother's mind was made up. Joe, my oldest brother agreed with my parents. He added that there were articles in the newspaper that indeed General Sikorski was forming a Polish army in the south even as he spoke. He said that there was nothing more in his dreams but to join such an army. We all thought how wonderful it would be to be in warm weather and maybe have better food to eat. After a couple of days, all of my family started to take inventory of our position and also what provisions we had put aside for dark days.

After two years of confinement, for some reason, we had accumulated more stuff than we arrived with. This probably happened because some of my parents' brothers or sister sent us some clothing and some dry food such as beans and other dry foods. This happened on three or four occasions. Mother decided that whatever we had we would take with us because nobody in Russia had too much of anything. My mother persuaded my father to bundle all we possessed and take it with us when we left. Some of my cousins made the same decision. Others were skeptical, they argued that some of this heavy clothing was not useful where we were destined to go. It made sense, but common sense dictated to take all and if it was not needed, then discard it later, but in the meantime hold on to everything you posses.

Once morning came and it was a nice, warm sunny day, you would think it would be some very special day? Well think again, because we could hear the clacking of wagon wheels and the noise of horses' hooves. Alleluia! We could see the caravan of horses and wagons coming toward us. The happiness overcame all of us and we began to sing spiritual songs like Bogurodcica and finally the Polish National Anthem, Jeszcze Polska nie zginela (roughly translated: "Poland will never perish while we are alive"). Along with the caravan of horses and wagons there were some troops and the KGB. We were assured that they were present to resolve any problems with the occupants of Kamionca in case a disturbance would occur.

The evacuation began peacefully. The children and older people were put on wagons with the bundles of peoples' belongings with joy and singing, kissing and hugging. It was something to witness! It took a while to assemble about two hundred happy campers for the departure. Departure to the unknown . . . . to the horrors of imagination. But as our leaders told us, it is better to explore the unknown than to stay in this misery and death trap. At least we will have a better chance for survival. Not long after the horse-drawn wagons arrived and packed us in as much as could be packed with our belongings, the rest of the people started the walk to freedom.

Since it was still in the early morning when the caravan arrived, we started to walk before noon. The distance to the railroad station was about eight or nine kilometers so we could reach the station by three or four in the afternoon. Walking along the pot-holed road, all of us talked about expectation, what it will feel like to be back in the cattle cars once again, and to reminisce about the previous ride from Poland to Siberia. It didn't take that long to arrive in Piniuk.

There were cattle cars waiting for us, but there was not even one soldier to supervise our entry to the cars. Sure, there were bunks inside the cars, and there was a potbellied stove in the middle of the car and, of course, the hole in the floor. It sure looked like old times. Our family tried to stay together such as the Bereaznicki, Leszczynski and other Bereznicki and Ostrowski. As you can see, we had a big interrelated family in this slave camp in Kamionka so we all tried to stay together.

It was getting dark as we got inside the cars, so it was hard to distinguish different things. We were told by the official to stay close by because we could depart soon. Before any of us got inside this boxcar, there were a lot of people, so we made a roll call. It turned out that we had close to seventy people inside this compartment. It turned out we occupied three cars to the tune of about two hundred people. That is about the same ratio as we came with to this God-forsaken place. But this was different. The doors on both sides of the box car were open and no guards. Before long there was a big bump and it was easy to recognize that we were hooked up to some train. Slowly, then ever faster, the train started to move.

All started to cheer, and we also offered the prayer to our Lady of Chestohowa, the Queen of Poland, the Mother of our Lord Jesus. Some people prayed for their deliverance and for the safe journey to our destination. As we started, it was the beginning of the evening so a lot of us were hungry and thirsty. Our family and others prepared food: sandwiches, jars of soup and other foods. Then after the meal it quieted down. Lanterns were turned off and after a long day and anxiety, all were tired and wanted to rest and await the next day and what it would offer to us. The next morning came and the doors were still open to the delight of all of us, it seemed that, indeed, we were free. What a good feeling to get up in this crammed box car and to feel good.

Inside the cattle car

When morning came around and we found ourselves alone in this crammed boxcar, we had something to eat for breakfast. We had a lot to talk about and reminisced about our past, in that awful place that we just left. For one thing, how can you be happy to suffer in this place and be happy about where you are? But certainly it is thinkable. As the morning progressed and daylight became brighter with the doors opened to be able to focus, we were able to read some inscriptions with their names on bunk decks in different languages. It appeared to us that some names were Latvian, Estonian, Lithuanian, Ukrainian and others.

Because of so many of us in this environment, and some could read many languages, the conclusion was that these boxcars were used many times over. The sad thing about all these discoveries was that totalitarianism and communism doctrines did not work. Not only people from Western Europe suffered but also their own citizens suffered as well. Traveling north to Kotlas which was a major switching railroad station serving the north Siberian state of Archangel, the serenity of beauty was indescribable. The forest and the meadows were just beautiful. You see, nature does not discriminate between democracy and slavery. It serves all the same way. It was a pleasure for a change to see the glorious scenery from this awful boxcar traveling to unknown places and to be able to see all the beauty God placed on this land.

The next day we once more arrived at the city of Kotlas. We had passed though this city on the way to Kamionka. The city was very dark even in daylight. Buildings and surrounding areas were in disarray. We assumed the darkened buildings were because they used a lot of coal to sustain their heating and lighting needs. It was a very depressing sight. The people of Kotlas were genuinely concerned about our situation.

Some never heard that Russia occupied Poland, however, they were sympathetic towards us. Some helped us buy supplies at lower than regular prices for our further travel. Our purchases consisted of potatoes, cabbage, onions, garlic, but no meat was available. Some of our fellow travelers were able to buy some grain such as barley and wheat. The time in Kotlas was limited, and we had been warned to stay close because we could depart at any time.

The speed of travel was quite slow, for we stopped at all stations similar to a milk route, so going was slow. We should not have complained for we knew in advance that we booked the lowest priority travel available. The weather at the time we left Kotlas was quite cold and very unpredictable. It might be warm one day and freezing the next. So we were exposed to the unknown in many respects. In the evening on the second day of travel the train stopped. It was getting dark while the train was still stopped, so I decided that I had to relieve myself, so I jumped out of the boxcar and being very young, I elected to go to the side that was darkened. As I proceeded to relieve myself, the man who examined railroad cars for cracked wheels (by using a hammer banging on such wheels and listening for a different sound, which would mean cracks), came upon me, saying to me, "child be careful and get back in your car because the train is about to start at any time." Well! For me from my past experiences "anytime" meant it might be one minute or one hour.

The minute he warned me about, well the train indeed started and I had no chance to cross the tracks to go into the family boxcar. So I decided to jump out further to the other side and because the train started at a rapid pace, I had no chance to cross the tracks to go in. There was no way to save myself but to catch up with the emergency car, which could apply brakes to the train in case of emergency. Being down on the other side of the train, dressed only in boxer-style underwear, I was getting cold, so I started to run in the direction of the train. As I was running as fast as I could, thinking that if I miss my opportunity to catch this box car, I may as well be willing to freeze to death.

So what other choices did I have? My family were probably worried about me; but preservation was most important at this time, so I ran as fast as I could and grabbed the handrail of this box car. As I lifted myself to the first step, I felt as though I saved my life. It was getting dark, as the days in the Siberian latitudes are short this time of year. As I got to the stairs of the car, I climbed to the top deck. I started wondering, "What am I going to do now? How am I going to get to the car in front of me?"

The Angel of the Lord was with me. As I looked around, I saw that behind the braking wheel, on the brakeman's seat, there was a person dressed in a white fur coat, seated there, looking at me. I found myself looking at her wondering where this person had come from . . . . for this is evening and the weather is very cold. "What is this person doing here?" As I looked at the person in front of me, the thought came to me, "What am I going to do now" It is getting colder, I am shivering and being almost naked, I might freeze to death."

In the meantime, the person seated behind the braking wheel said to me (in a woman's voice), "Young man, why don't you come to me and sit in my lap. You and I will stay warm together. When the time comes and the train stops, you can go find your family because you will survive this night." All this time I envisioned that I could easily climb up on the roof of the car and jump from one to the other and get to the car where my parents were. As the evening progressed and the weather got colder and freezing became more apparent, I decided to sit on this lady's lap, for she had a fur coat and we could keep ourselves warm. As a rule, the train never traveled for more than a few hours—not this time!!

Two of my fellow Polish travelers on the "cattle car" heading east towards Siberia.

For some reason it traveled until daytime so when it stopped it was dawn. The minute the train stopped, I jumped out of her lap as though she had some kind of disease. Down the ladder I quickly climbed and ran forward toward the boxcar where my parents where. As I knocked on the door and was surprised to see my parents, brother and sisters, who greeted me with royal fanfare. Everybody was happy to see I had survived. My mother asked me why I was so warm and red-cheeked and wanted to know how I spent the time outside that night. I told them how I climbed the ladder to a braking platform about three boxcars behind and how this lady invited me to sit on her lap. They insisted on more details. I explained that this lady hitched a free ride on our train to go and visit her family and that she was all alone.

The lady had asked me to tell her my story, which I did and where I came from and why we had come to Siberia and what my parents had done to deserve to be sent here. She was very persuasive and I was suspicious whether she was on the level. Anyway, we had time to exchange information because I had many questions to ask about her life and lifestyle. She was not very informative, so I didn't learn much about her. Of course, the night soon came and I suppose I fell asleep, for I was hungry, tired and cold and my eyes would not stay open. When the train stopped it was all over. My parents were quite impressed with how I used my initiative and plans for survival. At one point even my brother Joe was pleased with my conduct for he was very reserved when it came to giving me a compliment.

After my Mother learned what happened to me, she told me to go and bring this lady to our boxcar. So I partly dressed and went out to ask the lady to come to our car so my family could personally thank her for what she had done for me. As she came with me and I introduced her to my parents and the rest of the occupants of our boxcar. My mother prepared some hot tea and a slice of bread so she could refresh herself. After some talk she traveled with us further and then she exited our boxcar at her destination.

This was taken at the Concentration Camp in Kamionka, in the northern region of the State of Arcengel, close to Kotlas in 1940. Not a pretty picture except for me grinning on the left of the picture. Guess what, I never failed not to smile . . . . see for yourself and you be the judge.

Let me write about my little sister Stasia. She was born in June, 1934. I was then six years old so I remember her birth. She was a very blond little girl with black eyes. She hardly ever cried. When she was asleep, her arms were folded over her head. I loved her from the day she was born. As we grew up she was always at my side, well almost always. Her face was sad while we were in Kamionka. She was never happy. I remember nights in those barracks when cockroaches would come out when the lights were turned off. They would climb the walls and ceilings by the thousands. When complete silence would come, the roaches would prey on some people more than others. They didn't bother me, but boy they sure loved my little Stasia.

She would wake up in the morning full of welts all over her body, she was always in agony. Poor Stasia had another problem . . . . lice in her hair. My poor mother used all kinds of remedies to get rid of the nasty lice, but nothing seemed to work. Some people suggested that my mother should use some kerosene and soap, but that didn't work either. Eventually when my parents became overseers of the bathhouse and Stasia could be bathed daily, the lice departed. What a miracle, daily baths.

As for my brother Joseph, what a wonderful disposition he had for a man. He was very quiet, self-possessed, never eager to argue—just a very nice man. He was tall, blond with blue eyes and handsome with much intellect and character. My older sister Stefania was born on December 25th, 1925. She too was blond with blue-green eyes. She had the same character as Joseph except she was a girl, and we used to pick on her, but it was all in fun. I was a different story. If anything was broken in the house, it was Franek's fault; if something was missing or lost, it was Franeks' fault; it came to the point that this poor Franek (this is my loving name, short for Franciszek) was always to blame.

And guess what? They all were right! Was I sorry about all this blame? No I was not for I was always mama's boy; the other children were daddy's kids. So I was who I was and the whole family loved me for what I was. I was never a bad boy, but I was born with a smile and mischievous and I have never outgrown my demeanor. Now that I have discussed my brother and sisters, I could set it straight, because we were a very close family; nothing could divide our lives.

As we traveled "free" in our boxcar south in this huge country of Russia, we saw marvelous countryside. the Ural Mountains on the left of the train were spectacular with all the beauties which nature provided them. As we traveled day by day, our original food supply dwindled down to nothing. We began to worry about how we could replenish our supply. This tragedy not only happened to my family, but also to the others, such as Bereznicki's, Leszczyinski's, Strutynishi's, Bachrywowski's and others. The assignment of us young boys and girls was that whenever the train would stop, we would run to other open freight wagons and scour for any edible food such as grain, potatoes, beets and other such items. If anything was found, we would bring it back to our train and divide it as needed.

Well, the very next stop we ran out and scoured other trains for the possible "catch". As we went we found an open car filled with wheat. We were not prepared for such a large bounty. How could we get some of the grain back tour families? I suggested that we undress and fill our trouser pant legs and shirt sleeves and carry them full of grain back to our boxcars. It worked just fine; we made a few trips, and now we were supplied with pillowcases so we could bring more for our consumption, even while we kept a watchful eye on our train, to stay close so we would not be left behind. The success of the day was wonderful. You probably wonder what good was the grain? Well, get some water, drop in some grain and boil until the grain gets soft. With a little salt you have glorious porridge to fill your stomach and satisfy your hunger. Man what a life when you are hungry and can get your belly full.

This food hunt was not always successful; some days there was nothing to be found, so we had to rethink our way and maybe go to the bakery and buy some bread and other things. The money that we saved in camp was dwindling. We didn't know how long our trip would last so we had to have some reserve. After a few days of travel we stopped at an unknown station, but there were no other trains. We went out to look anyway for something or other. Well, low and behold there in front of us was this pile of potatoes!! Our eyes glittered with joy for here is some serious food.

When we came to pick them up, they were all frozen. Frozen potatoes become mushy, so we dug in to find some unfrozen. Surprise, surprise, there inside the pile were perfectly good, fresh potatoes. We must have filled about twenty pillowcases full of this delicious food. This supply lasted our families for a number of days, so the hard work and expectations paid off. We could afford to travel further south to our destination.

As we moved further south warmer weather was welcomed by all of us. The cold months and long northern nights were getting to all of us. Each day was different from the other, and one day someone would pass away from one cause or another. When the first such incident happened, we were all very concerned because no one knew how to dispose of the body. At our next stop, the relative of the deceased person contacted the railroad authorities and soon the body was picked up and taken away. How the body was disposed of we could not learn because the train moved on.

The worst part of traveling in a freight train is the unexpected stops and starts. There were no schedules and most often the train would stop far away from a main station where we could obtain some food or other items, so we were very restricted. Some necessities had to be purchased, such as milk and bread and, of course, tobacco and matches for my father, but spending money for some things was not available. Even though we had some money, we had a long journey in front of us. The estimated travel time was about three months. One day, a lady came to our car informing us that she found a building, someplace or a stand at the railroad station and bought a pot full of this delicious soup with meat in it for only two Rubles, which was very reasonable.

Of course, my mother could not resist the temptation of a bargain, so she went out with the pot to purchase some soup with meat in it. As I mentioned before, whenever we would sidetrack at a station, it meant the train could be parked there for some time. Well, well surprise. The minute mother went out to purchase this soup with meat in it, the train whistle blew and the train started to depart. There was nothing we could do to stop it. Well, we traveled for about six to seven hours and finally side tracked at another station. Again we parked far away from the main station. In the meantime, not only our family started to worry about mother and how she could find us, but the people in our car were in sympathy with us. All the people in the car liked my mother.

As soon as our train parked, my father and some members of our car went to the station to inform the railroad personnel that our mother was left behind trying to purchase soup right by the last station. They asked the officials to please unite her with our train. The officials assured my father they would do whatever they could. They also mentioned that they would call that station and alert them about our situation. With that kind of assurance, my father and the others returned to our car.

On returning to our train, the men, including my father, had no other option but believe all would come out alright. The next morning our train was hooked up to another train and we were on our way south. Sticking to our plan, at every stop our men would get out of our train and seek out any lost or confused Polish lady that was left behind on her train which departed a day ago. There was no luck finding her at the next stop, so our train took off and after about six to eight hours would come to another stop.

Meanwhile, all of our people were wondering if we were ever able to find her in the midst of this large territory. As we traveled for some time, we stopped in a little town. This was a very quick stop, but our men were out again looking for my mother. This time, God's blessings were on their side, for my mother recognized one of the men and was running toward them to show that she was alright. The reunion was quite full of enjoyment and gratitude and we celebrated her reunion with us. Incidentally, she was able to come to us with a bowlful of soup. How wonderful this soup was for us to celebrate her homecoming. We celebrated her return with prayers to our Lord and Blessed Mother of our Lord Jesus, that He was willing to return her to our midst.

The next morning, God bless, our train was hooked up to some other train and we were on our way again. The destination was, as we learned from the train authorities, was a major station called Alma-Ata. This particular rail configuration was the end of the track. Hence it made a triangle turnaround and headed back in the opposite direction. At one point in Alma-Ata we were told to disembark because this was the destination for which we paid at the station of Piniuk when we started our journey.

To our disbelief we were approached by some so-called "Russians" but later learned they were representatives of the Uzbek Republic United Farming Community (KOLHOZ) and that they were recruiting able-bodied persons to work in their collective farm system; the workers they wanted were to be able to pick cotton. This would provide us with accommodations and some pay if we would work, not by hourly wage, but on piece work; meaning the harder you work, the more money you would earn. On the surface it sounded very inviting, meaning to our elders that this system would get us out of poverty and possibly to something more fitting to our future.

After all the wrangling and discussion about what we were to get from the collective farm representative, our people agreed to accept their offer. To our amazement several donkey-drawn carts with only two wheels (unlike European four-wheeled carriages) came to pick up only some of our people. In all there were nine carts which could accommodate about six to eight people with their belongings; belongings of our family amounted to two bundles—that is, one blanket bundled all of our clothing and another with food supplies and dirty laundry. After traveling for hours, we reached a small village called the Kolhozor Collective Farming Community.

The road from Alma-Ata to this community was very narrow, surrounded by cotton fields. They were on both sides of this road, seeming to be as far as you could see. The temperature while riding in the cart in the daytime was very hot; probably in the low 100 degrees Fahrenheit. As we reached the community, we were assigned to little adobe huts. An individual hut contained so-called two rooms' eating/sleeping combination and a so-called family room which was in reality a sleeping room. In this little hut there were no beds nor chairs nor tables. There was no kitchen facility as we were accustomed to have in our home in Poland. But there was a bucket in one corner in the "eating" room. There was no other accommodation for any restroom facility in this little adobe, two room home. But there was one opening hole to act as a window (or ventilation) to provide fresh air and light to the environment of the interior. As we settled into this adobe, we realized that, although we were free to do as we could to support ourselves, we were really oppressed under their socialist way of life.

The next day after arrival, we were informed that the work assigned to us as a family had to begin. This collective community farm system required that each resident had to pick cotton to sustain us and earn enough rubles to provide a living for their families. This meant that the harder you worked the more compensation you earned on a piecework basis. Early in the morning, my father John, mother Maria, my oldest brother Joseph and my older sister Stefania and I went to work, while my youngest sister Stasia stayed home in the morning and was later taken to a so-called home day care.

Stasia, a little blond child was as fragile as she could be. When my parents would come home from a long day's work, they would question her about how she spent her day and how she was treated and what she had to eat during what was a long day. The answer was always the same, "I don't know", and she would add that she was hungry and would begin to cry.

The first day of work didn't seem as bad as we were issued linen sacks to put the cotton in that we had picked from the plants. Cotton plants produce many pods, and when the time is ripe the cotton pods open up and provide cotton to be picked. The picker picks up the pods and places them in the linen sack, which is about ten feet long. After filling this sack, the picker would empty the sack and proceed to fill it up all over again. And so it goes. Remember the heat of the day is so severe that water for refreshment was not available very often, making work very difficult and tiresome. This is a very short description of the very first day of our work schedule. We started work in the very early morning and worked until dark.

When we got back to the hut (our home so to speak) we found that there was no food to eat and no water to wash our faces or to drink. We were told to obtain a bucket and get some water from the well for our use, but what about food? Well, we were informed that as free people, we had to earn our money and we should be able to provide for our needs for food and all other commodities for our livelihood just as well as the rest of the citizens of the Soviet Union.

This was quite a shock to our Polish people for we were treated as slaves of the Soviet Labor Camp all over again. Sure, we were given this adobe hut, but we were charged for renting this accommodation, with no kitchen facilities, no bathroom facilities except our house and the bucket in the so-called "kitchen" to wash our utensils and then dump the dirty water outside our hut. The condition of work and living was about as bad as you can envision.

All of us were very sad that we came to this situation, that we were exploited to be slaves for the Soviet Union. This situation lasted for a few weeks; things did not change a lot and the hot sun and weather persisted. It depleted our strength and our ability diminished. Then we discovered another difficulty. We all developed eyelid problems; we suffered red crustaceans of our eyelids and much redness of the eyelids. This problem grew worse day after day. We contacted doctor's aid from another community to inquire about our eye problem. To our dismay we were informed that the past observations of this condition occurs to non-local residents. It always happened to Western European residents who are not immune to cotton pollutant dust which causes irritation to their eyelids for some unknown reasons.

For some of our people would still go to pick cotton balls to earn rubles to sustain themselves and others, including my family, to gain enough finances to get away from this selected slave camp. The so-called doctor's helper (intern) advised us, as well as my family, that to stay in this place and labor at picking cotton would severely affect our lives and at the end we could all be blinded by this condition. He advised us that for the best of our health, and to avoid this condition, we should leave this region and move somewhere else. As bad as this place was to survive, we became accustomed to life in these terrible conditions—no food to speak of, no sanitary provisions, no cleaning of our bodies, and no comforts of living to which we were accustomed in our native Poland. What is our next option?

As sick as we became, we planned to leave this cotton picking place and move on to the distant unknown in order to survive and to live on. My father and mother after consulting with us, all decided that to stay in Kolhoz is to doom our existence, so to survive we have to move from here and seek an improvement. As things got worse for the rest of our Polish people, and we all were ready to leave this cotton place, some news from somewhere by some unknown source came to our attention—that somewhere in Uzbekistan there was a Polish group forming a Polish army and they were inviting Polish Soviet slaves to join this movement.

With this exciting news, all of us in our community in this cotton picking village decided to go to Uzbekistan and seek the opportunity to join the Polish army. Well, the opportunity was not as easy as it sounded. To travel to Uzbekistan would cost an enormous amount of money, money which we did not have nor could obtain in a short period of time either by working or other means. Our friends, or elders for no other description available, decided that we should get all of our monetary resources, put it all together, pay our fare on the train and travel east in the direction of Uzbekistan.

The travel expenses would take us somewhere as close as we could get to our destination. The rest of the way we would travel without pay and put ourselves in the hands of the railroad authority. The reasoning was how could we be worse off if things go wrong? How could the government or the Soviet Union punish us more than they have so far? None of us realized where our destination would be, where we would locate ourselves. Nor did we realize that we came to the place that was so far from the place that we heard about in the hope that we would be recruited into the Polish Army formed under the authority of General Sikorski. The maps of the Soviet Union were not available to common citizens for obvious reasons. After our arrival in Alma-Ata and the consequences of staying in the midst of Kolhoz picking cotton, we were very disillusioned as to what would be the consequences of our struggles to come out of all this alive.

The decision was to go to the new destination as planned and seek out this Polish recruiting post in the town of Kermine in Kazakhstan. We discovered we were very far from our destination, but the decision was made and we would do whatever was to be done to attain our goal.

When we purchased our travel tickets for our family we had enough money to travel about one-third of the distance towards our destination. What would happen after that we didn't know, but we would worry about that at that time. As we settled in our cattle compartment, we discovered that the same people were with us on the same train. No wonder, as all the people took the same train thinking and trying to escape the tyranny of this republic. We traveled for several days to the west toward the Caspian Sea toward our destination in Kermine. But as the days passed, the food got scarce and we would have to abandon our train to seek food for further travel to reach our destination.

The elders of our group decided that we could go another day or two forward, and we could scout some food to sustain ourselves and keep going. The Elders dispatched young boys to scout empty railroad freight cars to see if there was any food to retrieve for our consumption. Sorry, there were no open cars with any grain to relieve our plight. The next day, we would have the same consignment to seek food for our survival. This time, the young girls as well as the boys were sent out to seek food. As we traveled on our way, day after day, we finally came to the station in some remote place.

God was on our side, we discovered some barley in an open railroad car. Joy that it was found and we will live! In the final six or seven days, we could bring some food to our loved ones. Barley, when it is soaked in water, expands to double its size; when it is cooked it is delicious plus very nutritious and filling. The journey went along and all the occupants were happy with the outcome. By this time, about the sixth or seventh day of travel, we were not confronted with any type of questioning about our tickets or identification. All was very satisfactory as was planned by our elders, and who knows . . . . it may be a successful trip if it turns out as planned. The journey to our destination would be very long because we had traveled very Far East not knowing where we were going.

At the time when we left our camp in Siberia (Camp Kamionka) it didn't much matter where we would wind up as long as we would escape that prison. Now that we found ourselves in this new dilemma, we will have to pay for this mistake with our miseries. You see, Alma-Ata is most likely about one thousand miles east of the Caspian Sea; our new destination is close to the Caspian Sea and that is where the Polish Army forces are forming. This is why we are headed there. As I have mentioned before, we want to escape the Russian terror and mistreatment. This is why we sacrificed our time and our miseries, sicknesses and deaths on this endless journey in this stinking condition where you sleep on bare floors, and in hunger—no fresh water to drink or prepare something to eat.

We had endured enormous misfortunes to be here. Our sanitation was non-existent and we were beginning to look and act like animals. One day our mother, bless her heart, which was a very strong woman, was mad when we awakened. So she gathered us together since she wanted to speak her piece. She said that this behavior had to stop and we should start behaving like the civilized people we were. She started with the prayer, Our Father, who art in heaven, followed with our Mother, Mother of God, pray for us for we need you and keep us in your prayer to our Lord God Jesus. When the prayer was over, she began to unload her grievances on us as she could not bear the entire family load and that we had to help her keep her family intact and whole.

You see, we had just come out of the cotton fields, very much overworked and sick with an eye problem. We still have to care for the eyelid problem; the crustaceans need some medical care to which we had no access and I suppose there were other problems that the younger children, including myself, were not informed. Now I can sympathize what my parents must have gone through. As ever before at the railroad stations, my brother Joseph and I would jump out and search open railroad containers for any kind of food to bring back to our family. Days went into weeks, but we are getting closer to our destination. The miracle to all this traveling was that we didn't have to change trains or put up more money (which we didn't have) and also no one got sick aside from the problem which we were somewhat accustomed. We did stop at one station, and mother had the chance to obtain some Vaseline to smear over our eyes which helped us a lot.

However, it appeared to all of us that after mother talked to us, our lives changed somewhat, and we started to appreciate our family more and we became a much closer knit family. But our search for food was for naught as we came back empty handed this time. God willing the next day will be better. The next day, to our surprise, we entered this big city called Tashkent. Tashkent is probably the biggest city that I had ever seen, and we were going west right through it in the bright morning. What a beautiful sight to see people hurrying up and down the streets, and us in these cattle cars with doors open watching them as they are hurrying to their destinations.

Since we were moving slowly, because the train made frequent stops for some reason, at one point we saw some Russian soldiers marching close to us. As we watched them, we observed that some of them were carrying their rifles without leather straps. Instead they had ropes attached to the rifles. When I pointed this out to my father, I asked him why this is so. "Well", he said to me, "Franek, this is Russia and not all is as well as it seems. Propaganda is one thing and life is another." He pointed out that these people have no better life than we have, this is a poor country but is dramatized as a powerful multi-ethnic nation; and the Government doesn't care whether the citizens of Russia are employed or not. He also said to me, "Don't think about it too much. It will only confuse your mind."

My father was not very talkative. What he would say was very direct and meaningful, this is not to say he was neglectful of his children, but he was not as expressive as mother. Uneventful days followed one after another. Thank God the weather was very cooperative in our travels. As we traveled further west and the closer we got to the Caspian Sea, the more desolate the countryside became and the railroad stations became scarce. The food we had gathered in previous stations was running out. It is very difficult to adequately describe our situation. Water, grain and patience were running out. It became evident that something had to change. I recorded that Stasia was crying, her cries this time were not because she was hungry but because she was lonesome and abandoned not by us, but by other people. As hungry as she was when she stopped to complain, she would only lie on her blanket and sleep.

On sunny morning the train stopped at the station in an out-of-the-way place. Well, we decided to explore our possibility to obtain some provisions for our future travel. Joseph and I jumped out of the train and started the search. Nothing happened for some time and we had almost given up. As we strolled back to the train, we spotted a new arrival; this train was long and the wheels were still hot. So I said to Joe: "maybe this new arrival has something to offer?" As we climbed the open wagon our eyes opened wide; we could not believe what was in front of us: potatoes, potatoes tons of potatoes were there for the taking. So we proceeded to stuff our shirts and our trousers with these potatoes.

It was very far from our train so we made several trips with these delicious potatoes. We filled several sacks for our future consumption. After some rest, after the very laborious work, we decided to scour the same train for additional food. On the way from our train, there was a railroad conductor. We asked him if he knew when our train was scheduled to depart. His response was plain—probably the next day. He interrogated us as to why we were inquiring. Joe said that we were going to the main station store and that we didn't want to miss our departure. Well, his answer made sense and the conductor left us alone. "Joe," I said to him, "maybe we have some time to find more food." so we climbed several more wagons and found some steel material, some electrical motors, and some manufactured items in which we had no interest.

It was now getting close to evening and there was not too much interest in searching for more food. As we came closer to our train, I spotted some people or young boys carrying something in gunny sacks and pointed this out to Joe. He suggested we go and explore what they found that was worthy of their efforts to carry it all. To our amazement this open car had tons of this little round grain of gold color, not bigger than a pinhead. I asked Joe if he knew what on earth this seed could be and what could be done with it. He said that he knew what it was and that it was a good seed, but he had to think about it to remember. After a while, he declared that his mind went blank and that whatever it was, it was worth our while to take some and that mother would find a use for it.

Again we filled our shirts and trousers with this precious golden seed and carried it to our train. When we loaded our find in our car, mother asked us what we had found. "Well", Joe explained, "we found this small grain but I don't remember what it is, but I have seen it before in Poland." Upon inspection, she shouted with a joyous voice that it was delicious and nutritious lentil seed. This treasure would save our lives for some time. Needless to say, we had a splendid supper, boiled potatoes and lentil soup. Glory to God for this gift. We prayed before and after our meal, it was a good feeling to go to sleep with full stomachs for a change.

This station, Novokozalinsk was good to us and like it or not, we were ready to go at any time. The next morning, the nice conductor, as he passed our wagon, said to my parents to prepare for a long journey west for there was nothing on the way. He added that we would start in about an hour. Joe and I decided to bring some water for our needs. As luck presented itself, we could get it close to our train. We succeeded by being well prepared for travel westward to our destination.

My father's health was worsening. He needed some medication to help him breathe, by doing so maybe he could gain some strength. Not only was our family worried about him but there were others, like the Leszcynski family as well as the Bereznicki family (who were related to us), as well as other people who were traveling with us. Life was getting easier because our food supply was in hand and people were more talkative. In a few days in our travel west we had the bad news that one of our co-travelers was getting very sick and it could be very serious. At this point, no one could assist him because of lack of professional experience. The only option was to disembark at the next station and seek a doctor's care.

This decision was hard to make because it meant that this family would most likely never get to the place where the Polish army was forming and if you don't get there you would most likely forfeit your chance of getting out of Russia. The decision was very difficult, but the man was too sick and needed medical care, but the family needed to continue the journey also. There was no easy solution. The decision was to continue the journey and pray that the situation would work itself out—whatever happened, was in God's hands.

It worked for awhile, and we traveled westward for about ten to twelve days. We were nearing the place called Kermine, where the Polish Army headquarters were located. It was a small railroad station, but it was the crossroads of two or three different directions. For this reason the Polish headquarters decided to establish this as a central place to grow. At some point when the train stopped we inquired how far away and how much longer it would take to reach Kermine. The answer we got was that it was probably around two hundred kilometers away but that it may take two to three days to get there. This news was very good for us and we were all happy to hear it.

The end was nearing for us to disembark and wait and see what the future would bring. This migration started about three months earlier and looked as though it would never end; for some people it did end because of starvation, sickness and other causes. My family had done the best we could. If it was not for my brother and occasionally my sister Stefania I am sure we would not have survived. The rummaging and searching through trains for food and finding some on different occasions is what saved our lives and we were thankful to God for that. In the next couple of days, we were nearing Kermine Station. We were anxious to see what was there which brought us from Kotlas (Siberia), for three months of misery, starvation and sleepless nights.

As it turned out, the train never slowed down in Kermine and it continued to go south. We reached the station which we had waited for so long and now, but the train did not stop there so it was most disappointing. There were rumors that it was a big ploy to lure us out of Alma-Ata and displace us in another God-forsaken place. Things didn't look good; everybody was skittish and worried about why this train didn't stop at Kermine. Of course, some reasons that not everyone in command of the train knew that we planned to stop there. Oh well, we could not change what happened and decided not to worry.

It was getting to be about mid-afternoon and the weather was quite warm. The terrain was sparse of trees and looked more like a desert. The word "desert" wasn't in our vocabulary, for we had never seen such a place, but now we were in the midst of it. The train finally stopped, not in our traveling lane but on the side of it. There were some people approaching in our direction. Soon they reached our wagons and informed us that the authorities knew all along that we traveled illegally, as stowaways, and that they let us do it. Now it is the time to disembark because they arranged transportation for us to relocate. They said they were the authorities of the Soviet Union and never let their people be abandoned, and that they would help us. At some point a donkey-drawn two wheel cart came to take us to an undisclosed place. There was about six to ten such carts to pick us up. So we slowly started to pack and bundle our belongings in a blanket, bundling whatever we possessed, along with very little food which was remaining from the big find in Kovokazalinsk. We were very thankful to God and his blessings to allow us to find this food. I am sure that we would not have made it this far without.

As we loaded our family on a cart with our bundles, we proceeded on a very narrow road. Well, this was no road at all, as we know it. It was a two-track, which the high wheels made and in the middle of the two tracks was a donkey track. We were unaccustomed to travel in two-wheel cars, except in Kazakstan when we were taken to the cotton farm. But the ride was much better than walking. The pace or speed of travel was about the same as a good walking pace. So after traveling for about two hours, we neared a building in which there were several rooms that looked like classrooms. There weren't any school benches or other commodities and the rooms were empty. All of us were gathered together awaiting someone with authority to say something to us about why we were brought to this place.

Soon a man came in, calling himself Commissar, meaning he was of authority in this place. He told us to sit down and that he had some instructions for us to follow. He started with such things as, that the Government of the Soviet Union knew of every move that we made, and that they let us pilfer food on our way here, and all the other things that even we could not remember, as this was another page in our lives. He spoke very good Russian and presented himself as an intelligent person. He said this would be our place to live for a while, and we should accept this place and make the most of our lives for a long time to come.

He also told us that the native Uzbeks who live around us will bring us food to eat and welcome us to their community. With those words he wished us luck and departed. There was much confusion amongst us. The older members, that are family mothers and fathers, started to talk and evaluate our position in this new place. The biggest puzzle was: How did they know our whereabouts and if so, why didn't they do something about it instead of leaving us alone? Another thing—why did they bring us here to this small village and make the use of the school for us. So many questions but no answers. Soon people from the surrounding community were coming with small bundles in their hands and were bringing some stuff for us, as was promised by the Commissar.

As they placed their gifts for us in the empty room, the aroma of hot prepared food reached us and it was glorious. The native men and women greeted us individually in their broken Russian. All of these people were dressed in picturesque dress, such as baggy trousers, etc. and almost all the men had beards and different jackets. The ladies had long dresses and black babushkas (scarves) and looked at us with some compassion. These friendly people urged us to fill up our plates and to start eating before the food got cold.

To our surprise, the bread was not a bread but more like thin pancakes—round things about one-quarter inch thick, somewhat like Mexican tortillas. There was soup with meat, rice-like meal and other goodies to which we were not accustomed. Eat all of this wonderful food? We surely did and liked it and were very grateful to our host people for doing this for us. We hadn't had such good food in a long time. God bless each donor of this food which they prepared for us.

After the meal, all the natives departed and left us alone. As we rested for awhile and digested this food, some men started to evaluate what just happened. With a generous reception, these Uzbek people showed us that things might get better for us. With these words each family occupied their place in this three room school house and retired for the night concluding with evening prayers asking God for His guidance and His care. The morning surely will bring us new surprises to deal with.

Sure enough, morning came and as we awakened there sure were more surprises because practically all of us awakened with stomach problems. It turned out that all the meat and other rich food the night before was too much for us to cope with. So we had to slowly adapt our diet so we would not get sick. Someone in our group suggested that we drink a lot of water to dilute the food we ate the night before. Well, all ended for the better. This day the leaders of this community came to where we lived, suggesting that we should start collective farming in order to support ourselves. Our elders inquired from the village people how to find out what sort of jobs were available, the answer was quite vague, for in reality there was no work of any kind to speak of. There were some farmers who would employ one or two people a week for some odd job for minimum pay and that would partially sustain a family. Anyway, we decided to tough it out and stay there for a while because of our mission to join the Polish Army.

After about a week, we inquired where the town known as Kermine was located and how far it was from where we lived. It turned out that it was quite near us. It was about ten kilometers away as the crow flies, or about six miles or so. At this point, my brother Joe, or as we called him Juzek, said to our parents: "I will venture to Kermine and scout what is available and whether or not all the propaganda about it is true." If so, he would then come home to us and then we could make a decision which way to go. Let me tell you why Joe reached this decision so quickly. It is because our future didn't look so bright. Joe and I were quite close and he was a good brother to me. He was five years older but he was very smart and a good scholar; he only had five months before he finished high school. At our time in Poland, it was a rare occasion for a farmer's son to finish high school (because of the need to help on the farm), and Joe surely would have done so. So for this reason he was protective of me. One evening he sat down with me and explained what his intentions were. He said, "Franek, I will go to Kermine and join the Polish Army and most likely I would be able to help the family sustain itself."

Early one morning Joe summoned our family together and informed us that he was going to Kermine to find out all there is to know. If things went well, he would join the Polish Army and come back to have us see for ourselves that it was true about the army. That evening my mother went out and borrowed some eggs and boiled them to make a little lunch for Joe so he had something to eat.

After hugs, kisses and goodbyes, Joe was gone into the unknown. Days passed and there was no news about Joe. My mother decided to go and look for Joe because we were all on edge wondering what might have happened to him. After crying and kisses, mother left one early morning to look for him. To the surprise to all of us in this abandoned school house where we all lived, that same evening my mother returned home to us. With wide and happy smiles she announced to us that she had indeed found Joe and that he was alright. Happiness is no small matter. We were singing praises to God and thanking him for large favors.

Mother told us, "Joe walked in the direction of Kermine. The terrain was quite difficult so it took him two to three hours to get there. When he got to the Army post, there were signs in Polish and arrows indicating where the recruiting office was located. When Joe got to the Recruiting Office, it was easy to enroll into the ranks of the Polish Army." At that point, he decided to enlist and stay in the army and maybe, who knows, he would be able to liberate our beloved Poland and at the same time help his own family. We were all happy for Joe. We all were happy for them. We went to visit Joe and other cousins in the vast populous of the Army, which must have numbered in the thousands.

Winter was approaching and the chill in the air was getting colder. We had to find a way to heat our quarters. The trouble was that there was a shortage of wood or coal. Jesus! There is always a shortage of food, medicine, water, wood and everything that sustained our living, not mentioning clothes or shoes. How can we go on in such a country where living is misery? The only way to heat our quarters is to scour the desert for camel dung or donkey extracts; when these things dry out they give a lot of heat. All of us would go out to find this dung and bring them back home. It wasn't easy to find these things so we had to venture father and farther away from our place hoping to succeed in finding some.

Well, we did find some dried dung to take home with us. After about a dozen of them, we decided to turn back home but by a different route. On the way back we had to go over some drainage ditches. Being young as we were and that "boys will be boys" we played a game of who could walk inside these ditches the longest. At one point there was a scary scream. We all ran to the area of this scream to learn what was the matter. It turned out that there were critters in their shells moving very slowly. Someone in our group said these critters might be turtles. Well! Let us take them home and see how we could deal with this find. It turned out just fine because one of the natives came to our place for a social visit, informed us that turtles are better eating than chicken. "Just boil water in a big pot, throw them in and when the turtle expands take it out of the hot water, cut in between the top and bottom shells. It is an easy task to shell all the fine meat and cook it like chicken." What a find for us to live on!!

The fire from the dung was quite hot and slow burning; most amazing as there was no distinguishable odor. We youngsters had future jobs to do to help our families. Yes, we had to share whatever we would find out here—"share and share alike." The winter was approaching, but it was not winter months as we had known in the past. This winter will be quite mild for it rarely snows around here. This is south of Russia and the weather is milder. Nonetheless, nights are cold and require some warm bedding. Joe was gone for quite some time now and we all missed him terribly. Mother would go to visit him not as often as she would like but she did go now and then. Joe was forbidden to leave his campground. The army feared that some unknown bacteria could be spread among the army population.

At one point after talking with my parents, I decided that I would go to visit my big brother. After careful instructions from my mother on how to get there safely and after some food provisions for my maiden journey to Kermine, I was out to explore the world all by myself. I did take some time to get there and after some inquiries on how to get to the Seventh Artillery Division (that was what Joe belonged to), I finally located him.

The reunion with Joe was great and he was much taller than I remembered him from the past. His face was much darker from all the field exercises, but he was as thin as ever. So I asked him: "Joe, is there enough food here for you to eat?" His answer was, "Yes, but the army drills are quite hard", and spending long hours on the field took everything from his body. Joe said that things were looking better and that the program of learning the maneuvers was near the end. He proceeded to tell me about life in the army. It sounded good from what I heard.

I asked Joe if there was a possibility for me to join the Polish army. His answer was really what I wanted to hear. He said that I was quite young yet for the army duties but to try to see what might happen. After a short visit, I had to head back home because as winter approached the days were getting shorter and I was worried that I might get caught in the dark hours on the road back. When I arrived home, I was greeted as though I was gone for a month or so. Even my little sister Stasia jumped up into my arms and hugged me.

It was nice to be back home with my family. Of course, I had to tell my family and others in the room how I explored the countryside and how I found Joe, and how we talked about everything and how happy I was to see him. I also announced my thinking about joining him in the near future, possibly after the new year. You see, on my way back I was thinking of my possibility of joining. After the new year, I would be in the fifteenth year of my life and most likely it would be easier to join—it sounds better to be fifteen years old than fourteen years old. So that was my decision. Then if I was gone, there would be one mouth less to feed and to worry about.

Life didn't get any easier but brought different adventures. One day, we had a native Uzbek visitor come to our school compound to visit us for the first time since we arrived here. He said that he was sorry he had not come and visited us sooner but that he was busy and it just wasn't the right time. He welcomed us to his community and at the same time invited all of us to come to his home to celebrate with his family because his son reached thirteen years of age and therefore, an adult in their religion. I am not sure, but it sounded like their religion was Muslim, but I had never heard of the Muslim religion. You see, by this time I hadn't looked at a book for two years or held a pencil. I had been too busy helping the families to survive and therefore, did not have any formal training. The other children also had been denied any formal education or direction to train their young minds.

The celebration in our friend's house was more than excellent. There was food on the tables everywhere, meat to eat, and all the other native dishes that we had never seen. It was all very good. The celebration lasted hours and hours. At some time in the afternoon, all of their party started their ethnic dances and singing in their native language. The whole celebration reminded us of our times back in Poland. It was one of the best experiences we had since we left our home in Poland.

Time came to end this wonderful party where we spent the time as well as getting acquainted with some people of our own age and we could relate our troubles to them. These people were very sympathetic towards us and they could relate with and sympathize with our needs. Soon some young boys could come over and just speak to us and try to learn who we really were. It was very difficult for them to believe that we were imprisoned in Siberian concentration camps, and especially that we were Polish citizens. At one point one boy, a little older than I, came into our home and asked my older sister Stefania and me to come to his home to share his lunch with his family. My sister Stasia was a very charming young lady. She was seven years old and she was as beautiful as a new rose which had just begun to open. This Uzbek young man most likely had never seen a blond beauty in his life, so he was very happy to entertain us in his family home.

There was some nice food, but what especially caught my attention was this baking stove (oven), heated with camel dung. This stove had a dome built over the hot coals. The young Uzbek man had some kneaded dough and made it look like tortillas. He would sling his tortilla into this dome and it would stick to the surface. After about a minute or so it would start to fall down and he would expertly catch it while it was falling. It was very clever the way he showed off. With a little butter over this tortilla/bread it was very delicious to eat. The man gave us quite a few pieces of this bread and we departed on our way home. (Incidentally, I refer to going "home"—well, "home" was where you came from last). Upon arrival at "home" our parents wanted to hear what we had done, where we had been and all other things that we did. It was very difficult to explain what we had seen, especially baking of the bread. How do you explain to someone who hasn't experienced seeing how this bread is baked? It is so simple and down to earth, but then you have to see it to understand the process.

After the initial wonderful welcome and reception, things got worse. The winter was taking hold of our environment; the colder it got, the worse it was for us. All of us youngsters and all able-bodied had to go out and scour the countryside for camel dung to heat our quarters. This turned out not to be an easy assignment, for it took us a long way out of our living perimeter to seek this precious fuel. But this had to be done. Some lucky days some of us would bring this dung, but in addition the very lucky ones would also being precious turtles to feast on. These turtles were the ones which had saved our lives in the past, as I previously mentioned. In addition, the government had subsidized our livelihood by rationing this food which they called "jugara" which was across between barley and rice. It was especially good when you cooked it and then added sour milk and it was very filling and nutritious.

The ration of "jugara" was about one-half a glass per person per day. It was difficult to survive, trying to work whenever possible, save whatever you could and trying to feed your family on this ration of jugara. This didn't get any better. Some people got sick and others tried, just tried to get along the best they could. Christmas time was bypassed because it was impossible to celebrate the birth of Jesus. It was time to reflect on what happened when Jesus Our Savior was born, but aside from that fact, the days went on as usual. The celebration of the New Year of 1943 didn't bring any jubilation either. What was there to celebrate? Another year of oppression and miseries. What would this New Year possibly bring to us? Many of our people in the midst of our school compound were sick from the cold, hunger and lack of food. There wasn't enough dung to heat the whole school compound, so we had to move closer together to conserve the heat and give up the privacy of our families. So things didn't change much, but we gained some intimacy and conservation of heat.

Well winter was from about the middle of January, 1943 until the time I planned to go and join the Polish Armed Forces under the command of General Wladyslaw Anders. He was the supreme Commander of the Second Polish Army. Under his direction and under the directives of the British Forces, we were to join forces to defeat the German Third Reich. Thus, after some talking to my parents, we agreed that it would be the best for all of us for me to join the Polish Army. I am not sure I happy about this decision since I was still a very young adolescent boy, but was streetwise. There was a good change I could make it on my own. Besides, I would be guided by the army discipline and would be regimented to do what I was told. Looking at my parents, at my older sister Stefania, and then there was my beautiful, little blond sister with her dark eyes looking at me with a very sad expression because I was going away. At some point, at this moment, I could change my mind and be resigned to stay home and roll with our chances. There was no rush to hurry my departure and I wanted to think this over—whether or not I was going or whether or not I needed to get more counsel from my father. After many questions, he simply said, "Franek, goes, try, enlist. It is not the end of the world. You will be there for awhile. If things don't go the way you like, you can always come back to us."

The next morning I cleaned myself, hugged my mother and she kissed me several times and blessed me and quietly said that she would pray for me. My father was not as emotional, but he too kissed me and blessed me. Sister Stefania, as well, kissed and hugged me for the longest time saying that it would be a long time until we will hug again, and with that she let go. My baby sister Stasia really didn't quite understand the emotions which were exchanged, but she jumped up and straddled her legs over my hips and began to cry. She knew that I was going away, but not sure if I could come back. I, too, was emotional and was crying. At one point, I turned toward the door and said goodbye to the rest of the people and they, too, cried for me. I waved to all as I departed, hoping that I would see them all soon.

I walked for awhile towards Kermine. I was not very scared to be alone in this strange land. Would I ever survive on my own? I convinced myself that this was the right decision and that I should get going. After about two or three hours, I finally got to Kermine. Since I had plenty of time I decided to scout around and find the Induction Center that Joe was talking about. I finally spotted the arrow and a sign in Polish, indicating that this place was indeed the right place. As I neared the entrance of a dirty dilapidated building, there was a nice looking soldier with a clean green uniform, with very shiny boots which reached his knees. He wore a wide belt with a strap of leather over one of his shoulders. He had some stars on his shoulder lapels and a beautiful cap with some stars on the front of it. I was very impressed with this man. I figured out that he must be some high officer and that he deserved a lot of respect.

As I approached him, he looked at me and reached for my hand saying, "You must be coming here to join the Polish Army?" He never gave me a chance to say a word. Instead he said that it was about time I showed up because the Army needed volunteers, young and old alike and said he was welcoming me to be one of them. He personally escorted me to the inside of the building and directed the person inside to issue me an appropriated dress uniform and all the other things that I would need in the immediate future. As I got all the clothing to dress properly, he came back and asked me to follow him. As we walked, he asked my name as well as my family name. I said, "Sir, my name is Franciszek Jasinski and that I am willing to do whatever I could do to aid Poland and to return there when it is time."

He stopped, turned to me and looked at me and studied my face for a little while, then said to me: "Franciszek, I will attach you to the building where the company kitchen is housed. You will stay there for awhile because you are too skinny and I want to fatten you up a bit. So stay there and help out whenever they ask you. Do you understand my orders?" I said, "Yes, sir" and with this he was gone.

At the company kitchen, another soldier told me that for now I would be assigned to the kitchen. He also asked me how I found the Captain and if he was my relative because he was so unusually kind to me. I couldn't answer him, because I could not react to his question. He said that soon we will serve meals and that someone will let me know when it will be served. I closed the door to my little room, got down on my knees, and said some prayers to thank God for what had just happened to me. It is incredible how fast things happened. How could it be that within a short time, I was lost and now am inside this small room. Am I asleep and dreaming or am I so sick that I am hallucinating and all this was just a dream?

Just then the door opened and someone said to me, "If you are hungry you better get your butt to the Mess Hall and get something to eat." I was not about to be asked twice to go eat. I immediately got up and followed this person to the Mess Hall. As I entered, the aroma of all this food was overwhelming. I knew that this meal was going to be good. I was still dressed in my old clothes. Soldiers were looking at me as a crasher—what was I doing in their midst? As I approached the line to receive my portion of food, the first server asked me how come I didn't have my eating utensils. I told him that I just arrived and no one issued any utensils to me. After some hassle, I was given eating utensils, a fork, spoon and knife. Now I know that I am one of the soldiers. The containers for food were quite large and, of course, as I went through the line the servers were spooning food into the containers. As I savored the delicious aroma of all this food, I said a prayer for the good fortune to be here and to thank God for His guidance.

I filled my belly with this good meal of meat, potatoes with gravy and other things including delicious bread. I got back to my room and retired for my first night as a free man. The next morning a big surprise awaited me. Breakfast was announced to all and the Mess Hall smelled glorious—eggs and toast and porridge! To wash all this down we had hot tea (Indian tea). It was the best breakfast I ever had. Good Lord what a life! Thank you Jesus for all your guidance to bring me here. After breakfast, I asked one officer if I could visit my brother who was in the same division as I was, for I hadn't seen him in some time. Permission was granted, but I had to shed my old clothing and dress as the soldier that I was. This was a big problem for me. The pants fitted ok around my waist, but were too long. The shirt was ok, but the sleeves were too long. My jacket was a little bit too loose. My shoes and socks were ok to some extent, but quite loose. What to do about my pants and shirt?

I decided that the cook whom I met the day before was nice to me, so I went to the kitchen. Lucky for me he was there, preparing the noon meal. As he spotted me entering the kitchen, he came to me and asked if I needed anything. Well, I showed him my dilemma with my clothing and explained to him that I got permission from an officer to visit my brother, Joseph, but the condition was that I had to wear my uniform. "My pants are too long, my shirt sleeves you could roll up some and it would be ok." He said, "Go and put them on. I'll see what can be done." When I returned he made me stand on a chair and measured something, and said, "Go back and bring these pants back and I will fix them for you." I don't know what he did but after a while he called me to try on my pants to see how they fit, and they fit just fine. I was so grateful to him for his help that I bowed down and thanked him for this favor.

When I was all dressed, I went out to visit my brother, Joe. It was just about noon when I got to his company. An officer stopped me and asked me why I was in that compound and what I was doing there. I told him my name and that I came to visit my brother for which I obtained permission to do so. He then allowed me to proceed. My brother was in his tent when I entered it, but he didn't expect to see me, especially dressed in the same uniform as he. Not realizing who I was, he kept talking to his companion. I said to him, "Juzek, don't you recognize me? I am your brother." He then stood up, grabbed me, lifted me and hugged me, saying, "I knew you would join me, my little brother." He then asked me to go out so we could talk about my past experiences. After I told him the story of how I met the officer with stars on his cap and shiny boots that reached his knees, and all the other details such as the Mess Hall and kitchen, food and my uniform experiences. He said, "Franek, you are fantastically creative and lucky. Whatever you do, don't abuse your privileges that have been given to you. Be humble and listen and don't talk too much."

Then Joseph suggested that we have lunch together. We went to the Mess Hall where I lived. I introduced him to my friend, the cook, who said to me that they know each other and he was glad to know that we were brothers. After lunch, I showed Joe where my room was located. He was surprised that it was as I told him. He said he was very proud of me, that I was probably very lucky and resourceful, and it was fine with him, but he had to get back to his company. As I lay down on my cot, I was tired from all this eating so I quickly fell asleep. After awhile, I woke up and looked out my window to see what was happening outside. At one point, I observed that two soldiers were carrying something on their shoulders which looked like a casket. I could not imagine what they could carry in it. I watched for a while, wondering what was happening around here to cause this situation.

Well, the only one who knows everything was my friend, the cook Piotr (Peter). So I said "Pan Piotr (mister), I have seen two soldiers carrying a casket. Can you tell me what is going on?" He had gotten to know me quite well by now and I think he adopted me and was very willing to help me. He explained that many soldiers who enlisted in the Army were very sick people and this sickness from which they are dying is called "typhus", for which there is no cure. So many soldiers die and are buried in common graves. "Go and see for yourself. See what this country has done to our citizens. Don't let what you see there make you sick. But when the time comes, tell the world about this." Mr. Piotr became my mentor. I could tell him everything as I could tell my own father. He understood my feelings and emotions.

This same afternoon, I decided to go outside to see for myself where the soldiers were carrying the caskets. As I followed them to their destination, about two blocks from where my quarters were, I came closer to discovering something which I am not competent to explain. It was a horrible sight. God help me to write this episode to be truthful in telling the story of what I witnessed. As I looked at it, there was an open cavern with bodies placed side by side in narrow rows for about fifty feet. The soldiers poured lime liquid over them. The next layer was laid in the same way but laid in the opposite way, where the lower layer were heads, the upper layer of corpses were legs and the layers alternate until it reached about six or seven layers. Then this common grave was covered with dirt. There are many of these graves in this common cemetery because of the lack of food for our Polish people.

I came back to my room and visited my friend Pan Piotr. I asked him how it was possible that so many soldiers died. I said, "yes, he must have been appointed by God to save me." To this Mr. Piotr asked if he was one of my relatives or something to that order. I assured him that I had never seen this man before. That ended the subject. I asked if I could talk to him again. Mr. Piotr said simply, "yes". I said to him that I observed during our meals in his kitchen that lots of food was not eaten. His reply was, "yes". So

I asked him if it was possible to save all the uneaten bread so I could give it to my family when and if they come to visit me and my brother Joe so they could take it with them and feed themselves and the rest of the people who live with them. He promised me that he would do it and with that answer he said, "Dobranoc Franek" (Goodnight Frank) and left.

I couldn't rest for awhile, the day was full of different feelings which I had a hard time to deal with. After a few days passed, I was sitting on my bed looking out and wondering if someone from my family would come to visit me. My stomach was full, I had a comfortable bed to sleep in and I was warmly dressed, but I was lonely. I missed Stasia, Stefania and my parents, as well as the rest of the people in that school house. I could never have envisioned that the time would come when I would be alone at about fifteen years of age. In Poland, in school and at home, I would read in books that children had always lived in their parents' home under their supervision, so why is it so different with me? Who am I supposed to blame for this situation? As the evening approached and more caskets were carried to the common grave, I decided to go to bed and get a good night's sleep. I was tired as never before.

Hello morning! As I awakened, I knelt by my bed and said my morning prayers.

I got dressed and went out to the kitchen for breakfast; same old powdered eggs, toast and tea from India. Since I could eat all I wanted, I filled myself until I was content. As I was walking out of the Mess Hall, Mr. Piotr called me and said, "Franek, remember the leftover bread you asked me to save for you?" I answered, "Yes, I remember." He said, "I have a small sack that you could have." I came to him and gave him a hug. As tears were running down my cheeks I said, "Thank you Mr. Piotr and God bless you." When I reached my room I placed the sack of bread in my backpack for safe keeping, that no one would suspect what was in it and placed it under my bed.

Again I went out to visit my brother Joe. When I reached his Company, I learned they were out on some kind of maneuvers and didn't know when they would return. Disappointed, I returned to my room. It turned out that I slept through our lunch time. Oh well, I was not that hungry anyway. I can wait until dinner time for my next meal. As I looked out of my window, I spotted a woman far away from where I was. She looked and walked like my mother. Could this woman be my mother? I ran out of my room and towards her thinking if she wasn't my mother, I would run past her, not to embarrass myself. The closer I came to her; I could see her face and her sad look. I yelled at her, "Mama, I'm alright. Look at me, it's your son, Franek!" I suppose that she didn't recognize me for I was dressed in uniform and probably gained two or three kilos (four to eight lbs) since I left home. She then put down the basket she was carrying on her arm and ran toward me.

I don't have the words to tell about the feelings I had at this meeting. Joy and tears and mother's affection toward me were beyond explanation or narration. After awhile I said to her, "Mama, please come with me as I'd like to show you where I live, eat and sleep." As we reached where I stayed, she was very surprised that the Army took this kind of care of her son. "Franek, she said, "I always knew you were a lucky boy from the time of your birth. You were always very resourceful and I had no worry about your well being." I told her everything, from my departure from the school building, traveling to Kermine, the talk to that wonderful officer who helped my induction into the Army and most of all, about Pan Piotr. I also told her about visits to brother Joe.

As we sat on my bed she asked me if I was hungry. My answer was negative. I asked "Mama, what have you in your basket?" She said, "Not too much, but I have two hard-boiled eggs and three breads (pancakes). I asked your father if he knew what might have happened to you, but since we had other problems, I didn't have time to come and see you." At this I said, "Mama, you better start eating what you have, and I can go to the kitchen and see what I can come up with." As I entered the kitchen, Pan Piotr spotted me and said, "Oh it's you, Franek. You missed lunch. You must be hungry." I said I wasn't but that my mother came to see me, and I wondered if I could get her some tea or coffee. He told me to go back to my room and that he would bring something for her to eat. It wasn't too long before Pan Piotr brought her a platter full of sandwiches, some to eat here and some to take home. He said his goodbyes and left us alone.

At some point, I pulled out my backpack from under my bed and pulled out the sack of dry bread. I said "Look Mama, the other day Pan Piotr gave me this sack of bread because I asked him for it. Please take it home with you and share it." I also told her that I heard some rumors that there will be an exodus for Polish soldiers from Russia to Persia across the Caspian Sea. She confirmed that she also heard some tales about the same thing. She got up from my cot and said she should be on her way home before it gets too dark to walk home. Before she left me, we kissed and hugged each other. She left and turned back to throw a kiss to me and went on her way. The next day I went to see my brother, Joe, to tell him that mother was in the camp but time didn't permit her to visit him, but she told me that next time she would visit him first because she was confident that I would be all right here.

Indeed I was ok and was not short of any comforts. I ate good, had a good cot to rest on and I gained some weight and I wasn't too far from Joe, so I visited him quite often. Joe was always tired and didn't look good. I asked him on various occasions if he was sick or something like that. He always replied that he was alright and I shouldn't worry about him. What bothered me the most was the soldiers with the stretchers going back and forth, carrying dead soldiers to that common grave yard. One morning I decided to follow the soldiers carrying the deceased ones. On arrival at the cemetery I remembered from the past visit, I saw a new row was started. There must have been about six rows that were covered with dirt. I can't say how many dead soldiers were in one row, but I could estimate that there were at least five hundred. Having seen them before and seeing them now, there were about six bodies on top of one another in long rows. I was quite moved by this experience so I went back to my room. This was about the first of February, 1943. The weather was quite cold, but not as cold as we experienced in the north of Russia (Siberia); still we had to dress warmly to stay comfortable.

One day, about midday, we were ordered to file in to receive some new orders and directives. It was a scary day for me, for this was something new. I didn't know what to expect. We lined up in different companies and stood in silence waiting for something to happen. Who would come before the gathered soldiers, but the officer who helped me to join the Polish Army. I was so happy to see him again. If I could have, I would have run to him to say, "Thank you Mr. Officer for your help, you saved my life." But I stood in my place and waited for his speech. He stated that time has come for us to depart this place; our destination would be Persia (Iran), which is what it was called at that time. We would travel by train to Krasnovosk, which is a seaport on the eastern side of the Caspian Sea. We would board ships of various sizes. We would arrive at the Port of Pahlevi in Persia. From there we would travel by trucks to Teheran. All this would take about three weeks' time.

He indicated that all of us would be notified by our Company officers who would be on the first assignment to go and who would be assigned to consecutive departures. Would I be lucky to be on the first assignment? Maybe. But, just in case this would happen I went to see Joe and learn his impression of the whole thing . . . . what we had heard today. As he envisioned the situation, his observation was simple. You are obliged to follow orders and what happens is you have no way out, you just have to obey them. I guess that wisdom comes with age and I had to listen to him because he was much smarter than I was. When I returned to my quarters I rested awhile, then I decided to go and see Pan Piotr in the kitchen and ask him what he knew about all these new developments. He said, "Franek, I know for a fact that you would be on the first transport out of here." He said, "I hope your mother will come to visit you and say goodbye. Besides, I have some dry bread for her." I thanked him for his warm words to me and also for saving some bread for my family. The next morning we were told that the train will come into our railroad station of Kermine and all those notified would have to report to the station at six a.m. the next morning. This order was very firm. There would be no exceptions.

CHAPTER III

On the eve of our exodus from Russian into Persia (Iran) it was a good time to retire early for the night because morning would come quickly. Waking time probably would be about 3:00 a.m. Can you imagine going to sleep knowing that the next morning would take you to freedom . . . . from this tyranny, from this place of hunger, from poverty, from oppression and from death? And death awaits all who live in this place. Hunger and death know no mercy nor nationality nor gender. It takes all equally. It was hard to fall asleep; as young as I was at that time, I was wondering how I would ever get to see my family again. I was all alone in this room and I felt abandoned. I believe I cried myself to sleep. The morning came quickly and it became very noisy outside even before the trumpeter blew his morning reveille.

The breakfast at the mess hall was ready and there was no order who was to eat first. We ate first-come, first-served. My friend whom I became to love as a brother, spotted me and came to say goodbye and wished me all the best. He gave me a big hug and promised that if he sees my mother he would give her all the bread that he would save for her. He said that she would come to this place for she would not know that I would no longer be here. I said my goodbyes to my friend, Mr. Piotr and left the Mess Hall.

The train waited for us on the main tracks. As the soldiers were directed to different railcars, the crowd became smaller as the train filled up. The time came for me to get on the train. I was surprised, no end, to see there were benches along either side of the narrow aisle. I had never seen this kind of railcar. I had no occasion to travel on the train in Poland so this was my first experience to even see this sort of transportation. My previous travel was in boxcars with a small side window and a sliding door on either side, with wooden bunk beds built into the boxcars. This train ride will be luxury.

It was getting lighter in the morning and the train was almost filled up with our soldiers. I sat in my space next to a person who was much older than I who introduced himself, and so did I in return. We engaged in small conversation and I asked him what he estimated to be the total number of occupants in this train. He pondered awhile and said, "Well, Franek, I don't rightly know., but there are an awful lot of us exiting this torturous place." He said after a while that if only one of us could come out of Russia this would be a blessing. I pondered his wisdom and answered that I was happy to sit beside him. What a wonder and smart man he must have been. The train whistle blew to announce its departure. In a very few minutes the clanking sound of the train cars became obvious that it started to roll. At this moment, the occupants of the entire train started to shout with joy and started to sing in Polish National Anthem, "Jeszcze Polska Niezginela puki my zyjemy" and so on. Translated this means, "Poland will never perish while we are alive." It was a little after six o'clock in the morning.

As we traveled through desert-like terrain, there weren't any sights to admire, we were traveling from Kermine to our destination of Krasnovodsk, which is on the eastern side of the Caspian Sea—to be exact, the southeastern side in Turkmenistan. About noon, some soldiers came with baskets to distribute sandwiches (kanapki), mostly of deviled eggs and something else, possibly sausage? What a wonderful thing it is to ride the train and eat these wonderful sandwiches! This Polish Army is something else. It showed you what civilized people can do to make your lives precious. The terrain didn't change too much, but each minute we were getting closer to freedom, so no one was complaining. Our train ride was estimated to be about eight to nine hours. We were to reach Krasnovosk at three or four o'clock in the afternoon. The hours passed with the train making its clipping sound on the tracks and we finally reached our destination. Where is this city of Krasnovosk for we stopped in the middle of nowhere?

As we disembarked to gather together we found ourselves on white sand. Our Commanders lined us up in marching order. We proceeded to go to our camp to stay overnight before we boarded boats out of this dead camp and miseries. We marched about one-fourth mile to a makeshift transfer camp. Now I could see where the transportation of this vast Polish Army had many stages of planning . . . . and this was one of them. How wonderful to be part of this experience. We occupied tents that housed eight Battalions. No one took time to get comfortable. The next morning we were to board the boats or ships to cross over the Caspian Sea to the south.

The next morning I remember we had quite a different breakfast. It was white cooked rice and fish. What in heaven is rice and fish? Rice was not known in the rural areas of Poland. Fish, well everyone eats fish from the rivers or lakes. But this fish was different and the chunks of it were large and white as snow. Was the meal tasty? To some soldiers it was very different than what they were used to. To others it was quite disgusting, but food is food and you eat what is given to you. After this early morning breakfast we formed our marching columns and started toward the port of Krasnovosk. We marched for about two hours. The road to the port was sandy and for this reason it was difficult to walk on and keep up the pace. As we got close to the seashore we could see some vessels. Shortly, we were directed to one quite large ship and we proceeded to embark. We had a lot of people to board, and we wondered if there was enough room for all of us. We forgot that we had good people in charge of this procedure and their calculations turned out to be correct. Soon after we were all secured, the ship was untied from the dock, the biggest "hurrahs" and screaming could be heard for long distances. We were on our way out of Russia to freedom.

The weather was truly extra nice and all was well. The voyage would take us from Krasnovosk to the Port of Pahlevi, Persia (Iran). After about eight to ten hours we were proceeding close to the eastern coastline, but at some point we left the coastline to go southwest. The weather in this part of the lake took a turn for the worst. The ship started to sway from side to side as well as from front to rear. It actually resembled a toy boat in the bathtub. All of us started to get sick sour stomachs. As for me, I had never been on any kind of boat and I had never seen a big ship. As for the large body of water, I never envisioned that there could be so much water in one place. I happened to be on the top deck when this all was happening. I was getting sicker and sicker, emptying my stomach until I was getting dizzy. There was only so much rice and fish for me to expel. The weather was getting worse by the hour. The boat swayed to one side. I fell down and started to roll toward the side of the ship.

One of the soldiers grabbed me, took off his belt, and tied me to some pipe. This way he secured me from further rolling around. As I lay there partly conscious I didn't realize how much trouble I was in and how close I came to continue rolling with the ship. As the ship moved close to the shores of Persia, the weather changed and the sun came out. Our boat stabilized and all seemed to pass. I realized at some point that I was still tied to the pipe. What happened to me? Well, the soldier who had taken such good care of me was not a stranger. He said to me, "Franek, remember I saved your life." He asked if I knew who he was. I said, "Yes, you're Bronek Bachrynowski and you lived in our house with your new wife!" Well, this man Bronek and his family lived across the street from us. When he got married there was not enough room in his family home, so my parents rented him one bedroom for a short time to give this new couple a chance to get started. This happened about a month before World War II started. I asked him why he said to me, "Remember what I have done to save your life?" He said that he had repaid the deed that he owed to my family for letting them stay with us. He then departed and I never saw him again.

Realizing that the ship stopped moving although we were some distance from shore, everyone was asking why? Soon the announcement came over the PA system telling us that this ship is too large and the water too shallow for the large ship to enter the port of Pahlevi so we had to wait for the smaller boats to come to take us into the port. After some time, we transferred to the smaller boats and reached Pahlevi. As we disembarked we found ourselves free at last; free of that terrible oppression and at the start of a new life.

The first incident we had was very strange. There were some Polish people waiting for us on the beach. As we got farther way from the beach our people told us to undress completely; they confiscated our under garments; they shaved our heads and underarms (not mine, because I hadn't grown any underarm hair yet). They gave us fresh underwear, socks, tee-shirts, and had us go to the showers to cleanse us of any lice or other bugs which we may have had on us. We did save our army uniforms. As we came through this cleaning process we were escorted to newly erected tents and then taken to the Mess Hall for our supper. This day was the longest day in my life and the most memorable. After the meal we were dismissed for the night. The next morning was like a Sunday. There was no need to get up as all of us were too tired so were given some needed rest.

Our Commanding Officers got us all together to inform us of the procedures we would have to adopt. First of all we would start leaving this camp in two days. The British Command, along with the Polish Command, made the decision to hire local civilian trucks and drivers because the roads from Pahlevi to the capital city of Teheran, were very difficult to drive on. The roads were very hilly and curvy. You had to be a very experienced driver to drive one of those trucks with these difficulties.

Our Commanders assigned two platoons, about twenty-two soldiers, to a truck. The trucks were flatbeds with side and rear gates. They were open trucks, with no canopy to protect us from the sun during daytime travel and it took us a few days.

Many, including me were not only carsick but I was also sick from the curvy road, and the fumes from the exhaust pipe. "God help me," I prayed, "this won't last too long I know, but I am very weak and sick from both the boat ride and this truck ride. Please God, save me for I am too young to die." Not only was I sick, I was also very hungry but could not eat. At some stops we finally were served some hot tea, which was helpful. After a couple of days the drive over the mountain ridges ended and the road was much better and the curves less severe. At times we would stop and were served some sandwiches, oranges and sodas. The sodas were a real treat. Anyway, we were in better spirits.

From the start of our departure from Pahlevi it probably took about five days to reach Teheran. Our column of trucks numbered approximately fifty. We were taken to abandoned airport hangers which were very large and made of sheet metal. As we unloaded, each Company was assigned a specific space in a hanger. We made ourselves as comfortable as we could and retired for the night. The next few days our Company leaders started to interview each of us to separate us into certain groups. It turned out they wanted to separate young combat-able soldiers like me from other young people who were to be sent to school. This was done very systematically. To my surprise there were a lot of young boys among the population of the Polish Army. After the separation, the combat soldiers went out and left the young boys behind. The same thing happened every week or so. Before we realized it, the young boys' population had grown rapidly.

This created some chaos with what to do with these youngsters. So we were introduced to teachers who took charge of us, assigned each of us to various groups by age and ability, so we could be assigned to respective classes. One would have to realize that we missed two years of school while in Russia. We had better study hard to be able to catch up with our normal age group. As the weeks went by, hundreds of young boys came into our group. All of us had the same tales to tell. It was just before Easter, 1943. We had a few priests who encouraged us to prepare ourselves to go to confession and attend Sunday Masses. Since none of us attended any church activities, a priest started to give us some instruction to prepare us not only for confession but also for Confirmation, for none of us were confirmed in the Catholic religion. This was a big deal in our lives. I personally needed guidance on how to conduct myself during Holy Mass on Sundays and in general get acquainted with my religion which was abandoned during my stay in Siberia and other places in Russia.

Of course, my mother always listened to our prayers such as the Our Father and Hail Mary, but that was all she was able to attend to since she had to be more concerned with our survival. As the weeks went by, it seemed that we learned quite a lot about religion, but did we fully know what it was all about? I don't think so. We were informed by our priest that confession would be heard by many priests on the Saturday before Palm Sunday. Well, the week before Easter came confession. There in the open air in the city of Teheran, Persia, we were marched from the airplane hangers where we lived. We found many priests, maybe twenty to thirty, sitting on chairs, prepared to hear the confessions of the participants. As the line formed before each priest, I happened to be at the end of our company. As always, I was quite anxious to get things done promptly. I started to look for the shortest line. I finally spotted one line to a priest which was quite short compared to the others. As the line got close to the confessor, I noticed that this priest had a General Rank on his army uniform. I didn't know the significance of his rank, but it got me thinking about the event. As I knelt on the desert sand, I was prompted to say my confession in the proper order. I spent quite a long time with him confessing about stealing food, stealing other things and other sins that I committed during my two years of not attending Mass or confession. I was then given absolution for all my sins and he dismissed me after giving me penance. I walked away a renewed and happy young man because all was forgiven and I came out clean. It was such a wonderful feeling.

The next day, Palm Sunday, all the boys received Holy Communion. What a wonderful feeling it was to reunite ourselves with Our Lord. As we exchanged our experiences about our confession we all had different views to express; but as it turned out, we all had about the same outlook. During Holy week, the week before Easter, we were preparing for our Confirmation. It included marching in the open air because the Holy Mass took place on the desert floor, where there were a lot of Companies assembled to attend the Easter celebration. It was quite hot that Sunday morning. It took a long time to distribute communion. It was quite tiring but all went well.

This picture was taken in late 1943. As you can see, my Father was volunteering to join the Polish Army. He was in pretty Poor health so he was not able to join and civilians were not Called to leave Russia during the first exit. But because I left Russia on the first exit as did my brother Joe, they allowed him to join. When he arrived in Tehran (Persia) Iran, the Polish Army excluded him from serving.

After the Holy Mass was over, the troops were dismissed. All us young boys were escorted to the hangers where we formed single lines about three to four feet apart, about fifty boys in each line and there were many lines. After the short ceremonies, the priest, whom I recognized as my Confessor, had presided over the ceremony. It turned out he was the Polish Army Chaplain, Bishop Gawlina. As he walked before us, behind us were civilian men and women as our sponsors. We were issued nametags with our new Confirmation name. I chose the name of Jan, which was my father's name; I wanted to honor my father by taking his name as my Confirmation name. I was very unhappy that my parents were not with me to witness my celebration. My brother and sisters were absent also and I missed them very much. It has been months since I had seen them, and I have no idea when I will see them again, if ever.

After staying in Teheran for another week or so we had orders to prepare for transportation to the country called Palestine. The time came to move on to another new destination. Remember the year is 1943, all of us are still not in good health, suffering from malnutrition, homeless and in these uniforms. By all means we were abandoned or, more exactly, separated from our parents in our adolescent lives when we needed them most. For it is not natural to be separated from your parents in your young lives.

As we started our journey southwest through the hot desert it wasn't easy travel. We passed the Lake of Ahwas in Persia, then entered Iraq. Moving west we crossed a large river called the Tigris, stopping en route to erect tents for camping overnight. At the end of our caravan, trucks carried all the provisions to support our travels. The land of Persia and Iraq were about the same in color and texture, but when we entered Trans-Jordan (Jordan today) the desert changed from tan to black. Along the side of the road were big black stones, at some times resembling large black plates. The time was late April or early May. The weather was hot, too hot to travel in the open trucks carrying about twenty-five young boys. The conditions were very primitive, and the hardship at times was almost unbearable. We had no other choice in the matter. There was ample water to drink and the food was good. It took a couple of days to cross Trans-Jordan to get to Palestine.

Palestine is the land of the birth of Our Lord, Jesus. All we could talk about was that we were going to the Holy Land to see the birth place of the child Jesus in Nazareth together with all other holy places. I pondered all these new events and the realization that this young boy who was born in the small place of Kalush, Poland, was visiting all these places which were unknown to him. Was I lucky when I was born and what has happened to me because of World War II? Or was it predestined that I should experience what is happening to me? As we traveled through Trans-Jordan, then Lebanon, we entered Palestine. We established the main camp in the region of Haifa (Palestine), called Israel today. We stayed there for some time. The Polish Army Headquarters assumed responsibility for placing us young boys in the proper schools according to our abilities and qualities.

About 400 boys were separated and sent to different schools according to their scholastic abilities and other qualifications. When it came to me as to what I was able to be schooled in, I wanted to become either a mechanical or electrical engineer or both. Well, I encountered some difficulty. The assertion was this: I was told, "you are a farmer's son and maybe agriculture education would be more suitable for you." I would not have any of their suggestions. I wanted to study what I had imagined that I would grow up to be. In the past, I was reading some books about the glorious life that a famous engineer had and wanted the same kind of life. I finally succeeded and was placed in that kind of school. It had taken some time to erect the school, to staff it with competent teachers, and to supply the proper books. For this training was very new to the Polish Army as well as the Ministry of Education.

As we stayed close by the port city of Haifa awaiting further dispatch orders of assignments, we had a little time to ourselves. I took this opportunity to look for my brother, Joseph. Every day new transports arrived in the camps near us so it gave me the opportunity to go there to find my brother. There were no signs that his division was coming soon. As naive as I was, I didn't take "no" for an answer. I would go directly to the new commanders to inquire if the Seventh Division of the Army from Kermine had arrived yet and the answer was always negative. I became an Army nuisance; they all knew the name of Juzef Jasinski. I was a pest, but how else could I find my brother? The time in my life was progressing to the point where I was about to depart somewhere; I was waiting for my assignment to some school somewhere. As the days passed I was about on my last search for Juzef. As I came to the camp where newly arrived soldiers came in, I went to the place where the newcomers were registered and inquired if the name of my brother appeared on the roster.

After a while, I was told that the name of my brother was indeed on the current list and which tent I could find him. They gave me someone to lead me to the tent where he should be. Well, I entered the tent where I was to find Juzef. I could not see him so I expected he went out for some reason. I sort of panicked by not seeing him. I was getting very frustrated and asked again if I could find out if Juzef Jasinski was located in this tent. One soldier stood up and said he was Juzef. As I looked at him I knew he was an imposter; he was not my brother. As I went toward him, he embraced me and said, "I know who you are." In the meantime as he was holding me to his breast I started yelling at him and punching him, saying that he was an imposter and asking how he could impersonate my brother.

I was hurt that I didn't find him to be my brother. As he tried to quiet me down, he explained that he was my cousin on my father's side and that he knew all about me. He pleaded with me to calm down and listen to him. He said, "I know your brother from Kermine because we were in the same division, but he was left behind to close down the camps that the soldiers left." He added that my parents also left Russia but he didn't know any more details. Disenchanted from my expedition of looking for my brother, I left their camp for my own quarters. As I was going to my quarters I was very worried that I may never see my family again.

In the next few days, we had good news from our headquarters saying that we would be transported to different holy cities as part of our curriculum to learn about our religion and past histories. We traveled from Haifa, our post, to Nazareth, Bethlehem, Jerusalem,

Tel Aviv, Jaffa and other holy places, stopping at every point to learn all about them. The Dead Sea was unimaginable; the water was heavy with salt. It was amazing to observe how salt was clinging to the paperclips. It was the most holy way to walk the same way Jesus was walking with His cross on His shoulders. The alley was narrow and leading up the Hill (Golgatha). I was amazed at how Jesus could endure this hardship. Being as young as I was, I couldn't comprehend all the implications of Jesus' crucifixion. All I could understand was that he was crucified.

As I looked back, I compared His death with the deaths of so many soldiers in Kermine who were carried out to a common grave. Was Jesus one among the soldiers that were buried there? As we departed Jerusalem toward Haifa where we had our camp, I was reflecting on my family's conditions and the situation they were in. As we arrived in Haifa there was no news about our assignment. It was quite disturbing to me because the time was wasting for my studies. Well, I could do nothing about it.

In the meantime, I had located my cousins Frank and Joe Leszczynski, as well as my godmother, Paulina Leszczynski, who welcomed me as would my own mother. Paulina joined the Polish Army as a nurse. For that reason, she was allowed to leave Russia as one of the Polish Forces civilians. My godmother and her sons, Frank and Joseph and I went to Nazareth. Nazareth is located in a small valley. On one side of the hill there was a large church built there; it was quite large and in its towers were many carillon bells. What impressed me was the sound of these bells at noon when they played the melody of Ave Maria. I believe that this was the most glorious sound I have ever heard. To add to this experience we discovered that on the other side of this valley was a school for young girls called Junaczki (or young girls attached to the Polish Army). Sort of the same as Waves in the British Army. Wow, there were some girls the same age as we were. We did have lunch and dinner in their quarters' commissary. Who was the most intrigued . . . . all of us were lucky to meet each other, for we were lost to our generation.

It was not all play and exploration of Palestine. While in camp we participated in maneuvers, shooting rifles and always seeking new arrivals of the soldiers coming in from the Soviet Union. Because we were stationed close to the City of Haifa, all convoys were coming our way. For this reason, I still was looking for my brother and learning what was happening to our family. Later we received information from the school board about the location of the school we were about to be sent to. As it turned out, some boys were allotted to cadet schools to study army regimentation, others to some other curriculum. I was assigned, to my liking, to engineering school. How gratifying it was to be able to study this enormous endeavor. To learn how metals can be produced, how gold is different from lead and how electrical power is produced and then consumed. It was like a fairy tale.

As the orders arrived, we were all summoned to attend certain quarters to obtain further instruction. So, as it turned out, I had orders to go to Egypt to attend school in Tel el Cabir which is close to Cairo, the capital city of Egypt. Our closest small city was Ismalia, located next to the Suez Canal. In all, there were about 200 boys to attend this school. As we arrived at this site in the desert, the perimeter of which was an empty sand-colored desert. We should have to transform this place into something resembling a school environment. We disembarked from the train and some British soldiers transported us to our place, where there were many tents and sleeping cots, as well as kitchen and cooking supplies plus temporary lavatories. With the instructors to supervise, we did a good job of erecting tents, with cots into comfortable living quarters.

These so-called dormitories were here to provide us with quality living conditions as well as a quality school environment. All of us were full of enthusiasm to get this all done quickly. In the next few days the tents were erected in straight lines and looked good. There were about thirty tents erected in a square, leaving the center for army drill activities. For a change everything was going my way. I got to attend the school I wanted and finally come to a place where I could settle down and get to work on my future. All the time I spent in Palestine, which was some time, I could not forget about my past, especially my beautiful sisters, my parents and my brother Joe. It had been about six months or so since I left Kermine and the last time I saw my family. It got quite lonely without them.

I often thought about all of them and I deserted my own family just to better myself. For that I blamed myself, if I had stayed with my parents and sisters, I would probably have been of some good to them. Instead I chose to leave them in that awful place. Still, there was nothing I could do now but to better myself and become somebody, not only for myself, but for all the family, so they could be proud of me. The classes started as soon as the books and other equipment arrived, which was almost immediately.

I remember as though it was yesterday that the chaplain arrived and we had open Mass in our square between the tents. As the Holy Eucharist was distributed we all were very emotional about this time. As the Mass ended, the priest blessed us and wished all of us a fruitful time in our school endeavors. What a wonderful way to restart the learning process. As the school days went by, I liked what I was learning and I was hungry for more learning. It was fun to listen, to read, to write and above all to attend classes. Was I a good student? I would say that I was very good. After the classes, I would go to the school library and take out books to read, some old Polish classics, some poetry books, and I would go and sit outside by my tent, lean back against the wall of the tent and spend hours reading. It didn't matter what book I would grab to read as long as it would activate my brain, because I missed more than two years without having anything to read and learn. As my studies proceeded, I was maturing not only scholastically and emotionally, but also growing up and getting some meat on my bones and life was good. I really enjoyed school and was happy to be there.

Occasionally some of us were split into three different groups or companies. Each company had about seventy pupils and each company had ten tents. Each tent had seven pupils. The seventh one was in charge of his tent. It was up to him to see to it that all was well inside and that order was kept such as night curfew, quietness and obedience. Such was the order of our lives.

On some occasions one or more of our schools would venture outside of our quarters and be driven by trucks to different cities such as Cairo, Alexandra, Carnak, Luxor and other places. The first such tour took us to Cairo, the capital city of Egypt. Cairo was a big city. On the west side of this city we could not fail to see the three giant pyramids of Giza, as well as the Sphinx. Wow, what a surprise to be able to see those wonders . . . . these huge buildings of large stones piled up one on top of another. Spectacular! What a colossal experience to stand beside them and wonder how the Egyptian Pharaohs were able to build them some five thousand years ago.

One cannot really see the wonders of this work until you step back from about one hundred to two hundred yards to observe the heights and the size of these pyramids. As we went to see the Sphinx, it was a most unusual sight; part lion and part human, the head of this monument was huge. Some fifty years ago one could go close to all these artifacts and touch or climb on them. With box cameras we would take pictures to remind us that we indeed were there to observe these marvels. When we returned to our camp, we were asked to write essays about our trip and to evaluate our impressions and emotions about the past civilization of Egypt. All went well. How can one complain about our trip to Cairo to see these remarkable sights? Still it was nice to come back to school where the mind gets more training.

As weeks went by, we got accustomed to the regimentation of the school curriculum and became accustomed to daily chores of school living. It was fun because everyone was at about the same level of education and we started to compete to see who would excel in our grades. As the days went along we still had Holy Mass every Sunday offered by the Army-appointed priest, with Confession heard before Mass. It became a ritual for daily and weekly living. At some time during this period we learned that we would be take to the Port of Alexandra. Well, this would be a highlight. Every one of us looked at the map of Egypt to learn where exactly the Port of Alexandria was located. When the time came, we took the train from Cairo and in a few hours arrived in the port which housed enormous camps.

There were Australian, Canadian, Indian (English Empire) soldiers and many more. We learned some English from our overnight stay. In the early morning, we were treated to the seashore of the Mediterranean Sea, to swim and enjoy the white beaches. Is this the life or what? As the day progressed, we met other young people, boys and girls alike. Well, this created different problems for us as girls were present among us at the beach. As for me, I don't remember seeing a girl in a bathing suit before. What does it mean to see one? It turned out they were English-family girls and they could not speak Polish.

What a shame that we could not communicate with them. After our evening meal, we asked our teachers to teach us some English. This created some big problems. The Polish Army Academy School, which was a pilot program overseas, began to tackle this problem. There was one English teacher of Polish origin who was appointed to our school to teach us some simple, basic English phrases, such as "Good Morning," "How do you do?", "May I help you?", "Thank you", and so on. When we returned to our camp in Tel el Cabir we started this new language—English—so what? Who knows when we could use this language? The sooner the war ends, the sooner we will go back to Poland. Who needs this English language?

As things went along, the days were more and more complicated. We passed through almost one year of this school year and were we better off at this point in time than we were a year ago? I would definitely say "yes!" I, for one, gained knowledge of life, observing such things as pyramids, and the Port of Alexandria. What a way to go. Here I am from the suburbs of Kalush in Poland to Alexandria, Egypt, on the shore of the Mediterranean. This is almost the scripture of Jesus coming in this world to redeem His people. Has he failed in His conquest? I say he didn't. Nor will we fail in our conquest to free Poland from its oppressors, such as Germany and the Soviet Union.

History proves our belief and history repeats itself as a rule. While attending school in this lovely environment, I got nice meals, hot or cold and slept in a quiet environment with a nice bunch of guys. The teachers were very knowledgeable and life could not be any better. Gone are the days of hunger and shivers of coldness. Every so often we took train rides to far away places, like Luxor, to explore the tombs of the Pharaohs (Kings of Egypt). As we traveled on the train along the River Nile, it was breath taking to see an oasis in the shadows of the river, small villages and hamlets nestled along its banks; people cultivating its grounds and harvesting. These people worked hard, but they looked happy and not shabbily dressed. The Egyptian people looked quite dignified.

As we arrived at the cemetery city of Luxor—well, this is a story by itself. There is a huge obelisk, reaching eighty to one hundred feet in height, measuring about eight feet square at its base—huge beyond imagination. There were rows of lions twice the size of live ones leading to a huge temple—about forty lions in each row. Huge temple pillars and some collapsed walls were giving testament to the huge successes of the past Egyptian civilization. We visited some Pharaohs' graves carved in symmetrical, straight columns fashioned and smooth as today's sheetrock walls. Deep inside these mountain rock caverns were kings' quarters, where he was laid to rest. The hallways and the room were elegantly painted with graphic caricatures to proclaim the life of their Pharaoh, Kings and Gods. We visited many fascinating graves and sights. We learned that we were not as smart today as they were some five thousand years ago.

We usually stayed on an outing for three or four days at a time. This gave us, the young boys, a chance to explore the different aspects of life. This was part of our curriculum. When we returned to our camp/campus in Tel el Cabir, it was to return to hit the books. Among other things we had to write about our excursions to those sights and what the experience taught us. The days of learning were not unpleasant. I must have read a dozen books, some novels, some past history and some military tactic books pertaining to the military history of Poland.

But I was grieving because I had no news about my family. Frankly I was beginning to believe that I would never see them again. The longer I stayed away from them, the more I felt isolated. Who knows what happened to my father, whom I left in poor health, or my mother, who was so worried about how to protect her children, or my sister Stasia with her black eyes and blond hair who was starving or my sister Stefania who was very withdrawn. How could I have such a good time here in faraway

Egypt and have no concert of what was happening to my loved ones? This was not a natural life, I was as alone as one could ever be.

What was my other option? I didn't know. I tried to go to the headquarters in the Seventh Division of the Second Polish Corps, in Cassasin, which was located about thirty miles from our campus. When I arrived at the headquarters, with the help of one of my teachers, I inquired about my family and explained my situation. All they could say to me was they would dispatch a inquiry to Isfahan, Persia; and if some news comes back, they will let me know. It was not the answer I wanted to hear, but that was all I could do. As I advanced in my studies, I was learning some applicable skills such as drafting, welding, designing, and making use of available tools.

This all was part of learning. I advanced in some skills to be able to evaluate work which was needed on some army equipment, such as tanks, heavy duty trucks, all terrain vehicles, and various transportation equipment. We were given the task of evaluating and passing the grade on all the equipment with which we had contact. We had to write how to improve the quality of the equipment. This was very difficult for us to undertake. We were told that we might see some things with our young eyes and minds that some other people might overlook. So give it a go and do the evaluations for better or worse.

Mechanical Company 339 on our yearly vacation on the shores of the Mediterranean Sea town of Alexandria, Egypt in 1944. I'm on the upper right of the picture.

Well, the days and weeks went by; the school decided that we should visit the Port of Alexandria on a second visit. All of us were delighted to go visit this historical city before all this work was undertaken. It was not hard at all to postpone our assignment. We needed this time out in our lives, considering what we went through. Alexandria was quite a different city to see; the blue waters of the Mediterranean and the beaches were nice to look at, as we were located in the British camp there.

We stayed there for a few days and returned to our campus to resume our studies. Our progress in school went along just fine. I was still reading books about Polish history and other works of famous writers such as Mickiewicz, lying on the outside of my tent, enjoying good weather and good books. Many times I thought about my family back in the Soviet Union. What can I do? Or where can I turn for solace? I decided to write to the Red Cross to renew the search for my family. I talked with my teachers as well as to the School Commandant about my dilemma. I was told that all my companions were in the same situation, and that we had to wait for the results of their inquiries.

Some weekends we were able to visit the closest town of Ismalia, which was about thirty miles away. Ismalia was located near the Suez Canal, which connects the Indian Ocean and the Mediterranean Sea. We could either take a bus which traveled between Cairo and Isamlia or hitch a ride on an army vehicle. We went on frequent trips to Ismalia, not only as an excursion but also to obtain some goods for our use. On one occasion a bunch of us went to town, but instead of going to Ismalia, we decided to go for a swim in the Suez Canal. Well, all was well until we decided to swim across this moving body of water which was probably about two hundred yards wide. Two hundred yards didn't look that far, so we decided to cross the canal, rest awhile and return. As we started our swim, we figured the current would take us about two hundred feet or so downstream, not knowing a ship was coming our way. As we came to this realization, we began to swim more aggressively so as not to be caught in its tow. As the ship was closing in on us, it blasted its horn for we were directly in its path. What a dilemma to be in! It seemed it was the end for us.

As it turned out, we managed to avoid the collision and were saved. We finally got to the other side of the canal. We not only rested for awhile, but were on the lookout for another ship traveling our way. We swam back across the canal and walked back up the street to get back to our original point of crossing. This episode was published in our school bulletin, warning what could happen to others. I was proud of the fact that we could have saved some lives.

Everything was going well for me. On one hand I was very lonely for my family, but on the other hand I attended a good school, was well fed and clothed and had plenty of recreation plus exploration of many ancient places. Our school housed about two hundred or more students, so at first you don't know all your fellow students. One day as our assignments were scheduled, a fellow who was unknown to me, whose name I don't remember and I were assigned to inspect army vehicles such as tanks, canons and others to examine the towing hitches so we could repair any which were showing wear. One of our drivers in an American-made Jeep drove us to the assigned location and we started to look for defects, monitoring each vehicle which we inspected and noting its assigned number. All went well for a few hours. We sort of talked about small things and I was comfortable with his companionship.

Suddenly from nowhere he came up to me with a pistol in his hand, saying he found it in a tank, adding that he wondered if it was loaded. He then pointed the pistol at me and before I could react he fired it. I could see the flash of the explosion, hear the noise, and feel the burn on my face. I did not know what had happened to me. All I remembered was that here were many people talking loudly and I was lifted and jostled around, but I have no other memory of what had happened. When I awakened from the incident, I was told that there was a British hospital close to Tel el Cabir and I would be taken there.

I did not realize what had happened to me nor how serious my condition was. I was dazed for many days. An English doctor who was a major in the British Army said he would take care of me. I later learned that his last name was Thompson, Major Thompson. He took care of the left side of my face, which was burned by the powder from the pistol. He could not conclude if the pistol had a live bullet or was filled with practice ammunition. After some period of time, my face began to heal and he told me everything would be alright. He had to perform surgical scraping of my face to remove the burn marks but told me the powder would remain under my skin. I can't remember how long I spent in the hospital, but the interpreter who translated the doctor's procedures to me said he was satisfied that all was done properly and eventually I would be released from the hospital.

When that time came, Major Thompson invited me to go to the Suez Canal for rehabilitation. This sounded very nice to me. The hospital provided me with swimming trunks, towels, night wear and clothes to go for this rehabilitation. It all worked out well and I began to adjust to what happened to me. I was then returned to my school environment. I was asked at first, but I was questioned over and over by my close friends as to what had happened to me. I was not willing to talk about it since it happened so suddenly and I was not even sure what happened. I asked my teacher what happened to the fellow who was with me on our assignment. I was told that he was transferred to another school and would not be coming back. I then asked them to tell me his name; but his identity was never revealed to me.

By this time it was the end of March, 1945 and I was a changed young man. The torment of what happened to me was constant. I wanted to find out how this could have happened for I didn't know myself how this incident occurred. The constant mental turmoil affected my thinking and concentration in the classroom. I decided to go to the Principal of our school and ask him to transfer me to the Polish Army as a soldier, which I wanted to be to begin with. He hesitated for awhile because he told me I had great potential and would forfeit my future education. But after reviewing my situation, he agreed to let me transfer to the Polish Army. As it turned out, I was ahead of the times.

I was placed in the Mechanical Company which was Company 339 of the Seventh Division and Captain Socha was in charge. He welcomed me as the newest man in his Company. After reviewing my file, he assigned me to troubleshoot problems with the electrical systems on the army vehicles. The sargeant in charge of this department welcomed me to his platoon. I was very happy to be in that environment. I was somebody needed to perform his duties. As time went on and my qualifications became known, I was one of the Company, an individual involved and respected. As days passed, I was called to visit the Company Commandant, Captain Socha. When I entered his tent, he invited me to sit down as he wanted to speak to me. He said that he was very satisfied with my services and my eagerness to help with his problems and he wanted me to secure better living conditions for his Company. At one point he said, "Franek, I want you to think how you can help us improve the environment for our men." I came out of his tent feeling I was someone entrusted with this big vision.

Some days later I received a letter addressed to my old school which was forwarded to my present Company 339. The letter was from my mother, Maria. A letter from my mother!! My Mother! I opened the letter, the first letter I ever received in my life. What could it be in this envelope? How long did I hold it in my hands before I opened it? It was a letter from my mother and how I had longed to hear from her. I was happy I had a family and I had this letter. It said on it, "From Maria Jasinski, Isfhan, Persia." As I opened the envelope, which was quite bulky, I noticed there was part of a newspaper in it. I unfolded the clipping and there on one side was a picture. I paused and looked closely. There was a picture of about sixty boys in uniform, and I spotted myself on one end of this picture.

I had never seen this picture before but then after awhile it came to me that, indeed, sometime back there was a photographer taking pictures in our school. I unfolded several pages of my mother's letter and slowly tried to digest every word form it. Mother greeted me with God's blessing and that she was very happy to find that I was on the faraway Egyptian soil. She informed me that my father was quite well, Stefania was doing well and had grown to be a beautiful sister to me. She wrote that it took them three months after I left Kermine (Russia) traveling the same way I did. She said my father also joined the Polish Army in Kermine but when they arrived in Teheran he was discharged from the Army because of ill health.

Then she gave me the bad news, saying that brother Joe, during liquidation of the camp to which he was assigned, was getting ill and lost a lot of weight. She tried to help him with some special food whenever she could but it was not enough. After some time, the Army doctor diagnosed Joe with liver problems and complications so the Army sent him and some other soldiers to Teheran, Persia where there were advanced medical facilities to help them. After a week or so Joe couldn't regain his weight and passed away. He was only about 20 years old. His death certificate said he died from malnutrition. He was buried in Teheran, Persia in the military cemetery.

The other bad news in the letter was just as awful. As mother tried to soften the blow in my young life, she simply wrote that my younger sister, Stasia, also passed away from the same cause. As my mother with my two sisters arrived in Teheran, Stasia was almost unconscious. She was taken to the hospital immediately but the doctors told mother there was no chance to save her life. Her liver was gone; she was only eight years old and only about thirty kilos (66 lbs) in weight. The Polish Army allowed Stasia to be buried next to brother Joe. Mother was very sorry about what happened in my absence. She did not blame me, but praised me for the help when I provided them with food. She and my father, as well as Stefania, missed me very much and hoped that we will or could meet again soon.

At the end of the letter she added that she was not very sure if the letter would reach me, but if I would receive it to make sure to write back to her because they missed me very much. As in the beginning of the letter she blessed me again that the good God would keep me safe for them. It took quite a while to read her letter; I did so many times for I could not believe what happened to my family in my absence. Here I am sixteen years old, abandoned so to speak, having to take care of myself for almost two years and now this. How do I cope with this news?

After I composed myself, I decided to take this letter and go see my Commanding Officer, Captain Socha. When I first arrived at his Company, he said that not only was he my superior, but counselor as well and that if any of us had some big problems, to bring them to him first. As I walked across the company parade square and got to his tent (all Polish forces in our Division were called Cassasin Camp), I called in with the permission to enter and he called me in. As I entered his tent, he took one look at me and said: "My God, Franek, what has happened to you?" Well, that was the wrong thing to say to me because I started to cry very hard. I could not control my emotions. He, the Captain, was of small stature, but very big in understanding. He came to me, took me in his arms, and held me without saying a word.

When I again composed myself, he asked, "What has happened to my young soldier?" I handed my mother's letter to him. He permitted me to sit down while he read it. As he was reading the letter, I watched his expression. He, too, was wiping his tears. I don't remember how long it took him to read, but when he finished he got up from his chair and said to me, "Soldier, this is war and that's why we are here. Things like this happen all the time and we can't do anything about it. You are lucky you are alive and well off." He also said I should go see our chaplain and get his advice. "As for me, I sympathized with you, but remember that you are a soldier in the Polish Army and that you have to endure life as it presents itself." He then shook my hand and dismissed me. I said, "Thank you captain" and left his tent. When I returned to my tent, I told my comrades of what had just happened to me. They sympathized with me and were sorry to hear the news that I received. This was my problem and I alone had to take it.

The next evening I went to the Social Hall to write my family that I received the news. I had no choice but to go to the Social Hall since we had no chairs, tables or electric lights in our tent. As I finished several pages, telling them what I endured after leaving Kermine, I did not mention the shooting incident, nor would I ever. (Even today, I have not recovered entirely from this incident, nor do I think I ever will.) I continued to try to be on my best behavior and advance myself.

As weeks rolled on I was very crafty with my hands and very innovative. I was asked at one point if I would like to be in charge of the Machine

Shop and also take care of the electric power plant for our Company. The power plant was in a Leyland five ton truck, built in England. It was a beautiful and practical truck or lorry, as the English call it. I answered that indeed I would love to do what was the best for the company and our workshop conditions. You see, we had to take care of trucks, cars and heavy equipment so there was a lot of work to be done. I was well trained to do lathe work, welding, and electrical work. As days passed I was successful in effecting the mechanics' work and some remanufacturing. I don't know whether or not the mechanics said something to the Sergeant in charge of our shop, but he told me I was doing a good job. Well, I was praised by my superior. Wouldn't my parents be proud of me hearing this?

A handsome Frank was promoted to Lance Corporal in the Polish Army, Company 339, 7th Division. Picture was taken in 1944, Cassasin (near) Ismailia, Egypt. As I was told by my Commanding Officer, Captain Socha, that I was the youngest non-commissioned officer.

Winter was approaching and the desert days were getting shorter; dusk and night were getting longer. So, after some thought I made some schematic drawings to wire our camp to be able to get lights installed in our Company 339. I handed this proposal to our sergeant to see whether he approved of it and to get permission from our commander, Captain Socha, to do the job for our Company. A few days passed and I lost my enthusiasm because I didn't receive any news about my project. One morning I was told that Captain Socha wanted to see me.

As I approached him with a salute, he asked me to be at ease. He started to question me about my idea for installing the system for our Company. The first thing he said was, "Franek, you know that you are a very young boy. Yes, I know you had some schooling, but this? This is a big undertaking. You really think you can do this job?" I was kind of scared at his questioning, but I stood my ground. My answer was simply this, "Sir, Captain, have you reviewed my drawing and if so, then maybe you agree with me that such a thing is attainable?" He said that he would review my proposal further and let me know. At this he dismissed me and I walked away feeling quite good about my presentation. As I walked away, I started to think and it came to me, "What am I trying to accomplish by doing this? What is there in it for me?" But my spirit and drive for the betterment of my comrades was what mattered and that was enough for me.

In the next few days my supervisor, the Sergeant, came to me and said, "Franek, I don't know where you are coming from but you are transforming this camp into a better place to live." With that, he said that my project had a good chance to succeed, and "if you succeed it would be wonderful for you." The darker the days got the more excited I became to wait for the big answer. It didn't take long before I got called to report to Captain Socha. As I reached his quarters, I announced that I was responding to his call. We talked about the project and he agreed with me that if it was successful it would increase our productivity and would make us look better to our superiors. With that, he said to go to the Purchasing Department and give them a list of materials necessary to complete the assignment. He added, "I am doing this because you made me believe in your idea. Please don't let me regret my decision."

I walked away from his tent and began to wonder if I was doing the right thing. Then I convinced myself that this was an easy task and that all would come out ok. As I came in to the procurement desk to place my order for wire, switches, bulbs, insulation and other small items, the man taking the order said that he would have to clear this with Captain Socha. I said it was ok with me. After receiving my supplies I went to see my supervisor, the Sergeant, and asked him to give me a helper for the project. It didn't take us much time; within a week we wired all twelve tents in our Company. It was a great feeling to have Captain Socha pull the switch which was connected to the Leyland electric power plant. After the count of "one, two, three" the lights went on to the applause of our comrades. He then came to me and said, "Thank you, Franek."

I was very proud of myself for being able to accomplish this task, helping our company to have a more enjoyable lifestyle during evening hours. My friends thanked me personally for my deed. All went well for awhile until one day my Sergeant in charge called me to do some more hat tricks. He asked me to do the same thing in our workshop area. He said, "You know our days are too short and the workload too large. You could help make our task a lot easier." It didn't take long to finish the job to his satisfaction. It made me especially proud, since I was only 15 years old at this time.

Company 339 in Cassasin, Egypt
(that's me on the left)

As for my life in the Army, I was very happy because everything was going well for me. I had written many letters to my parents and received many back with some good news. In one of the letters I was informed that my sister, Stefania had found a nice man. He was an American soldier stationed in Isfahan, Persia (Iran) where my family lived and worked as kitchen workers as well as dining room servers for the army. He and Stefania were very serious. In subsequent correspondence, I was informed that they planned to get married. In one letter my sister asked if it was possible for me to attend her marriage ceremony.

With invitation in hand, I went to see Captain Socha to obtain permission to attend the event. His answer was, "Franek, I like you and what you have done for our Company. I wish I could let you go to see your family, but this is wartime and I can't let you go to a distant country. There is no certainty that you could come back. Permission denied." I later learned that Stefania's wedding was successful. I was very happy to know that she was scheduled to go to the USA to a town on the West Coast called Alameda, California. She also mentioned that her husband, Robert, was transferred to Cairo, Egypt. She said in her letter that Robert would contact me in Cassasin where I was stationed, which is about sixty miles north of Cairo.

Some time later I received a short note from my brother-in-law telling me that he indeed arrived in Cairo and that he wanted me to come and visit him. He explained that I was more familiar with the country than he was, and that it would be better for both of us to spend time in Cairo than in the desert camp of Cassasin. It was quite challenging to read his note for me for my English was quite limited. But armed with my Polish-English dictionary, I was able to decipher his note. "Oh God, how can I communicate with this man? Oh well, we'll see what happens." With this letter I went to see Captain Socha and he asked me to sit down. I presented him with the letter from my brother-in-law in which he said he would like me to visit him, so we could get to know each other.

Captain Socha was surprised that my sister got married and that she would go to America to better herself. He said, "I will let you go to Cairo for two days. Get the keys for the Company jeep. I'll give you some money to help you with meals and a hotel room for one night and wish you the best of time with your brother-in-law." I walked out of his tent floating on clouds. What an understanding man this officer was who was in charge in our Company. He even helped me with finances!

It wasn't very hard to find the American Army compound. As I approached the entrance gate, I properly identified myself as a Polish Army soldier and presented my ID and the letter from Robert and was escorted to his barracks. When he and I met, we just looked at each other for some time. He extended his hand to me and with a brief embrace said how happy he was to see me. He asked if I was hungry, which I was, so we went to the dining room nearby and had something to eat. He then pulled out a stack of pictures to show me of the wedding ceremony, as well as other pictures. Well, I was quite taken aback.

Seeing my parents, Stefania, and the wedding pictures as well and seeing some relative who emigrated from Russia together with my parents and Stefania. They surely were changed in theirs looks and appearance. Some tears were rolling down my cheeks but I was happy to see my family. My limited use of English was not a big problem. We managed to have a good time together. I even took him to visit the pyramids and the Sphinx because I visited these sites before. He was glad to see them with me and we got along quite well. He also impressed me with his looks and intelligence. He was about five years older than I. We even took some pictures together at a fast-photo booth where you wait five minutes and get them back to see what they looked like. It was fun to do. I didn't stay in the hotel overnight because Robert made arrangements for me to stay in their visitor quarters. We got to know each other somewhat. This was early in 1945. The next time I would see him and my sister Stefania would be in February, 1951.

After my brief visit with Robert, I reported back to duty as Cassasin. I gave my Captain the hotel money he gave me because I didn't use it. He was very surprised at my honesty. The longer I stayed in Company 339, in the repair facility, the more experienced I became and more trusted by my comrades. As world tensions eased up, things were quite different. I heard from some sources that it was easy to travel from one country to another. In the meantime, I received a letter from my parents informing me that Stefania was finally scheduled to go to America to her husband's home and also that the Polish civilian camp in Isfahan was dismantling and they were scheduled to move to Lebanon, close to Beirut. My mother was the inspiration to me for she was in charge and was informing me about their situation. It was not long after her letter that I received another letter that they had been moved to a village close to Beirut. Without further delay, I had the notion that I have to go see my parents there!

It seems that I frequented my Captain's office on a regular basis. Well, it was not so. However, this time I wanted to go to Lebanon to see my parents whom I hadn't seen in almost four years and I deserved to see them! Well, he agreed to give me a pass to Lebanon for three weeks at the most! The next day he informed me that I had to travel with my rifle and ammunition, and with all my gear, carrying civilian clothes. When I got to Haifa, Palestine, I had to surrender all my gear, including my rifle and ammunition and change into my civilian clothes then travel by taxi to Beirut. All my papers were in order for me to start my journey.

I got to Beirut at dusk so I went to the nearest hotel, called Kit-Kat, where I spent the night. In the early morning, as directed by a hotel employee, I took a taxicab to the bus stop. After a while, I boarded this awful looking bus, which was carrying a cart of chickens on top of it, along with other animals and it was crowded with people. As I nestled in the back of the bus, we proceeded. At the time, I did understand some Arabic so I was able to communicate with my fellow passengers. I had to travel about one hour to reach my parents' village. As we were going up the hills on curvy roads I got car sick. Well, people around me helped me with my sickness.

My first contact with my parents in 1945, holding a letter from Stefania from the US. Please notice above my parents are pictures of me and Stefania on the right. This picture was taken in Beirut, Lebanon.

I finally arrived at my destination. When I got off the bus, I had to inquire where to find my parents. I suppose my mother had told her friends that I was coming to visit them. Before I knew it, there were other Polish people in this village in the same circumstances as my parents. I couldn't believe it, but in a few minutes my mother was there to greet me. She took my hands, looked at me and smiled and said, "You've gotten tall and handsome." She hugged me and kissed me all over my face. "How I miss you, Franek," she said to me, "how much we love you only God knows." She said I was the only one left in her life.

We walked to the house which they shared with another Polish family and the owner, a Lebanese family. The family spoke perfect French, but couldn't speak Polish. My father greeting me with a hug and a kiss. He said to me, "Franek, you have grown up. I have not been able to support you in your growing and maturing, but I can see that you have done alright. I am pleased with the way you look." My father was very much to the point. He spoke when something needed to be said. My mother could not do enough to please me. We had something to eat and then talked some and left other items to talk about for the next few days. I was very tired because the trip was exhausting so I slept until noon the next day.

As I was waking up, I overheard my parents talking about me. How much I had grown up, how mature I became and how I was very handsome. As I got up, I repeated, "Well, mother and father, do you approve the way the world helped me grow up?" And added, "Do you know how abandoned I felt when I left Kermine?" We all felt reborn and reunited. We could not stop looking at each other. The next day my Mom said to me, "I have something for you that I saved for a long time." She then reached and pulled out a box. On it said "Hershey Chocolate." She said "It's for you." As I opened this box it was full of chocolate bars.

This is the Mechanical Company, 399th Division, 7th Polish Army in the Middle Eastern country of Egypt. I am standing in the left top row, third from the end in July of 1944.

I had never tasted Hershey bars and they were out of this world. It was a wonderful taste. She told me to take it easy because too much chocolate could make me sick. We talked about how we crossed the Caspian Sea and crossed the mountains toward Teheran. At one point, as I recall, I asked my mother, "Remember when at one time, before I left Kermine for Persia I handed you my knapsack full of dried bread? What happened to it?" She had told the people in the school where they lived that I, her son, was going away with his Division of Polish soldiers to Persia and that he gave all this dried bread to us to share. So my mother distributed a few slices of the bread to all the occupants. Well, this did not look too good to my little sister. She tugged at mother saying, "Please don't give all that bread away. Please leave some for me for tomorrow." Mother began to cry recalling that incident. She recalled that they were all starving. It was hard for me to listen to my mother tell about how Stasia was behaving, but I could also recall how it felt to be hungry day in and day out.

This picture was taken in 1945 on my first visit to Beirut, Lebanon

I surely had a wonderful time with my parents. We went down to Beirut to explore the city and see the splendor of Lebanon and the capital city, Beirut. At one point, we came to the center of town where the alleys of shops selling gold were on display, such as rings, necklaces, bracelets, and all other artifacts. As we approached some other counters she turned to me and said, "Franek, your father and I would like to get you a gift. Would you like a nice watch?" I said, "Could you afford one?" She then took my arm and we went inside the watch store. She pointed to one of the watches and said, "How about this one?" I picked it up and it was a nice watch, an Omega. I said to her that I would like to have it if it wasn't too expensive. She said, "Son we have never given you anything over these years and you deserve it, it's yours." I was very grateful to have received this expensive gift from my parents.

When we got back to my parent's home we had something to eat, then we talked some more about how I met my sister's husband, Robert, and how we got along and how glad I was for Stefania that she found a good man for a husband. But I also said that not only had I missed her wedding, but I also missed seeing her. Now that she is in America, who knows when or even if I would ever see her again. I was told not to worry. Mom said, "You have overcome all these difficulties so why do you even worry what will come tomorrow." We will find a way to see her again, one way or another. You will see." I had a very good time with my parents.

I also got acquainted with the son of the owner of the building in which they rented the two rooms. His name was Kamil and he was about my age and we got along just fine. He took me sight seeing to show me some new places at different times in the city. I recall that one evening we sat on a rock, with a view of Beirut. It was spectacular. It seemed that the Mediterranean Sea surrounded Beirut like a diamond-studded city reflected on the water. It was an almost unbelievable sight to see. One day my new friend Kamil said to me, that we didn't communicate efficiently. I spoke a little Arabic and a little English and he in turn spoke French and Arabic but a different dialect yet we could kind of make out what each wanted to say.

We went out quite some distance to the other side of the hill to observe the railroad train climbing the mountain via the gear-driven method. It was a very unusual way to travel up the hill. What an invention to travel up and down the mountain. Kamil and I remained friends for some time, but time separated us because of lack of communication and the lack of a common language. After some time with my parents, I had to get back to Cassasin to my mother Company 339. What a good feeling to get back!

Late in May of 1945, for my contributions I was promoted to the rank of Lance Corporal. This made me the youngest soldier who was promoted. All my comrades were very happy for me because they said I deserved it for helping others. It didn't take long to write my parents telling them of my promotion. I was no longer a Private, but now a Lance Corporal. I was very proud of it!

When the war ended in 1945, things changed at a very fast rate. The news circulated that soon we would break camp and move on to England in preparation to return to civilian life. The war was over and the Army was not needed. We, the Polish Army soldiers, were puzzled for we didn't know who was the winner or liberator of Poland. Russia and its cronies were in charge of the Polish Government. Polish Communists were ruling and oppressing Polish citizens. Things didn't go the way we expected. After all we sacrificed, thousands of our Polish soldiers fought on all fronts to gain freedom for our people. What we got was a division of Poland, oppression by Communist Russia and lots more nonsense. I'm not going to dwell on the politics of the treaties in Potsdam when Mr. Roosevelt, Mr. Churchill and the leader of Communist Russia Mr. Stalin, divided my country, but the decision was made and we had to adhere to it like it or not. The fact that the war was over meant we had to close our camps, turn all our equipment back to English authorities, and prepare ourselves to go to England for disarmament.

It took almost three weeks to travel via Navy ships from Alexandria, Egypt to Southampton, England. In Southampton different divisions were given different destinations. My Division was sent to the York city area for preparation for civilian life. In order to be discharged from the Polish Army we had to sign an agreement with England to stay with the British Resettlement Corps for two years. During this time, we would be trained for civilian life; at the same time we would study English.

Within these two years we could find jobs within our qualification or liking. The English classes went along slowly but constantly. Some older men and/or women had a lot of experience in their fields and they were able to find work faster than others. Some spoke English well and they too, had jobs presented to them. Others, including me, had to learn English to get the job which we were seeking. In the meantime, we stayed busy doing odd jobs in our camps. As time passed, I had to get out of the Army uniform because I too had to find a job in the textile factory as a spinner, making thread.

It was an ok job, but not the job I would hold for a long time, but it was something to do and be on my own, pay for room and breakfast, and still have some money left over for spending. I must confess that I was not a very stable person. I wanted to see England for what it was worth and try to get a job in my field. This was not an easy thing to achieve as everybody was looking for work. After the war was over about one million people were discharged from the military services including the Polish military, so the times were difficult. All this didn't stop me from exploring possibilities for traveling. At the time of my stay in England I must have changed living quarters and jobs about forty times. Was I a vagabond? I would say "yes". Did I have good times? I would say "yes" to that too.

In the meantime my parents followed me to England. They settled in a town called Ely. Ely was located close to Cambridge so occasionally I would go to visit them and of course I would bring a bag full of dirty laundry. My mother was happy to wash them for me. She would say, "How come you don't have many socks to wash?" Well, I couldn't tell her the truth because socks at some stores were very inexpensive so I would just throw old dirty socks away sometimes. I would communicate with my parents by letters only. I also stayed in touch with Stefania in America. She would write to my parents often. On one occasion she announced that she had a baby boy who was born January 27, 1947 and that she named him Edward. So my parents became grandparents and they were very excited. Some time later we got the news that she was expecting another child. It was all joy in the family.

Since I was discharged from the Polish Army, I joined the Polish Veterans. I was able to receive communication from the Veteran's Office about any news about our status in England. As part of our discharge from the Army we were promised that the English Government together with the Polish Government would pay for transportation to any country for which a veteran could obtain a proper and valid visa. With this news, I wrote to Stefania and asked if she and her husband could get us such an invitation. I forwarded her instructions for what was necessary to obtain visa to the USA. I advised them there would be no cost to them for our travel because the tickets would be free for the whole trip.

I suppose the US Government favored former Polish servicemen because it granted 20,000 visas for this purpose. This proposal was signed by President Harry Truman. It further stated in the document that each visa was good for one former Polish military man who was honorably discharged and his or her family regardless of the number. The news was good for all ex-service people. It didn't take long for other Governments like Argentina, New Zealand, Australia and many others to invite us to their countries to settle down. Some of my friends did go to those countries. I chose to wait and see what would happen to my family. As it turned out we did receive an invitation to come to the US from my sister and her husband Robert. With that paper, I went to visit the US Consulate General in London. Upon presentation of the paper for me and my parents, the usual reply from the clerk was that we will let you know as soon as possible. With that I left the Consulate with a good feeling. I then wrote a happy letter to my parents, telling them what I had done and assured them that all was looking well for us.

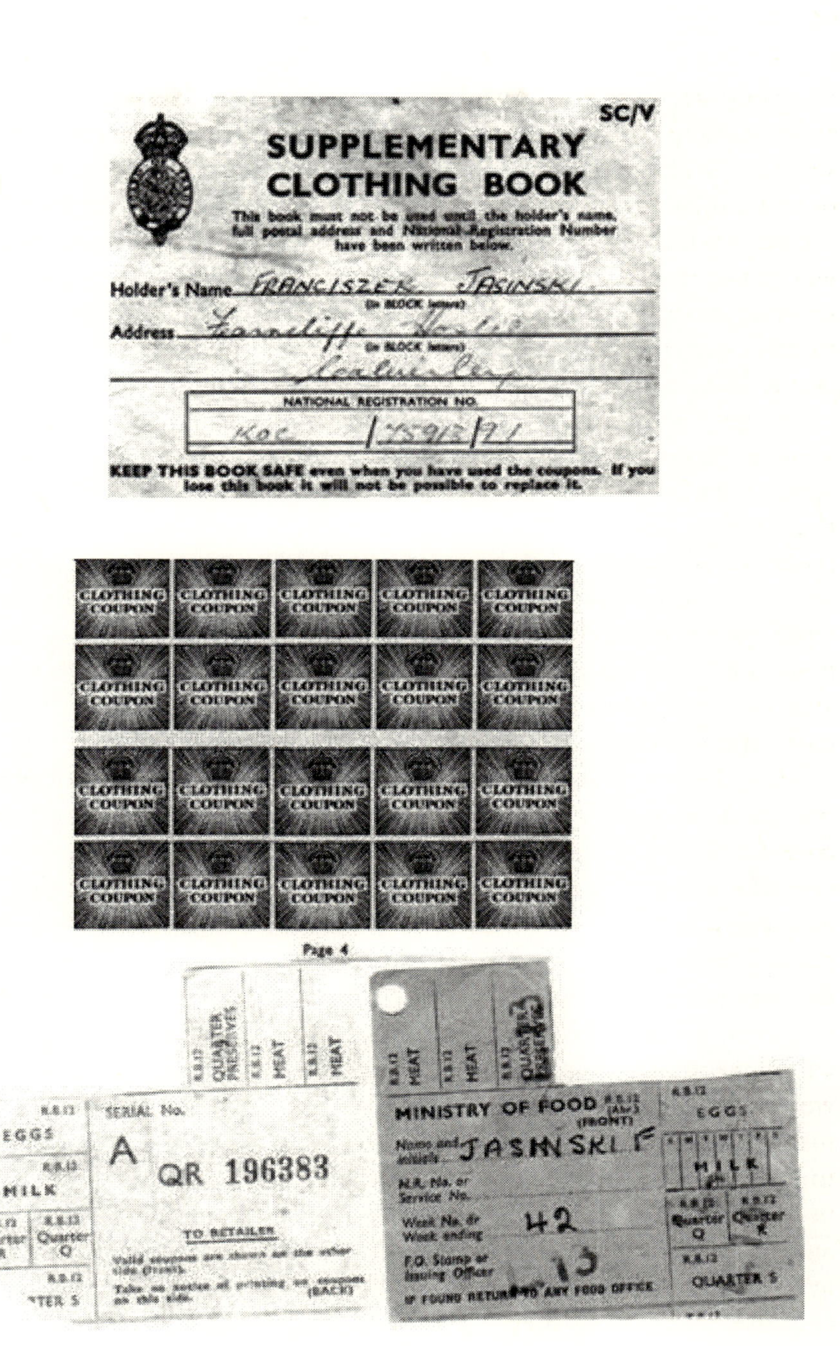

SC/V

SUPPLEMENTARY CLOTHING BOOK

This book must not be used until the holder's name, full postal address and National Registration Number have been written below.

Holder's Name FRANCISZEK JASINSKI
(In BLOCK letters)

Address [illegible]
(In BLOCK letters)

NATIONAL REGISTRATION NO.
KOC 175913/91

KEEP THIS BOOK SAFE even when you have used the coupons. If you lose this book it will not be possible to replace it.

CLOTHING COUPON	CLOTHING COUPON	CLOTHING COUPON	CLOTHING COUPON	CLOTHING COUPON
CLOTHING COUPON	CLOTHING COUPON	CLOTHING COUPON	CLOTHING COUPON	CLOTHING COUPON
CLOTHING COUPON	CLOTHING COUPON	CLOTHING COUPON	CLOTHING COUPON	CLOTHING COUPON
CLOTHING COUPON	CLOTHING COUPON	CLOTHING COUPON	CLOTHING COUPON	CLOTHING COUPON

Page 4

QUARTER PRESERVES
MEAT
MEAT

EGGS
MILK
Quarter R
Quarter Q
QUARTER S

SERIAL No.
A QR 196383

TO RETAILER
Valid coupons are shown on the other side (Front).
Take no notice of printing on coupons on this side. (BACK)

MEAT
MEAT

MINISTRY OF FOOD (FRONT)
Name and initials JASINSKI F
N.R. No. or Service No.
Week No. or Week ending 42
F.O. Stamp or Issuing Officer 13
IF FOUND RETURN TO ANY FOOD OFFICE

EGGS
MILK
Quarter Q
Quarter R
QUARTER S

A copy of Frank's Food & Clothing ration coupons given out at the Resettlement Camp in York, England in 1945.

In the days to come I wondered how my life would change in the USA. Sitting at home, in my room, after a day's work I reflected on the time when I arrived in York. I did not react too well to the conditions in which I found England. There was a shortage of food, for which I was issued food coupons for the privilege of purchasing some food such as meat, butter, bacon and all other food to sustain one's life. In addition, I received coupons for clothing and coupons to allow me to purchase shoes, outer clothing such as jackets, trousers, overshoes, etc. It excluded such things as underwear, socks and other things. Would the USA be the same as England?

Stefania never mentioned that there were shortages of any kind. I was quite satisfied that we would be doing the right thing and would not worry about it anymore. After pondering about all these coming events, I decided to do myself a favor. I went out to the grocery store to purchase some food. I gave my coupon book to the grocery clerk and asked to fill my basket with my weekly allowance of food. After I paid for it, I went home and inspected what I was allowed. I found there was enough food for one good meal so I made one meal to satisfy myself. The rest of the week I lived on fish and chips and other food from Lyons Fast Food Stores. While in England I personally didn't feel I was welcome. I was looked at as a foreigner, sometimes I was called a "bloody Pole." I was offended by that kind of treatment, but what was I to do about it? I just kept hoping that when the time comes, we would go to the promised land, USA, and that all would be alright.

All this time, I continued learning English. I purchased a Polish-English dictionary and found that during the learning process, it was difficult to perfect this weird language. I was telling myself "Frank, you do speak Polish, Russian, Ukranian, some Arabic and some German. How is it that you can't overcome the difficulties of learning English?" It was obvious to me that after I analyzed the problem that I was using Polish most of the time during work and leisure times with my friends. This had to change because when the time comes to emigrate to the USA I have to have a command of the English language better than I am doing now. So I decided to move again to a different district of London where there were fewer Polish residents and I changed my job.

I landed a job at Lyons Bakery where there were no Polish people working. I had to learn and speak only English and it helped me a lot. I was wishing I had done this a long time ago, but it was better late than never. It was time to go visit my parents in Ely. When I arrived by train I was warmly greeted and, of course, I delivered my dirty laundry for my mother to help me with the wash. My parents told me that they received notice that the Ely camp was closing and that they had to move. Their new destination was to be somewhere in Yorkshire.

In a very short time, they were transported to Yorkshire and relocated in another camp for refugees. I did not participate in their relocation at all. It was all done by the Polish Resettlement Government Plan. Some things turn out for the better. In this case they were reunited with relatives from next door in Studzianka, Poland by the name of Bereznicki. My mother's cousin Mikoai Bereznicki died in Russia. His wife Petrunia was at the same camp as my parents. She had a daughter, Hania and son Broneck. The reunion was great as they had lost contact since Alma-Ata in Kazakhstan, USSR, so they had a lot to talk about and compare notes.

Unknown to my parents, Hania had a suitor who was serious about her; a man called Stan Labuda and he was a nice man and my parents were very fond of him. As it turned out they were going to be married so my mother and Hania's mother, Petrunia, were arranging the wedding and reception. The food was still scarce because of the coupon problem so my mother asked me by mail to conserve my food coupons for the coming even. So I was invited to Hania's wedding.

My cousin Anna Bereznicki's wedding to Stanley Labuda in York, England 1948. In this picture is Stan's bestman, my mother Maria, myself (Frank), and my father Jan. Don't we look like human beings and happy!

This was a long distance to travel because they lived in Yorkshire and I lived in London. It was a train ride of about eight hours. As I was preparing to get my wardrobe together for the possible departure to the USA, it became obvious to me that I had good enough clothes to go to Hania's wedding. I wasn't worried what I would wear. The only thing I worried about was the time might come quickly for my departure, and I had to save some funds for traveling to such a distant place as the USA. I was not very excited about going to Hania's wedding. I hadn't heard from the US Embassy about any visa possibilities as yet so I was quite confident that there was a good chance that I could attend the wedding. However, as I wondered about the possibilities to go to the USA, I decided to go to the Embassy to inquire what was happening about our possible departure. I was told that the procedure might take months and I should not expect quick results.

I was confident that things would come to a satisfactory conclusion and that all will turn out alright for I have trusted God all this time. How could he let me down now? As my English improved, I was getting work with better pay. I perceived from the English people (natives) that if you couldn't speak English you were a dumb foreigner. In my mind I didn't think that I was dumb; just because I could not speak their language didn't make me stupid. I remember when I first came to England and I had to take the bus to my next destination, the conductor asked me for the bus ticket, and I said I didn't have any and she was very annoyed, so she asked me for some money. She said I owed her four pence and three farthings or something to that effect.

I'd heard of a penny, but what was this farthing? She explained that one penny is worth four farthings. Hurray for England and their currency! As I entered any bus in which I was trying to get to my destination, I would put my hand in my pocket and pull out a handful of change and reach out to the conductor to pick out coins that where appropriate for the fare. Was I dissatisfied with the English system? I would say not. I was placed in the situation where I couldn't function in a civilized fashion.

So I tried to better my conduct and respect their way of life. I told myself that I'd better get civilized and get to mimic the lives of the English people if I wanted to get ahead in my life. I decided to comply with their system. Since I was able to understand some English, I began to learn as much as I possibly could, so I would pick up a newspaper. Regardless of whether it was old or current, the words in each one were the same. I was making some progress. I promised myself that I would learn some English to prepare myself for possible emigration to the USA, because I wasn't going to dig ditches or do some work that I wouldn't like. I set myself a goal to better myself.

The time came for Hania and Stan to get married. All relatives and friends were invited. The date was February 26, 1948. This meant that I should spruce up with some new clothing and shoes because who knows who is going to be there. After all, I was somebody! When the time came, I was there to celebrate their wedding, but I had to contribute my food coupons. I had no problem giving them up. This was my first wedding since I left Poland and yes, it was a very big event for me. It would have been a bigger deal for me if I had been able to attend my sister's wedding, but that's the way life goes. I was very happy to be with my parents to enjoy Hania's day. I was with family having a good time. I also got together with other cousins like the Leszczynskis, Bereznickis and others.

The eldest son of Leszczynski's was Karol. He lived in Edinburgh, Scotland. He invited me to go visit him there and I promised him that I would do so as soon as time permits. We all had a lot to talk about and compare our past. The same thing happened to all of us. After the wedding, or let's say family reunion, we had to return to where we came from to earn a living. It was hard to say goodbye because who knows if we could ever have another opportunity to have such a reunion. Back in my room in London, I was at home in my surroundings. Work lately was ok and I had nothing to worry about.

My stay in London gave me the opportunity to see a lot of different sights. On my days off, I would venture to different parts of London and get some education from this old city. I would go to Hyde Park's Speaker's Corner and spend all Saturday afternoon listening to a lot of speakers talk on all sorts of different subjects. Although not understanding much of what they were talking about, their expressions and body language would amuse me. Not only were they entertaining, but they were required to stand on some kind of box to say what they wanted to say. On other days it was the exploration of Big Ben. This was a great treat. As I stood at the base of Big Ben, it struck on the hour.

It was ok but a bystander next to me said, "Did you notice the sound plays tricks on your hearing?" He gave me his small radio to listen to. After a few minutes the bell rang out again. "Listen to me," he said. "The radio signal is well before you hear the sound from the bell." I said to myself, "This is a fantastic phenomenon and how could it be so? I haven't heard about this before." As I went to the place where I lived, I was thinking about the noise traveling through the air and through the radio waves and it finally made sense.

On other occasions, I would kill time by going to the Thames River and walk on the old London Bridge. This was quite a treat walking on this historical work of art over this wide river. What a sight! I had never seen such a bridge, and was very impressed with the construction of the big crafted stones and its beauty. This bridge was well used not only by automobiles and trucks but also by people using it in the evenings as a lovers' lane promenade. It was a nice day spent and I wondered how it was erected in that place.

To me, it was like having wonderful cookies to eat every day of the week. On other days, I would get tickets for the underground subway from Piccadilly Circus to some distant station, see the country sights, and get back in a few hours. It would be a fulfilling afternoon for me, and sometimes I would go to see Buckingham Palace. One time it was a special day to watch the guards guarding the Royal Palace and at the same time watch the artist creating wonderful images of all sorts of things in colored chalk on the sidewalks. These creations were something to admire and ponder—how an artist could spend so much time creating this craft only to have it washed away with the evening fog. But I suppose that's the way artists' lives go on. Here now and gone way in no time at all.

During my time in London I spent a lot of time exploring and trying to find better work for myself and earn more money. A friend of mine told me that he worked at this cardboard company where cardboard boxes were made. He suggested that I go there to get a new job which provided better pay. I lived quite a distance from my job so I moved much closer to the work. Because my new place was farther away from the center of London, the rent was much cheaper. So here I was a winner and the move was profitable for me. After some time working for Thompson Cardboard Company, I somehow developed a hernia in my right groin. It necessitated going to the hospital to correct the problem.

Being in a London hospital was like being in the army barracks. There were about forty patients in one ward. It was noisy and reminded me of a train station. Doctors and nurses ("sisters" as the nurses are called in England) were mostly running back and forth to take care of the patients. After the surgery, I spent about fourteen days in the hospital. I was discharged, and went back to my place to recuperate. It was ok, but I wasn't very happy about losing four weeks' wages, although I got some pay as sick leave. The life after that went on as before. I made sure that I would see all the important places as possible for who knows when I would see them again, if ever. Back at work I was assigned to light duty and I was doing well working and earning some money.

In the meantime, I wrote to the US Embassy to inquire on the progress of getting visas for my parents and me. A few days later I received information from the Embassy that everything was going on schedule and that good news should be coming to me soon. I wrote my parents about the progress and offered them the advice that we should be preparing ourselves for departure to the USA. As soon as my mother got my letter she wrote back and asked me to come visit them. They wanted to talk about the possible departure. The next weekend I purchased a train ticket to the town of Ely, and after a few hours I was there to see my parents. I didn't see them as often as I would have liked, but it was always nice to visit just the same. My mother had a problem of stopping hugging me and she would also cry because I was home again, but that made her happy.

We talked about our possible departure. Mother informed me that she went out and purchased some presents for their first grandson, Eddie, and she wanted to send them to Stefania in the USA. My mother lost all she ever worked for when we were sent to Siberia, so now she sort of began to purchase all that she missed in the past years. I told my father that if and when we went to the US, we would be limited to what we could take with us so he and Mom should limit themselves to about two suitcases and my suitcase. The distance from London to Oakland would be about seven thousand miles. About one-half of that would be by train. I advised my mother to please dispose of all things which would not fit in two or three suitcases at the most because I would be in trouble carrying them in the stations whenever we would change trains. She said that she understood and that all should be alright.

By Sunday afternoon I had to return to London to get back to work. On the way back, I was wondering what it would be like to be in the USA, to live and work there. How much better off will I be there? Everyone I talked to about going to the USA without except said that I was lucky to be going. As I got back to my place and back to work, all was ok for me because I was working and could not think about going or coming. A few days later I received a letter from Karol Leszczynski, my cousin from Edinburgh, Scotland inviting me to come and visit him. He and his family, along with his brother Franek and his youngest brother Joe were getting ready to emigrate to Edmonton, Alberta, Canada. This would be the last chance to see each other. Karol's mother was my godmother as well as our cousins and neighbors in Kolonia, Studzianca back in Poland.

Not having too much money, but enough for the ticket, I told my supervisor of my need to go up to Scotland and asked for a few days off. He had some problem with my days off, but in the end said it would be ok with him to do so. I thanked him, and on Friday of that week I went up to Scotland. It took most of a day and a half to get to Edinburgh. As I got off the train it was weird to see this big city darkened by smoke and soot. The city nestled in a valley and had this beautiful building. As I walked out of the station, I was amazed at what I was seeing. Some men were dressed in skirts, with elaborate hats with all kinds of medals on them. I finally found a phone booth to call and tell Karol I was at the railroad station. He advised me not to wander around but to wait for him.

It didn't take him long to come on the bus to get me. When we arrived at the place where he lived, he introduced me to some lovely ladies, the owners of the house where he was renting. I was quite surprised how they treated Karol and me while I was there. The next day Karol and I went out to visit this beautiful Scottish city. The first thing Karol did was to take me to the Scottish castle to show me all the artifacts from this Scottish King who married a Polish princess from the 16th century from the dynasty of Bolshlaw Chlobry. The Polish King Chlobry gave a big dowry to the King of Scotland. All these artifacts were displayed there. Both Karol and I were very proud of all the fine things that the Princess brought along with her to Scotland. We visited some churches and a cathedral, some museums and other places. The trip to Scotland was worth it plus I could visit Karol who I haven't seen since leaving Russia. He was about three years older than I, but still we had the same interests in life. I spent about three days with him; then I had to go back to London for work.

My celebrating was soon to be over for I had to tighten my belt and save some money for some clothes to travel to the USA. As I boarded the train heading south back to London it was early in the morning so I could see all the scenery along the way. A few hours after leaving Edinburgh I went past the City of York. This is the first place that I came to stay when I arrived from Egypt a year ago. It looked the same, but I had changed dramatically since I first arrived here. Time went fast, but the longer I traveled by train the more my memory was reliving the train ride from the Siberian Forest to Kazakistan. I was very happy to be on this train with my belly full and sitting on a cushioned seat in a comfortable environment.

Going back to work felt good because work gives me stability and a good feeling. I had saved a little money for the possible departure to the USA and that there will be a time when I will have to purchase new clothes for travel. When will this time come? I didn't know. Not too long after I got back from Scotland I received a letter from Karol saying that his parents and two brothers managed to get affidavits of support from Edmonton, Alberta, Canada, from some distant cousin of Mikolaj Leszcznski, Karol's father. Because of this affidavit the English Government granted the Leszcznski family permission to emigrate to Canada. This happened in late, 1950.

I was surprised when I learned about the departure of my cousins so I went to the US Embassy to inquire if there was any news about our visas. I was told that the Embassy was reviewing the application and evaluating the sponsorship of my brother-in-law Robert and Stefania. Once the review was completed, the embassy would notify us of the results. About that time, my parents received some wonderful news in the mail about our application to go to the USA. Enclosed was a copy of the affidavit of support, if one was needed, so the Government wouldn't be burdened to support us if for some reason we were unable to support ourselves. I suppose this was like an insurance policy. This was done to satisfy Government requirements in order to issue visas to enter the USA.

I was very happy to receive this news indicating that all was going well so far for our departure in about two days or so. I received another letter from my mother informing us that my sister, Stefania, delivered another child. This time it was another boy who they named Randolph or Randy, as they called him. Mom wrote that she should have to add something for her second grandchild for she could not face Stefania if she came in empty handed. She wrote that she would add little more to the luggage, like it or not. I wondered how it would turn out with all this planning. As always things take care of themselves if given a chance. Since I lived close to the American Embassy, I decided to go there again only to inquire about the progress of our visas. What did I have to lose if I inquire? In my mind it was good to show the US Government that I was eager to go there and offer them my talents.

Anyway, the Embassy treated me very nicely, and that made me feel good. This time as I was invited to sit down and talk with one of the personnel, I was told that the visa was in the works, that the decision was quite near, and that the outlook was positive and emigration was imminent. I thanked them for this information and walked away—or maybe I danced away. As

I left the building I jumped up and yelled something with appreciation for the event. As the days went on I was getting serious about going but since winter was coming I went to the department store to find a coat and other warm clothing for the trip. This took some time for I was always short of funds. I had to go from store to store to find something more reasonable to fit my budget. Finally I purchased a new coat, scarf, gloves and a hat. It almost broke my pocketbook, but what could I do about it?

It was early December, 1950. My mother wrote me that some important papers arrived and that I had to come up to see what they were all about. The papers were from the American Embassy. The very next day I was on the train north to see my parents. The papers informed us that the visas were approved and that we should schedule our transportation and pick up the appropriate papers for such transportation. The news was too good to be true. My father opened some bottle to cheer our new endeavor with the possibilities we could settle down someplace and become a functional family again. We could not stop talking about what happened to us since the war began and how our lives changed. Is this too good to be true?

I told my father that I had to go back to London and contact the Polish Veteran's Office to tell them I possessed a valid visa for the USA and that I needed transportation to Oakland, California to which I was entitled. I had to show them all the documents to verify that it was so. I was advised by the Polish Veterans' Bureau that this was possible but it would take about two months to arrange transportation and provide me with tickets for the train to the port, the ocean vessel and the train in the USA. They also advised that when the transportation was arranged, I would have no window of delay for my departure. So it would be wise to start making arrangements for possible departure in early February, 1951. Well! The news was good and I wrote to my parents about all I had learned at the Veterans' office. My mother had close contact with Stefania so they communicated closely about our plans. I learned from my mother that Stefania wanted to wait to christen Randy for me to become his godfather. Me becoming a godfather for my sister's son—what an honor!

Until now I hadn't seen Stefania since 1943, which was almost eight years. How will I know her? We were strangers—what would I say to her? We don't know each other as adults after such a long time. It is hard to vision ourselves getting together and get reacquainted as brother and sister after such a long time. On the other hand it might be all so easy when we see each other.

When I got to Ely to see my parents, they showed me the correspondence from the American Embassy. There were some documents, but I could not read them and in several places I could only decipher the word "visa" and the dates. It was very promising for it was valid news. I told my parents that I would take the documents to the Polish Veterans' Office since, if this letter suggested that we were granted visas to emigrate, the Veterans' Bureau would need to know about it and work out our transportation. When I returned to London and went to the Veterans' Bureau they indeed acknowledged that the visas were granted for our emigration. Hurray for Frank and his family! We will go to America, the promised land, where all people are created equal. I will see Stefania and I will become her son's godfather! We will be a family again under one roof.

I wrote to my parents that the letter I took from them was our salvation and that we will go to America as soon as the Veterans' Bureau could obtain transportation tickets. As it turned out, I got a notice to go to the Veterans' Office for consultation regarding our departure. The Polish Veterans' Headquarters was located in the center of London. They owned the building called Bialy Orzel (White Eagle), named after the Polish national symbol—the flag which has the white eagle in the center with a red background. Thus the eagle adorns the Polish flag, just as the eagle is the American symbol of freedom for its strength.

As I entered the office and was taken to the appropriate desk to arrange our travel, I was informed that the American Embassy already contacted them and that arrangements for making our reservations were already in the works. They told me to come back in a few days to check with them about the progress. All through the days watching movies about wild America, such as Indians and wars, and cowboys, about Al Capone and other major criminals made me wonder how I would cope with this new frontier. But by reading Stefania's letters she never complained about what I had seen in the movies so I concluded that the "wild west" was only in the movies. When I went back to the Veterans' Office to inquire about the status of our travel arrangements, I was told that all transportation was arranged and all necessary tickets would be available within the next few days. The man in charge told me to get ready to depart from Southampton on February 5, 1951, on the Queen Mary, the ship that will take us to New York.

I was determined to do all I could to make all rough roads smooth. I wrote to my parents that all is well and please start making preparations to depart for America from Southampton on February 5th. I told them that I would be there with them, and we would travel together and we will have all the transportation tickets in hand. "You have about three weeks to get ready." My God, how lucky we will be to be there with Stefania and her little family! I recalled the time from our departure from our home in Poland in 1940 to go to that camp in Siberia, and now we're ready to go to this free nation called America. How is this possible? Is God preparing this trip for us? Are we ready to deal with His Providence? What about all the other people who are left behind?

I had to think how to prepare to quit my job, how to finish shopping for clothes, how to coordinate getting to Ely where my parents lived, and then depart from there to Southampton where the Queen Mary was berthed. All this had to be planned ahead of time. To make sure I was on the right page, I went to see the Train Master in London's main station and explained my problem. In no time, they gave me a schedule of dates and times for departure from Ely, including the change of trains, in order to get to Southampton on time. I was very satisfied with their instructions. Well, I suppose these English people were not as bad as I had perceived them to be.

The longer I lived here the more accommodating they became. Maybe it was that I had just imagined them to be arrogant towards me? Well, I will not hold them as being against me as a Polish ex-serviceman. Now was the time for all of us tohustle and bustle. I had improved my English quite a bit and I was happy about that. Up to this point I had learned several languages such as Polish, Russian, some Arabic (Egyptian), and now I am learning English. How wonderful life can be. At the age of twenty-one, I am multi-lingual and going to America!

In my preparations I had to work to make some money to sustain myself and make arrangements in the meantime to go to America. As time got closer to February 5th, I went to the Veterans' Office to see what was going on because I had to quit my job and other commitments. When I got there, all the papers—visas, tickets and all the other papers pertaining to this voyage were ready for me. Before they handed them to me, the clerk informed me that all the transfers and other important tickets were included; even taxi cab transfers from one station to another were there and paid for. I could not believe that I was such an important person as well as my parents. I was treated as some kind of VIP. Was I in a dream world or what? The time came to go to Ely and pick up my parents and depart on this long journey to America. As I arrived at the transit camp where my parents lived, they were very happy to see me for the time to leave had come for the unknown.

I told the person in charge of that facility that we were preparing to emigrate to America and would need transportation to the railroad station. He informed me that whenever we were ready to depart, transportation would be available. The Lorry (truck) arrived and picked up our belongings, and the three of us and took us to the railroad station in Ely, Cambridgeshire. As we deposited our luggage in the baggage compartment and were seated in our car (this time there were cushioned bench-type two seaters on each side of the aisle), the train started on it's way to London where we had to transfer to another train to go south to Southampton. I asked the conductor what would happen with our luggage. He informed me that it was transferred to the train to go with us. What a wonderful way to travel! The luggage is handled by train personnel and we didn't have to worry about it. What a way to go!

Traveling south of London to Southampton took about five hours. On the way we could see some fantastic views. We got close to the White Cliffs of Dover and other sights. It was an unbelievable train ride. We were free, free at last, as one family together since 1942. How can we contain the joy of freedom and togetherness? This is what free people should feel like—with some dignity—instead of being treated as pack animals.

During our ride we were asked if we would like some refreshments such as tea and biscuits. Yes, they were free for train travelers. My parents were overcome with the service and so was I. This was a fairytale ride to the unknown. When we arrived at Southampton, we were told by our conductor that we had a taxi service coupon to take us to the Queen Mary along with our luggage. We were to leave our luggage on the dock, and it would be taken care of by the personnel of the ship. The ship personnel greeted us as Mr. and Mrs. Jan and Maria Jasinski and Mister Franciszek J. Jasinski. We were indeed welcomed travelers on board.

CHAPTER IV

to America

Once on the ship we were welcomed by people called Stewards. They escorted us to our cabins. My parents were escorted to the second level below the main level. They were to occupy one room with their own bathroom. I was escorted to the third level below the main level and shared the room with another man, but I never got to know who he was. I was intrigued about this man but I was preoccupied with my own family. I had to attend to my parents' needs, if they had any, because for the first time in my adult life I was able to assist them in any way I could. Just sitting with them and sharing their company was good enough for me. It made me feel good just to see my mother just looking at me, showing how much she loved me. My father as usual was very reserved. He would just look and smile and nod his head, indicating that he was happy.

As dinner time approached, we were called to go to the dining room. Well, this dining room was so large it would probably accommodate more than one hundred passengers. The tables were very funny because they had ledges around the tops, which prompted me I wondered why. There were porcelain plates as well as cups and saucers including silverware. All this was done in a very appealing way. Were we some kind of celebrities or what? The dinner meal was more than good. There was soup, salad and a dinner plate covered with baked potato with butter and sour cream and a big succulent beef steak. Oh, what a meal. Frankly this was the best meal in my life. Then ice cream with sugar wafers and hot coffee was the limit of my expectations. When we finished this superb meal, my parents were speechless, so was I. How could some people live in these riches and others were starving to death? The answer was simple. This is the civilized side of the world, and things are so different here on this side of the freely governed world. Democracy is here—whether on land or the wide open sea.

How about the next morning meal? Hot tea, hot chocolate or hot coffee served with either ham and eggs or bacon and eggs or pancakes and eggs or maybe sausage, bacon and eggs, or the combination of all of the above with maybe pineapple and other fruits on which to feast yourself—for a breakfast meal. As I ate some of these things I remembered the times when there was nothing but hot water for breakfast, and I had to be content that it was hot and not cold water. My God—things got better each day. I told my parents this could not last forever that things could not get any better—ever! As this massive ship plowed through the water at a pretty good speed, it was wonderful to just sit on the top deck and see the wonders of the vast ocean of water. How mesmerized I was, sitting and watching what was going on around me.

About a day after we started this fantastic trip on this ocean liner, I spotted some rather large fish swimming alongside our ship. I still had my Polish-English dictionary with me, so I went down to my room to bring it with me to the top deck where I was observing these new fish. After inquiring from some people close to me, I learned that these fish were called dolphins. Well, the dictionary suggested that dolphins like to follow ships, because of the game they played with the moving object. In addition to the game, they would at some point, get some food while traveling alongside vessels. It didn't take long before there were hundreds of dolphins on either side of our ship and they kept us company for long periods. It was a daily phenomenon and I never got tired of watching them perform for us.

The trip was to have lasted about five days, from Southampton to New York. Well, for me it could easily last months, because the food, clean bedding, movies and games aboard the ship was everything that one could ask for. Yes, I did smoke some cigarettes. The metal box holding about fifty cigarettes cost about twenty-five American cents. I gave most of them to my father for he loved to smoke, but he insisted on rolling his own. I went back to the kiosk where you purchased tobacco products and asked them if they had some loose tobacco and some cigarette paper. Well, they indeed had some, so I purchased these things for my father. I called him "Tato", that's what I called him in Polish. He was very happy when I gave him his loose tobacco and papers. I think he was very impressed with me by getting him the things that he liked.

About the third day of our travel the weather changed somewhat and things started to affect our smooth sailing and the waves started to rock our ship. It was progressing to rock this large ship more and more violently, and the ship was pitching from front to back. But there was some kind of device that would stabilize the pitching by rolling some heavy objects at the bottom of the ship. We could feel and hear the rolling motion as the ship rocked from bow to stern. After a few rolls the ship would stop pitching. The problem was the swaying and people became seasick. That's what happened to my parents. They wouldn't come to the dining room because they couldn't hold any food down. A lot of people didn't attend the meals. Some of us were asked if we wanted additional portions of food because there was an excess and it would be thrown out. So I think I solved their problems by having some extra food to eat. Why not? The food was lovely and very tasty, so I ate all I could, for who knows what lies ahead of me?

The weather lasted for a couple of days' and the wind and rain were quite cold. This was wintertime—the beginning of February, and one should expect this sort of thing. But by being on top deck you could still see hundreds of dolphins escorting our vessel as it plowed through the never-ending ocean. What a wonderful voyage it is to see all these wonders of the world and at the same time be treated as special people on this voyage. As night came and we were ready to retire, we heard over the public address system that the next morning we would pass by the greeting of the Statue of Liberty. This would happen about seven or a little after seven a.m. Those who would like to see this statue should wake up before that time. Well, I didn't know what the Statue of Liberty was all about so I looked in my dictionary to find the meaning. Those two words gave me a little indication of what it was, but it didn't give me the importance of the meaning.

As the ship docked and was secured, the ramps were attached to the ship linking us with the dock over the water. It didn't take us long before we disembarked onto dry land. My parents gave each other a big hug and gave me one as well because the voyage was a successful and safe one. As I looked around I noticed this tall man standing along a motorcycle observing the crowds. Looking at him for some time, I decided that he must be a policeman because of his uniform and a strapped handgun on his belt. To me he looked like a big gangster because I read something about gangsters in America. I was not scared by his presence but was overwhelmed because of it. It reminded me a lot of what happened to me while still in Poland and it was almost ten years ago to the day because we left Poland on the tenth of February, 1940. There were a lot of people waiting for their loved ones coming back from England. I overheard one of them speaking in Polish, so I went over to them and introduced myself in Polish. They were glad to talk to me and asked if they could help me in any way. I showed them our tickets to travel to California and said that I needed to find the railroad station to get to Chicago. The ticket indicated the Northwestern Station. The nice man who spoke Polish to me said the taxi cabs are all waiting to take us wherever we needed to go. So he signaled for a cab to come and take us to the station.

We helped the driver pack our suitcases in the trunk then we left the port for the train station. We arrived there in a very short time and the driver asked me to pay his fare. I asked him how much we owed him. When he said the price was fifteen dollars, I almost fainted. This was about half the money I had for our whole family. What could I do? I had to pay his fare and go on and board our train to get to Chicago where we would transfer to the Southern Pacific Railroad to go to Oakland, California. This train ride would take us about five days and nights, so here we go again, nothing but train wheels clicking on the rails, what a southing sound.

As we departed the New York station, it was quite a nice ride for the sights of New York were splendid. My father and I were surprised to see all these small cities so close together and all have their own architecture. We all wondered when we would see red Indians on their horses attacking our train for some ransom. It was something to talk about for this journey will be long and we might as well get used to it. We'd done it before so not a big deal now. As evening approached we were getting hungry, so I suggested that in the next station stop, I will jump out and get something to eat.

My dear mother was always so resourceful and she cared for us so much that I could not believe it. She said to me, "Franek don't go out because I have a surprise for you." She then pulled out of her bag these beautiful sandwiches. "Here," she said, "sit down and eat and when the train stops, get out and get us something hot to drink." Wow, what a meal that she gave us from nowhere! I asked "Mom, when did you prepare all these sandwiches?" She simply replied that "This time I didn't get lost because I went to get some soup. There were these sandwiches and I could not get lost because I was aboard ship."

Well, we had something to laugh about and to reminisce about our past. As we were traveling, the train conductor came up to us and asked us to show our tickets for our transportation. When he examined and punched some holes in them he simply said, "thank you" and went to do the same thing to other passengers. Not too long after his visit he announced that we were in the state of Pennsylvania. I said the same thing in Polish. So at this time my father said, "My aunt on my mother's side whose name was Strarczewski emigrated to America about 1885." But he added that he didn't know the city or the place where she had settled. I said it was a shame because we could stop and visit her. To that he said, "Franek, she would be dead by now and it would be of no use to stop and try to find her."

Anyway, it was something to talk about for I never heard that I had a great aunt in America before we got here. You always learn something new and it never ends. We finally arrived in the state of Illinois. The city of Chicago was ever so cold. There was no cover up or way to avoid the cold winds from Lake Michigan. We had to stay in the station in Chicago for eight hours to catch our Southern Pacific train to our final destination of Oakland, California. Eight hours in this cold, windy city was an eternity.

It didn't matter, cold or hot, you will get hungry and will run out of food. It was time to go to the store and get some supplies, not only for our evening meal, but also to prepare ourselves for the upcoming ride to California. I told my parents that I had to go to get some supplies. I had a lot of time to scrounge around to find a food store outlet instead of a fast-food outlet. I came upon an open store where there were some people shopping with the store baskets. Well, it looked to me as if this store was not too expensive, as the people in it were dressed comfortably, so I was at ease and picked up milk, bread, sliced meat (called bologna), and I spotted a jar of pickles which said on the label "Polskie Ogurki" (Polish pickles). Wow! Polish pickles in America. That must be something special!

As I approached the counter, I overheard the clerk talking to the customer ahead of me. It seemed to me that it sounded like Polish, so when my turn came I asked the clerk, "Did I hear you speaking Polish?" He looked at me somewhat annoyed and said, "No, I was talking Chinese." It seemed to me an eternity to realize that this man indeed spoke my language.

I was very embarrassed by the clerk's remark. So I told him that I just got to the US three days ago, and that I didn't expect this treat to hear my native language. He then shook my hand and said, "Brother, welcome to America where all people are equal." After I paid for my groceries, I went back to the Chicago Railroad station. I told my parents word-for-word what had happened to me in my experience purchasing our supplies. At this point my father said, "Franek, the City of Chicago has more Polish people than the capital city of Poland's Warsaw." Therefore, it was not so unusual to hear Polish spoken. Now you tell me. I was so embarrassed because I was made to transact the purchase in English, and because of that I made a fool of myself. I said to him, "Tato (father) why don't you tell me more of these things. If you tell me I would be better off." Finally the loud speaker announced that the Southern Pacific train on some platform would depart for California at some time.

When we boarded the train car, there were about a dozen people in the car. As I figured out, the fewer people, the more room for us, and because evening was approaching there would be more room to sleep. After awhile the train started up with a gentle shift. I said to my parents that it sure is different than on the Russian train. Tato gently nodded his head in agreement. As we started to gain speed and left the City of Chicago, behind us, Mother started to prepare something to eat as we were hungry. The train was warm and very comfortable so the food was good to prepare us for the night train ride and to sleep on the seats under the covers of our blankets. When the morning came we were some distance from Chicago. I monitored the ride on my US map and figured that we were well on our way to California.

As we passed some cities, I observed big buildings with big parking places, filled with hundreds of cars. I made this observation to Tato. He said that all the workers in the USA, or most of them, need transportation to go to work so that's why there are so many cars in the parking lots. As I tried to comprehend this concept I thought, "This must be the place where I want to live." I told myself that I must succeed when I settle down as this would not be another England. Here I must succeed for better or for worse. I will not fail, I will succeed! Was this just a fairytale or a commitment? No, I was dead serious. The vast territory that we were traveling day and night will have to embrace me and my family into its environment. As we got to Utah, I again noticed the same parking lots with many cars parked by the buildings. That reinforced my ideas and goals about my future. Because I was young and well trained in my profession and very eager to make myself into "a somebody", I was equipped with eagerness to start anew—and nobody will stop me in doing so. I will not fail!! This was a very strong promise I made to myself and I will live up to it.

As we passed through Salt Lake City and the salt flats, it sure resembled the Salt Sea in Palestine for it looked somewhat like white sandy rock. The train stopped for a very short time. It didn't look promising for a good chance to get some more supplies. As I looked at the map, our next possible stop was Reno in the State of Nevada. My mother assured us that all will be okay, and that we had enough food to last us to the next stop. The environment in Salt Lake City was quite hostile because the snow was everywhere. I was glad that I didn't have to get out of the train because inside of our car it was warm and cozy. So why go out and fight cold if you didn't need to? Besides, Reno was quite near our estimate of the length of our travel, so we will surely survive. There was an announcement that the next train station was indeed Reno and that the train would stop there for a very short time.

As the train approached Reno I decided that I would run out and get some supplies for further travel. As the train came to a stop, I jumped out of it and ran to the lighted building to purchase some provisions. Instead I found a mass of people in the building making a lot of noise that I had never seen or heard before. There was no food nor food counters. Instead there were tables surrounded with people shouting, hollering, and screaming. What is this place? Who are these people and what are they doing here? I left the building to go into another one and find the same environment, so I decided to go back and get on our train. I didn't want to miss it as my mother missed hers in Russia. I got back to the train in the nick of time. When I got to our compartment, my Tato asked, "Where are the supplies?" I sat down next to him and said, "Tato, I don't know how to explain to you what I have seen because I don't know what happened to me." He said, "Franek, we have nothing but time, so take your time and we will listen to you and maybe we will have something to say about it." After going through my experience in the City of Reno he said that it sounded like something that he had seen in the First World War when he was in the European Theatre of War, he was in France and passed through Monte Carlo. It was simply a gambling house. He helped to add to my story describing what the tables looked like and I agreed.

The next stop was the town of Truckee. It was about an hour's ride so no one was too upset about the lack of food. It was not the lack of food, because we had a dinner car behind us, but the prices were too high, so we had to wait for something more affordable when we get to Truckee. It was late at night or early morning when we arrived in Truckee. I had some success getting bread and milk and some cold meat to make sandwiches and the meal was more than great and very satisfying.

When we awakened the next morning there was still snow all around us and the mountains were also covered with lots of snow. But as the train proceeded to plow through the snow we would sometimes go through wooden tunnels or rock tunnels. It was something to admire and see the wonders of the world. As we traveled into California the sights were getting prettier by the mile. As we dropped below the snow level and forests we were able to see the valley in front of us. It was beautiful—all the greenery and beautiful golden flowers. It looked as a paradise might look. Not only my parents and I were overwhelmed with this beauty but the rest of the travelers were impressed too.

We were informed by our able conductor that our projected arrival time would be about 3 p.m. barring any problems. It looked like about 4 hours to go. Not bad for ten days of travel all the way from England. Years ago it would most likely take the most part of a year or more. Tato made a very good observation about the scenery. He said that because California was bordered by the Pacific Ocean and tucked against the high mountains on the east side, that it made the plains of California a very mild place, because the temperature would be mild. He was partly correct with his assessment. As we passed the capital city of Sacramento, California, I always envisioned that the capital city was Los Angeles, it turned out that I was wrong.

The City of Sacramento didn't impress me as being something special, but who am I to judge the cities. It didn't take too long to go west and reach the Bay Area, in this case, Oakland, the city across from the City by the Bay, San Francisco. We would finally get out of the train in Oakland, possibly for the last time in our lives. How much train travel can one take in one's lifetime? Well, this time the long travel we had coming to America was to improve our chances for a better life. Above all it is to unite ourselves with my sister, Stefania. I wonder who this sister of mine is? I had not seen her in the past eight or nine years. What will I see when we meet? Will she know how I look? What will we say to one another? I was scared to face this whole episode in my life. Or maybe this whole thing is just a dream and she is really just a fiction and is not here in Oakland, just like my brother Joseph and sister Stasia.

I have been alone for so many years of my life so why would things change so much now? I asked mother what she expected to say to Stefania when we meet her. I also asked Tato how he would act toward Stefania when he gets to hold her in his arms. He only smiled at this question and said nothing. What will I say to her? Will I recognize her and her husband Robert? Times will be hard to reconcile for we are strangers to one another. I came to the conclusion to take things as they unfold and be happy about it all. As our train rolled into the City of Oakland—well this city was not New York or Chicago or Salt Lake City. Oakland was quite gloomy and dark. It was still early in the afternoon when we arrived. But this is the place we were destined to come, so be happy and that's where you wanted to be. As we got off the train and gathered our belongings we were taken to the train depot by the attendant and our luggage was on the train platform. As we got there, well there was this man who I recognized to be my brother-in-law Robert. He made a gesture to me that he knew who I was. At the same time, there was this beautiful lady at his side. This must be my sister Stefania.

I looked at her for some few minutes. Is this lady really Stefania? Is this girl my sister and what will I say to her when I greet her? I don't know her as she is a stranger. We have not talked to each other in about ten years, or about half of our lifetime. I don't know what went on in my parents' minds but by their expressions, they were overcome with emotion. As we came down the platform to meet them, it was another thing. It seemed to me that from the moment I spotted my sister to the time I actually held her in my arms that was only an hour later.

As mother and father exchanged greetings, hugs, kisses and wiping their tears, it was my turn. I simply got close to her and grabbed her hands and held them tightly and looked at her face. The tears were rolling down my cheeks and hers too. I wasn't able to say a word for a while, just held her hands in my hands and looked at her. I spoke to her in Polish. I said how deprived I was not to be close to her and that we were cheated of our childhood to grow up together. I was astonished how beautiful she was and I told her so. She also expressed her lack of knowing me all those years and said how tall I was and also a good looking young man. I suppose we held hands for more than a few moments. I then gave her a big hug and kissed her on both cheeks saying how much I had waited for this moment. I also greeted Robert and we exchanged big hugs because we hadn't seen each other since 1945 in Egypt. He had matured as well as I had. It was a very memory-laden affair.

As we drove in their car from the Oakland railroad station to Castro Valley, which was about 25 miles, we could hardly wait to see their two boys, Eddie and their little boy called Randy. We arrived at their house in Castro Valley and went inside of their lovely home. It was not too large but it was nicely furnished. There we found these two gorgeous boys, the older boy Eddie was about 4 years old and very talkative asking who we were. On the other hand there was the baby Randy, in his crib, sound asleep so we left him alone in his dreamland. As Stefania prepared some tea and coffee and some finger sandwiches for our evening snack we had a lot of time to sit down and cover a lot of lost time.

The war brings lots of surprises and heartaches and it treats all equally. Sure we lost two of our family members because of the war but at the end who do you blame and hold responsible for it? Life has to go on. How lucky we are to be able to sit down and hold each other and have our family together again. Can't we just thank God for what we have instead of wondering why we don't have what we wanted? We will survive as we are getting closer to our goal. The future definitely looks a lot brighter from now on. As we were going to sleep in my sister's house after the long journey I felt very secure. As I was taking a shower before I retired for the night, I noticed that my ankles were very swollen, almost double the size of normal and this scared me. Besides I had to shower for I was quite dirty, not having the chance to clean myself for five days. No wonder Stefania stayed quite far away from me! After the shower, I showed my parents my lower legs and they concluded that it was just lack of exercise and all would be okay in a day or so, so don't be too concerned about it.

Next morning a wonderful breakfast awaited all of us—bacon, eggs, toast, hot coffee and tea, with some jams and marmalade. And good company! Stefania had a chance to present her boys to us. Eddie was quite shy, but quite receptive towards us. Although my mother couldn't communicate with him, he was quite willing to sit on her lap. As for me, I treated him like a big boy and he liked that, so we made friends quite easily. The younger boy was too little at 3 ½ months. He didn't know the difference between English or Polish so we all got along with him okay. Goo-goos and smiles were all that was necessary to communicate with him. The daily events were going quite well. I spent quite a lot of time covering events which I missed with Stefania. I wanted to know how she managed growing up and how she managed to be so beautiful. Above all I told her how lonely I was not to see her all these years but how it was all past and we were together again. Mother and Stefania could not stop talking, about what? I could not tell, but it was continuous and made them happy, so what could I care, let them come to know each other again.

My father was evaluating the grounds in the backyard of their house and he decided that they should have some fruit trees and some vegetables alongside them. I agreed with him but cautioned him that he should talk to Robert, for this was his house and his possession and that he needed to get his permission. He asked me why all the ground at the back of the house was empty of any growth. I explained to my father that his son-in-law was not a farmer, but that his profession was in golf and didn't have time for farming. Besides he wasn't a rich man, and a new house, two young boys and a new start in life didn't allow him all the privileges of luxury. He said that he will give him a hand to do something to help him have some nice fruits and vegetables. It was okay with me but I said that when I earn some money I would help make his dream come true.

The next day before Robert went to work he asked me to call him Bob, which is the shortened form of Robert. I told him all about what my father suggested about his back parcel of land. He simply said that he would love if somebody would improve his backyard (as he called it) because he didn't have time or ability to do anything about it. I told my Tato that he would have to wait because we didn't have any funds to invest in his dreams but when I find a job I would give him funds to fulfill his vision.

As I was talking about work, well I have been here three days and was rested so should think about going out and scouting for some kind of work. I recalled when I was still in England that I promised myself that I would get some good job and that I will make something of myself and that I would not fail. I again reinforced this pledge to myself.

Bob returned from his work on the golf course—he was a professional golfer and teacher. His hours were flexible so he could come home at different times. That evening I asked him if I could ask him some questions. In my broken English I asked him if he knew of any jobs I could undertake to make a living. I told him that I wasn't worried but that I needed to go out and find some work to support our family because sooner or later we will become a burden to him.

He insisted that he had no leads on work for me. But he said that as he goes to work he passes this plant were they manufacture big trucks, called Peterbilt. Maybe I could go there and see what they might have for me. Well, this was as good as anything I had so far, so I said that I will try to go there. The next day when we finished our breakfast and he was ready to go I asked him if he would take me with him. He simply said, "Let's go." When we came to the plant he stopped his car, got out of it and showed me the door which said, "Main Entrance" and I thanked him. He shook my hand, said good luck and left. Here I am standing in front of this plant.

As I stood there I said to myself "Franek, be brave, compose yourself, get in there and don't come out without fulfilling your mission. This is a great task. You have to fight for your existence!" With this determination I proceeded inside the building. As I entered the reception room there was a lady attending to a weird piece of furniture with lots of wires attached to it. It was continuously making ringing noises. She was very attentive to it, yanking the wires every which way and constantly talking to seemingly no one that I could see. So I just stood there, wondering what this was all about. I never moved or said anything. I just stayed there observing this entertainment. When the ringing noise stopped and she slowed down on pulling the wires, she noticed that I was watching her. She turned and faced me and asked how she could help me. I addressed her with the greeting, "Good morning, Madam" and said I was looking for any kind of work. She looked at me and said: "I'm sorry but we have no work at this time so we can't hire anybody right now."

The machine she was attending started ringing again. She was busy and left me alone. I spotted a bench nearby, sat down and waited. I told myself that I had to be persistent and not to give up. After all this is a big plant and they must have some work for me because I am qualified to do some work here. I will not go away, out of here, without work. I told myself not to be afraid as things will turn out okay. Not too long after she spoke to me, she turned around and looked at me as I was sitting on the same bench, waiting.

At this time the whistle at the plant sounded. She said to me, "Didn't I tell you before that we have no openings? Besides why don't you go out and have something to eat? Don't you hear the whistle? It announced that it's lunch time." I said that I couldn't go out because I didn't have any money to purchase something to eat. "That's why I have to get a job. Besides I have my parents with me and we need to have some funds to live on." She was again interrupted by another phone call so I was safe for awhile. After the call she put her coat on and left the building. I suppose she went out for lunch. I wonder when she ate her lunch with someone, what was she talking about? Probably said that she had some dummy in her office all morning long that couldn't speak English but persistently asked for work. Well, it didn't bother me what she might say about me. There was another whistle which meant lunch was over. I sat there warming the bench, waiting. About three o'clock the door on the opposite side of the office opened and a big man, about 6' 4" walked toward me. I was sure he wanted to talk to me so I stood up and waited for him to say something.

He slowly approached me and said, "Young man, I understand that this lady on the telephone told you that we don't have any work at this time." My answer was simple "Yes sir, she said the same thing to me." So he said, "Why don't you go away?" I replied, "Sir, I can't go away. I need a job. I just emigrated here from England with my parents. I need a job to support them and myself." He asked me why I don't speak good English since I just came from England. I said, "Sir, I am not an Englishman, I am Polish and I was in the Polish Army but because of communism in Poland, I could not return to Poland." He said, "You are a very interesting person, but I still have no openings at this time. Besides what qualifications do you have to work here?" I said "Well, sir, I attended four years of Engineering School while I was serving in the Polish Army. The Army sent me to Cairo, Egypt to study but because the war ended I didn't graduate, but instead had been sent to England. For that reason, I don't have any diploma to show for it."

He shook his head and asked me to follow him to his office, which I promptly obliged. As he sat me down at the table he asked my name and addressed me by calling me Frank. He asked what were my majors. I told him my first love was electrical study and then mechanical. He said, "Frank, can you read schematics and can you also draw them?" My answer was "Yes, sir, I can and I am very good at it". "So you can follow electrical schematics and you understand them?" I said, "Yes Sir I can". This man was always mumbling something to himself so at one point I could understand he was saying to himself, "I could use this man". He then asked me if I could draw a simple schematic about a starting system on a vehicle.

I did so in the shortest time I could. He then proposed that I draw a simple drawing of a light system, including a battery and the switch. I did this quickly as well. He then stood up. I stood up as well, waiting to be thrown out of his office. After a few moments he said, "Frank, I don't have any openings in your field but (my heart fell to the floor), how would you like to work for me temporarily assembling radiators. In the meantime, I will find an opening in your field." I think I screamed with joy and said to him, "That means that you gave me a job here?" He said, "You deserve to have a job. Be good and obedient and keep your nose clean." I asked him "How can I work on radiators?" I don't have any tools to come to work for you." He said, "You come in the morning, here to this office, and I will take care of you." I thanked him and said that I would see him in the morning and said "Thank you very much, sir. Goodbye, sir" and walked out of his office. As I walked past the telephone lady she turned to me and said, "Didn't I tell you before that we didn't have any openings?" I said to her, "Have patience with me for I will see you in the morning. That man gave me a job and I start tomorrow." She came out from her post, came to me, and gave me a hug, for she was happy for me. She said that I was a very determined young man and she had thought I would land a job here.

As I walked out of the Peterbilt building I was walking on air. I said to myself, "You are a lucky so and so." I proceeded to walk to Stefania's house in Castro Valley because I had no money for transportation. It was about seven miles. What was an hour and a half walk when I got a job on my first try. As I was going home I had a lot of time to think. For one thing why is it that I found my job so easy? Or was it easy? I could have walked away from that building at the first answer that I got from that lady but I didn't walk away. I suppose it's destiny. It seemed I was back home in no time. I forgot to eat something when I left Peterbilt. Oh well, that's not the first meal that I missed and I will survive.

When I got home my parents and Stefania were worried what had happened to me because I left the house about 8 a.m. and it was almost 5:00 pm in the afternoon when I just walked in. My mother looked at me and asked what was the good news, because she recognized my smile. I said, "Nothing new. Just was able to find a job." "New job they all asked? They were all excited. "What kind? Where? How far away?" and on and on. I had to tell them all that happened and how. My father asked Stefania if she had anything to celebrate the occasion. So we had a Schnapps for the good fortune that happened to me. My mom asked if I was hungry. I said, "just a little". "Are you this and that"? I hadn't had this kind of attention for a long time and I wasn't accustomed to it. Anyway, when Bob arrived home he asked me if I had any luck at Peterbilt. Well, I had to repeat my whole escapade to him. He was amazed at what I'd accomplished because he said that the times were hard and unemployment was high. "Frank", he said, "I was worried about you finding a job but I should not have been because you're bold and persistent." He told me that he was proud of me for getting work on my first adventure.

My first day at work was very pleasant. I was introduced to another Frank—he was of Portuguese origin and was very pleasant. He showed me his tools and I was issued a pair of overalls. I was to intern with him to learn the work within a few hours. I even found some shortcuts to assemble the radiators. Of course, all around me everyone was watching all my moves. I suppose even Mr. George Brombaugh, the Chief Engineer who hired me knew about my moves. "So what" I said to myself, "I am who I am and I'll do the best job I can to prove myself that I deserve this job." On my first full period they handed me my first paycheck. It was, after all the deductions, $42.82. My God this was a lot of money. I didn't get this much for one month of my labor in England. When I returned home I gave my check to my father. He looked at it and was surprised to see the amount. He said, "Go to the bank and see how much money they will give you for this note." You see, while in England I was paid in cash in little yellow envelopes which they called "sack". So I never received a bank note (or a check).

When I arrived at the bank, I took my turn in line (in England they call it a queue). When my turn came at the cashier's window, I handed her my check and asked how much she would give me for it. She said if you sign it I will give you $42.82. I was elated and said, "You will"? and she looked at me again and said "Yes!" I took the money and ran. This much in one week, wow, what a country! When I got home Father asked me, "Well, how much did you get for that note?" I said, "the whole amount." His head just moved from side to side in disbelief. It was hard for Bob to transport me to work in the mornings because he worked later hours, but I walked back home after work. One and a half hours to walk home from work was nothing for me. The next Friday when I took my check to cash it, there was a different cashier than the week before. I just signed it and handed it to her. As she looked at it she said, "I will give you $42.82" and smiled at me. I was so embarrassed because I made such a fool of myself.

I knew the whole bank knew about my first transaction. What a fool I was for asking such a stupid question. So when I came home I was quite disturbed about the fiasco of my father asking me about my first paycheck. He asked me how much I got paid this time. I snapped back at him and said, "The same as last week." He asked me why I was so angry. I said that he set me up to ask such a stupid question about the check. He then explained to me that in Poland before the war if one came into the bank with the note, the bank would offer a lesser amount than the face value of the check and if the recipient would not take the offer, he would then go to another bank and so on until he would consent to the offer. He then said he was sorry for my embarrassment.

The work at the plant went okay and I made some new friends among the workers. They were very eager to help me with my work and my new language. It made me feel very much like I was one of a big family. My co-workers and friend, also named Frank, suggested that I purchase a second hand car for coming to work. He was amazed that I was willing to walk all the way to Castro Valley, and said the time it took to walk those seven-plus miles could be better utilized to my advantage. He said that one of his neighbors had an older car which he might be willing to sell to me. I asked him if he would inquire about it and let me know.

Sure enough, the next day he told me that the car was for sale and I could get it for $75.00. He confirmed that it was a good price and was also a good transportation vehicle. I said that I would let him know the next day.

When I got home that day, I announced to my parents that I had a chance to purchase this car for $75.00. My father started to laugh and said to me, "Franek, it didn't take too long for you to become Americanized. Today a car, tomorrow a house and then what next?!!" I waited for my brother-in-law to return from work for I wanted to talk to him about the value of the used car. As he was eating his dinner, we talked about my new venture of being a car owner. He confirmed my viewpoint, that I needed transportation to go to work and added that if my coworker is providing this car as good transportation, then the $75.00 purchase price made a lot of sense and that I should go ahead and get it.

As it turned out, I had saved about $100 in my first few weeks, so after consultation with my parents, we decided that it was a good idea. So I purchased this 1937 two door Studebaker. It was a nice running car and it was quite unusual because in the back of the front seat there were two small folding seats. So here I am in the United States of America, and I am already in a position to own my car to go back and forth to work. I remembered the time coming across the plains of the US and seeing all those cars parked around factories. Now I was the same as all those workers. What a life I came to have in America! I was told by my coworkers that I had to get a driver's license to operate a car in California. I was in possession of such license but it was issued in England by the Polish Army.

It was valid now, so I drove to Hayward, which is a neighboring city to Castro Valley, to apply for my license. I said to someone in the lobby that I wanted to obtain a driver's license. Well, it was ok with them and I was given a long piece of paper with questions on it. I was shown tables where I could sit down and work on those questions. When I was finished, after checking my answers on the questionnaire, the lady checked all my answers as wrong. All the first four answers were wrong. She looked at me and smiled and said that it was not that bad. I missed getting a license because I had nine wrong answers. She informed me that I could try again next week and gave me a booklet to study and asked where I came from. I told her about myself and showed her my Polish Army driver's license. She was very sympathetic towards me, but said I had to come back and retake the test.

She said that she hoped I was not driving the car without a valid license and I promised that I would come back.

When I came back home everybody wanted to know how I had done. I simply answered that I failed the test. My father broke out laughing and said something to the effect, "What, my genius son failed a simple driver's test?" It is too long and complicated, and the language is unfamiliar to me. Instead of sulking, I picked up my booklet and started to study its contents. A few days later it began making more sense because some of the graphic signs and directions were clearer. So the next week, I was armed with more knowledge. I stormed into the same office and came to the same lady I had seen a week earlier and said that I was ready to take the test again. This time when she checked my test she smiled and said that I had only missed four questions, so I passed the test. Congratulations Mr. Jasinski!

My name was somewhat mispronounced but it was okay with me. Now I was legally on the roads of America. How privileged I was to be able to be one of the motorists on American roads. Both of my parents and Stefania as well as Bob were very pleased that I had passed my driver's test. On Saturday as I took my parents for a ride to see the area we could not believe seeing the different sights, towns, homes and parks. We were in paradise. As we drove along this wide road there was a homemade sign "Apartment for Rent".

I stopped the car and went in to inquire about the apartment. An older gentleman came toward me and asked if I was looking for a place. I nodded and said "yes". He then walked with me and showed me a one bedroom apartment. It was a nice place, clean and quite spacious, so I asked him how much was the monthly rent. He asked me, "for how many people and where do I live now, where I worked, and some other information?" After that he said that the monthly rent was $55.00, which included utilities, but the washing machine cost 10 cents per load. I said that I had to talk to my parents and that we would make a decision.

When I returned to the car, I said to Mom and Dad that we have stayed with Stefania long enough (about six weeks) and that we have to be on our own because there were far too many people in Stefania's house and that it was time to leave them alone. We all agreed that this was a proper thing to do so when I came back to talk to the man about our wanting to rent his place he was quite happy. I told him we had just come from England and didn't have any furniture to furnish an empty apartment. He said that he had some furniture and he would be happy to give us a helping hand, so I made a deal with him. He asked me for a deposit, gave me a receipt and said "you can move in any time."

When we arrived back at Stefania's house I announced to her what I had done this day and asked her not to be angry with our decision but that this was the proper thing to do. We had to make this decision because she had her little family to take care of and we would be in her way and interfere with her family life. Besides, we would move out of her house sooner or later for we had to have our lives to plan for our future. It really turned out for the better because she had time to arrange for little Randy's christening. We were so excited to know that at last we can be included in this glorious event. Besides, I was asked to be his Godfather before I came to America. After moving into our new apartment, Mr. Bierman (our landlord) asked me, "How come your mother stays home day in and day out?" I simply answered that she doesn't know how to find a job for herself. After a few moments he said, "Frank, I know someone at Hunt's Foods in Hayward who would give your mother a job. I, in turn, told him to talk to his friend about the possibility of getting her this job.

I told my mother about the turn of events and my conversation with Mr. Bierman. She was thrilled to know that she might get a job for herself. As it turned out, luck had it that indeed he talked with his friend and my mother was offered a job as a tomato sorter. I informed my Supervisor at Peterbilt that I would be late the next morning because my mother was having an interview at Hunt's tomato plant. She was told she was okay for that job and was asked to come to work the next day. We were blessed. I got a good job, now she can go to work and try her luck. What more can you ask for as a good beginning start in America? With my new (old) car I was able to take Mother to work in the early morning and then go on to my own job. She was able to take a bus home after work. My mother was still in her late 40's and very energetic. She was working on piece work at the sorting belt. She was good at what she was doing and was paid well.

A few weeks later Stefania announced that Randy's christening would take place in the next two weeks. All arrangements were made. One glorious Sunday afternoon we all gathered in a small Castro Valley Catholic Church to christen this little boy, Randy. Afterwards, we all met at Stefania and Bob's house to celebrate the occasion. Our families and Bob's family were able to meet each other; too bad that the language barrier made it difficult to socialize much, but a few drinks made it more sociable and it all turned out okay in my estimation. I didn't know what impression we made on the Fry family, but we are who we are and things could not be changed.

I was pretty well liked by my fellow workers and occasionally was invited to go fishing with them. Well, I never fished in my life so it was something new to me. We went one weekend to fish for catfish and it was quite an experience. My friend, Frank, drove to a place on the river bank, towing a small boat with a small motor at its rear. He told me I would love the experience catching these catfish. We did catch some of them and put them in a gunnysack which was attached to the side of the boat in the water to hold them until we got back from our fishing. Well, surprise! When we got back to the pier, and we pulled the gunnysack out of the water there were no fish in it! There was a big hole in the gunnysack and all the fish got away! What a loss of these beautiful fish on my first try. But, after all, we did have good time fishing. For me it was something new because I never fished before except when I was still a child and then I don't remember if I ever came home with any fish.

As weeks went by I spent time with my little nephews and that was fun. One day I was told by my Foreman that the main Engineer of the plant wanted to see me. When I got to his office he told me that he was pleased with my progress at work and in my English language. I was very happy with his compliments. He also informed me that starting the next Monday I should report to the Electrical Department and that would be my new assignment. I was also instructed that I should observe and make notes as to how to streamline the whole department some day. I liked what he said to me but I was not pleased to be in a position where I would act as a spy (sort of) and I told him how I felt about undercutting my coworkers. He then explained that it was not a "spy" type of job, but he wanted to do the work differently or to put it clearly, the work was done Model T style and he wanted production to take a new look. I said that I would take the job and map out my suggestions of what I wanted to change, and that it would take some time. He said it was okay with him.

As I got back to what I was doing my friend, Frank, asked me what it was all about. I explained that when I was hired I applied to work in the Electrical Department but since there was no opening they placed me to work with him. I told him I learned a lot from him, as well as learning to speak English. He then said, "I will miss you because we got along so well."

Finally when I showed up Monday morning for my new assignment, the Superintendent introduced me saying that this new man will be working with you and you will treat him as one of you, and that they were to show me all of the schematics, plans of wiring schedules, and all the other fine points of the operation. As we got ourselves introduced, I was surprised that they were all of Portuguese background, so I was one of six workers in our department.

As the days passed, the work progressed well. But it seemed to me that there was a lot of room for improvement. I would have to digest a lot of knowledge and experience before anything could be changed. So the work for me was a lot of fun because I was doing something I really liked. A few days later I was approached by another worker whom I had not met before. He called me by my first name and said he was the Shop Steward acting as a representative of the Union. He said it was time for me to join the Union if I wanted to work at this plant. My answer was simple and I said that I would like to join because it would benefit me.

It was quite an easy procedure to join the Machinists' Union. To this day I am still an active member, although retired. Just lately I was awarded a diamond studded pin, honoring me for continuing fifty years as an active member and in good standing. What a wonderful country to work and live in! Work was fun, and I liked my job and I was good at it. After being in the department for about four to five months, I was promoted to Foreman. That meant that I was responsible for all the work that was done under my supervision. A heavy task was loaded on my shoulders. Was I up to my new responsibilities? I wondered, but in my mind I was sure of myself, that with a little luck all would turn out ok.

With more work, I was rewarded with more pay and that made me and my parents very happy. They were so very proud of me. My father asked me at some point where I gained all this knowledge. I simply said, "Tato, I received these gifts from God and I thank Him for it all the time." Maybe it's payback for all the miseries I had when we spent the time in Russia and for the deaths of my brother and sister. Who knows? Besides, I didn't attend school just to eat lunch but to learn all that I could to prepare myself for today's life.

My mother and I worked very hard with almost an obsession to get ahead and prosper in the shortest possible time, and erase past losses and discomforts. With my mother working nights at Hunt's Foods and now I was earning higher wages, we managed to save some money. My old Studebaker was giving me more and more problems, especially brake problems. It became a little too dangerous to operate this old relic. Mother was after me to purchase something safer for us to drive in and to be able to explore the surrounding areas. It was approximately November, 1951, when my parents sent me out to purchase a newer automobile for us. I made my first stop at a local Chrysler dealership. Upon inquiring about a new car, I was told that new cars were scarce, and if they had one I would have to give them $500.00 as a premium on top of the purchase price. I said, "thank you" and walked away. I was not that desperate for a

Chrysler anyway. As I traveled toward Oakland from San Leandro, there was a Chevrolet dealership. I decided to go there and see what kind of cars they had available.

Not being very knowledgeable in making this kind of major investment, I was scared to even ask someone about a car because the experience at Chrysler wasn't that pleasant for me. So caution overtook my desire to purchase any car. At some point, a young person approached me asking if I needed any help. He was very pleasant, and it seemed to me that I could talk to him about the possible purchase of a car for my use. He walked me around the car lots and showed me what they had to offer. It looked to me that I should spot some car to my liking. As we proceeded to walk around, I spotted a white car with two doors. It had rear fender skirts, with whitewall tires. As we got closer to it, it looked fantastic. He opened the driver's door, showed me the interior and said that this car has an automatic transmission, radio and a factory-installed heater (radios and heaters were optional equipment). The interior was of gray material.

"My God," I said to myself, "this is the car for us. We could drive it anywhere without worrying about problems." I didn't say anything to the salesperson. He knew that I liked this particular car. I asked him how much the car would cost and he took the number of the car and invited me to follow him to his office. He then opened his file cabinet and looked inside; then he started punching numbers on his adding machine. He looked at me and said, "If you want to purchase that car it would cost you $2,150 with tax and license. What do you think?" I looked at the invoice slip, but I didn't know what it was all about, so I simply asked him what he was thinking about the price. He said that there was a shortage of new cars because of World War II and there was a great demand for them, so if you want to purchase a new car, you have to pay for it.

My God, this car is very expensive and Mom and I worked hard to save all this money, and it will take all our savings. On the other hand, my mother wanted us to drive in a safe car so what was I to do?" I asked my salesman to leave me alone for awhile so I could think about it. I never made such an important decision on my own, so how could I make one today on the spot. As I sat there it came to me that I had to make an intelligent decision. We had the money and we wanted dependable transportation. We could save some more money "God willing", so what more could I need to make this decision?

As the salesman came back, he asked me about my decision. I said I would purchase the car. He proceeded to write up some papers for quite awhile. Then he gave me this paper to fill out after some credit application. It contained a lot of questions which I didn't understand, so I said that I wouldn't fill out the application. He then said that I could not purchase that car, but I said I wanted to purchase the car. He again said that I had to complete the credit application in order to get the car, and back and forth it went. He then asked me how I would pay for this car. With my poor English I said I would pay for it "with money!" For some reason we had a miscommunication because he was raising his voice at me and I was repeating my answers, with this great accent, and I was going to pay "with money"!

Well, soon another gentleman came in and asked the salesman why there is a commotion in his booth. The salesman started to explain to this man that I was unwilling to fill out the credit application and that is what the commotion is all about. So this new man turned to me and said, "Why don't you want to fill out this application?" I said, "I just didn't want to." He said, "Then how will you pay for this car?" I answered, as before, that I would pay "with money!" He said, "and where will you get all this money?" I then stuck my hand in my pants pocket and pulled out a bundle of money and said to him that this was "the money" that I will use to pay for my new car. They looked at each other in amazement and then they looked at me. One of them said that they were very sorry for the misunderstanding.

Then the first man followed the second man outside, and after awhile he returned and asked me how I came to this sales office. I took him outside and showed him my first love, my 1937 Studebaker. He then said that he will take it from me and will pay me $150. Well, this was good news because I only paid $75 for that car, so there was some incentive for me. I told the salesman that I would pay for the car. So then I only had to give him $2,000. He took the papers out of his office and came back, and we went to the cashier where I gave them all my money. Oh well, it had to be done and I could drive this brand new car home and oh, what a wonderful feeling to be in command of this new love.

When I arrived home to show it to my parents, they were in awe. This is it! That's what you purchased for us? What a great country this America is. It had been only ten months since we arrived in this great country and we have managed to accomplish this much. My father came to me and gave me a big hug and said how proud he was to have such a good son. I was proud of what he said to me; I hadn't received praises from my father because I was absent from his life for about seven years, so I was yearning for his attention.

Days went by for me and I was in seventh heaven because I was driving this new car and could listen to the radio while driving. What an extraordinary way to travel. When I drove to work I made sure that I parked in a place where I could see it while working. Oh, what a wonderful feeling to look at what my Mom and I accomplished in this short time in America. As days at work went by, I kept a watchful eye on my car. Then one day one of my coworkers asked me what I was looking at. I said: "I'm keeping an eye on my car." He replied, "What is so special about your old Studebaker?" I answered, "I have another car now, so I'm keeping an eye on it." "Which one is your car now?" I said, "The white Chevrolet." He then looked and could not find it. I told him it was next to the fence and he replied, "Is that the brand new car with the sticker on the windshield?" I said, "yes, that's the car."

Well all the commotion started. He said, "my parents and all of my family never owned a new car so how come you have one? You just arrived here and now you have one. How did you manage to purchase a brand new car in such a short time?" From my coworkers' conversation in the past, they were telling me how much fun they have on weekends at local bar establishments and all the girls they had fun with and other activities, while I was at home learning English from newspapers and magazines, and thus I saved my wages. I told them my mother cooks for us for between five to ten dollars per week. She prepares simple Polish foods for pennies each meal.

So I explained to them, "It's not what you earn, but what you save". So don't be envious of what I do, but maybe what I try to get in my life." As things went along there were many jealous feelings since here I was a novice, hardly with a good command of English, and he was the Foreman of the department and was guiding the Peterbilt Company. At some department meetings, I was slighted because I could not speak perfect English. George, the Chief Engineer, would say, "This man can do the job he was assigned to do." He said that I implemented a numbering system for the wires because we used all black wires and because of numbering them we could easily trace any problem if the wires were incorrectly misplaced; he said that I implemented mass production from ordering to projected manufacturing. At the end of our meeting, I was well received by my division co-managers.

Things never ran without problems but we always managed to correct them. The production of the trucks was going very well. I suppose it went so well because it looked to me that the whole production was going through growing pains and it seemed to me that I was lucky to step into my position at the right time, and it made me look good. As my group came to know me, they realized that what I was trying to accomplish made sense to them as well. Although they opposed me when I first took over the department, they now tried to help me because they realized I was there for good. As time passed, our production improved and management was happy.

On one occasion, after I worked at the plant for some months, I was called to see the Plant Manager, Mr. George Brombaugh. This was the first time he summoned me to see him in his office and it made me very nervous. I was wondering what I had done wrong and because of that could I lose my job? As I entered his office, he pointed me to the chair and asked me to sit down. He then started to tell me about this new project which had never been done before.

OAKLAND · CALIFORNIA

April 30, 1952

Mr. Frank J. Jasinski
Peterbilt Motors Company
10700 MacArthur Boulevard
Oakland 5, California

Dear Mr. Jasinski:

We are enclosing herewith a photograph recently made at the Peterbilt plant in which you appeared as one of the workers who helped to make P-I-E's new Dromedary midget tractor.

We are forwarding this picture to you with our thanks and appreciation for your efforts in connection with this project. As you may know, it is our plan to take the newly converted tractor and the midget trailer on a tour of the territory served by P-I-E between Chicago and the west Coast. It is our plan to visit schools throughout the territory in the interest of promoting driver training and highway safety. Within the trailer will be contained all driver testing devices used by P-I-E in testing its line haul drivers who are employed by this Company. High school students and others will be given an opportunity to take the same tests and we hope in this way to promote the idea that in order to have safety on the highways equipment must not only be maintained in first class condition but that drivers, whether professional or private, should be properly qualified.

Again our thanks for your contribution to this project.

Sincerely yours,

PACIFIC INTERMOUNTAIN EXPRESS CO.

Parkman Sayward
Vice President, Sales & Traffic

PS:MS

Encl.

A thank you note from P.I.E. (Pacific Intermountain Express) for Peterbilt's great work

This big transportation company, called P.I.E. (Pacific Intermountain Express) asked the Peterbilt Company to manufacture a truck to half scale with all the fixtures for public school training programs and for advertising purposes. He asked me if I would help him design the electrical system because he planned to use a four-cylinder Jeep power train, and it differed a lot from a diesel power train. I was mostly delighted that he valued my opinion so much as to ask me for my help. My answer was simple and that I would do my best to be of help to him in this new endeavor. He then said, "Do some homework and design some schematics and get back to me as soon as you can." I thanked him for his invitation.

I walked out of his office with my head in the clouds. Instead of worrying about my job, I was reinforced in my future employment. That day when I got home from work, my mother asked me what was so good that I had such a big smile on my face. I told both my parents what had transpired in George's office. My father asked me if I was capable of doing this new design. All I could tell him was that I was capable, but what the outcome would be was questionable. He then asked me, "Franek, where did you learn all these new things? When you left us in Russia you were a young boy, and now ten years later you are a Supervisor of your department and now a planner for this new truck? So what has happened to you in all these years?" My answer, as always, was simple, "with God's grace he has given me this talent; without God's given talent I would be nothing." Well, all we talked about would not change a thing. I never talked about my duties and accomplishments in the Polish Army, so my parents were sort of strangers to me and I to them.

I would ask my mother to cook me some old Polish food such as Pierogi (sort of Raviolis) or Golabki (stuffed cabbage). She was so happy to do so, and she would watch me eating and enjoying her food, and in time we finally became a family again. Stefania and Robert, with their boys, were doing fine and would visit often. My project with the toy truck, as we would call it, was progressing just fine, and I ironed out the difficulties with the wiring even though it was quite complicated, but manageable. It took about five months to finish the project. When it was completed, there was quite a celebration such as picture-taking and newspaper coverage, and so on.

About a week later I was called to George's office again. I went promptly to see what it was all about. He sat me down and said that my department did a good job on the toy tractor, and he wanted to relay his praise for a job well done. Then he handed me this piece of paper and said, "Thank you Frank." On my way back to my department I looked at the paper which expressed gratitude from P.I.E. There was another paper and a check in the amount of $500! Oh boy, that much money for my participation in the project. Is this a great country, or what? "Lucky Frank" I said to myself. But then I was always lucky to some extent. I was never afraid to give of myself more than 100%, and it was always returned to me. When I showed the letter and the check to my parents, they were amazed at what I was able to do and show them what I had accomplished in the short time since we came to America.

It was not all my doing. My mother was working hard at Hunt's Foods, working nights on piecework. She was making good wages, so together we were doing fine. As in the past, with our new white Chevrolet we would go out for rides. On one occasion when we were out on some rural roads, we spotted a sign by the road with a Polish name on it. My father was longing to meet some Polish people so he could talk to them in his native language. As I drove on their private driveway, the first thing I encountered was a big dog, barking and barking. I didn't get out of my car. The lady occupant came out of the house, quieted her dog and approached our car. I then got out and politely asked her if her family was Polish and, if so, could they speak Polish. She said something to the effect that her husband's parents were from Poland, that the parents were gone and that her husband never learned Polish, and besides, he was out of town.

So I turned my car around and we were on our way to explore some more countryside. As I drove I related my conversation to my parents. My father was very disappointed that with such a Polish name they didn't speak Polish. He was heartbroken; he wanted to be back in Poland, but on the other hand, because Poland after World War II adopted Communism imposed upon it by Russia, he didn't want to go back and be subjected to that way of life. So he was stuck here in American without any other way of life.

As weeks went by, one day when I came home from work, my father said to me, "Franek, you know as I walked around this neighborhood I noticed some funny things." I asked him to explain. He then said, "You know when I was by some homes, there was this sign on the lawn, 'For Sale'," He said that the home had but four rooms. I almost laughed, but didn't because it would make him angry at me. So I simply said that it was a sign "for sale" and it didn't say "four rooms" as he understood because "sale" in Polish means "room" which he naturally interpreted as "four rooms". We had some fun with his discoveries.

The next day it occurred to me that sales of homes were available throughout the region. So it happened one Saturday that I went to the real estate office to inquire how one would purchase a house. I had one experience when I purchased my new car, but to purchase a house, well, this would be a new experience. As I entered the office, I was asked if they could help me. I explained that I was new in this country but was wondering how I could purchase a house. The response was simple. "Where do you want to live and second, how much money do you want to spend?" I was puzzled. I had no clue how much the houses were selling for, nor how much I would want to pay for one. But deep in my heart I wanted to own one. I explained that I worked for Peterbilt Truck Company, and I would like to live close by.

So after about forty-five minutes or so, after the person looked through piles of paper, he announced that there was a house for sale close to the factory. The price was comfortable, so after awhile he said that I could purchase the house for less than five thousand dollars. So I said that I wanted to see the house. After driving from the sales office for a few minutes we arrived at the house. It was empty, so we went in. It was two stories, had room for two families and was large enough for our future, as well as having an attached garage. I fell in love with this house because it was both affordable and close to work. I thanked the salesman, said it was a nice home and told him I would get in touch with him after I talked to my family.

When I got back home, I had to explain to my parents about my experience. The next day after church, I took my parents to the house. When they saw it, they said they liked it and as we figured, it would take us about three years to pay for it. They wanted to see the inside before we made up our minds. The next week we were shown the entire home. It had a large front yard that my father visualized as a flower garden. So we were all in agreement and set to make an offer on the home. The next few days we drove to the empty house and looked at it as our new home away from home. We made the decision that it was better to own a home than to pay rent month after month. It was a no-brainer for us to purchase this place, and it would be our first adventure purchasing a home. We had never seen another house so it was important to us that we purchased what we could afford and in the right location. I went back to the real estate office and told the salesman that I was willing to purchase the house and that I would pay four thousand, five hundred dollars. After giving him one hundred dollars to hold the purchase, they wrote a big contract which I signed.

My God, here I am, new to this country, I hardly speak English, own a new car, have this glorious job and am now negotiating the purchase of this home! Am I in a dream world? Well, nothing is so smooth and I received bad news. The seller wanted four thousand, nine hundred dollars. I was thinking this was four hundred dollars more than I offered. However, we finally purchased the property for four thousand, seven hundred and eighty-two dollars. I paid my five hundred bonus dollars, plus another five hundred dollars as a down payment. After final closing costs, we paid a little over forty dollars per month to pay off the mortgage. This was about fifteen dollars less than we paid Mr. Bierman for the apartment. So how can we go wrong? Here we are in America, not quite two years, and now we have a new car, two-story house, my mother had a good paying job at Hunt's Foods, and I had a wonderful position as the Chief Electrician at the Peterbilt Truck Factory. In what better position could we be? Life in America is great.

As I continued working for Peterbilt, I was advancing in my position, was making higher wages than when I started, and I had joined Machinist Union 1441. This was in 1952 and we made a grand start. We were probably in the upper 20% income bracket in California. With my mother working we would be able to pay for the house and purchase some furniture because we had none to put in the empty house. We were sure that things would go smoothly because we had the will and the resources.

The home we purchased was set at the back of the lot so the front yard was very large. My father was a born farmer, and since there was not that much ground to cultivate for produce, he decided it would be a good idea to have a flower garden. We went out and purchased lots of bare root roses and in a broad spectrum of color. So while he was babysitting, he spent his time planting and cultivating his roses. Each time I would come home from work he would show off his work of art. Before mother and I realized it, the better half of the yard was planted with roses. Mother was very happy with them but said to my father, "Jan, you could plant some vegetables too. Roses are not edible. We could have some tomatoes as well as some other goodies." Since my father was very agreeable to what mother asked of him, he agreed to plant some veggies.

Sadly, one day my sister Stefania's husband Bob was killed in a car accident on his way to Oregon and this severely affected her. As a result, she was admitted to Agnew State Hospital with a nervous breakdown and we all missed her and would visit her every week where she was recovering. While everything was going well for me and my family, we became guardians of her little boys, Eddie and Randy. She was quite sick and would look at the boys but wasn't very happy to see them. She was withdrawn and seemed to be in her own world. It made my parents and me very sad because she wasn't getting better. When I would talk with the doctor on duty he would only say that it would take a very long time for her to get well again and to make long range plans, especially for her sons.

Before we knew it, we received a letter from the Veterans Administration Office since Bob had been receiving VA benefits from his service during the war and the VA wanted to make sure that the benefits were being spent wisely and that the boys were being provided for. All of us were quite scared because the Government was getting into our lives. What could we do but wait and see what they wanted? A few days later, two of their representatives stopped at our home. After identifying who they were, we let them in. After a short introduction they went through the entire house, saying nothing. Since my parents could not speak English, they turned to me. I said that I was limited in English but could understand and speak it but not fluently.

That was okay with them. They praised us for giving the boys a clean environment and said that they looked good and clean and well fed. They also informed me that the boys' father had GI insurance and that we would receive monthly checks to take care of them. They instructed me on how to keep track of how the money was spent each month, and told us that we would have to give them a yearly accounting. This was okay by me because the money belonged to the boys, and I didn't have any objection to the system. As they departed, we were glad to be left alone. However, it was good news that we had some monetary help.

My father reminded me that it had been quite awhile since we visited the Polish Club in San Francisco. So he said, "How about going there and see what is going on." I realized that he wanted to talk with other Polish people and other news about Poland and Polish politics. Mother said, "you boys go ahead. I will stay home and take care of the boys. Since I work, I have some household work to catch up on." Friday nights were the largest attendance, because, as always, the boys played poker games while the ladies had their own agendas. We went to the Club early in the evening so my father found some men his own age who he could talk to.

There were just a few younger people where I could find some company. Our conversation was quite restricted because I was a stranger. I didn't know any local sports, such as baseball, football or any others so the talks were simple, such as, "Where did you come from" and other small talk. For this reason, I felt very uncomfortable as I was an outsider. I kept to myself until it was time to go home. As the evening went by my father said he was tired and it was time to go home.

As we were driving on the Bay Bridge and getting closer to the toll booth, I got my quarter out and paid the fee. My father said, "Son, you are getting with the program and I didn't have to bother you at all to give them the money." As I said to him, "If you get something you have to pay for it." We had some small talk on our way home. He sure liked riding in our new car, saying, "of all things that have happened to us, this was quite a pleasure going from one place to another." When we arrived home, the boys were in bed fast asleep. Mother wanted to know what was happening at the Polish Club.

Well, I reported that there was nothing new and, as before, some people played poker and that was about all. My father, on the other hand, had some other news, such as there would be some sort of traditional evening where there would be traditional Polish cuisine and some other programs, and we were invited to attend. This was news to me. I asked why he didn't say anything about it on the way home. He said that he didn't want to repeat himself, that's why. Mother was smiling about it. She said, "Sometimes you have to pay him for some conversation. You will see and get used to it because your father is a man of few words. You don't know your father yet. The longer you live with him, the more you will know him. But he is a good man."

Well, Mother was planning the trip to San Francisco to meet some new people and she was excited about the entire episode. I was also excited to go as well because, who knows, maybe just by chance I would have an occasion to meet someone as well, so why not take advantage of the occasion. The trip to San Francisco went just fine. As we walked into the Polish Club, we encountered the same crowd, some playing poker, some just gossiping, some were drinking beer, but mostly all we just having fun being together. Some people spoke English and those playing cards spoke Polish. Well, guess where my father was sitting! He could not have enough Polish from other people. Mother, of course, mingled among the other ladies and she seemed to be having fun. As for myself, I was having great fun just watching my parents enjoying themselves speaking to their own age group.

It was time to go back to San Leandro since it was about midnight so we were not in too much of a hurry. The lights of San Francisco and across the bay looking at Oakland were all lit up. It was a pleasure to cross the Bay Bridge. As we approached the toll booths to pay our twenty-five cents, I started to reach for my wallet. I could not find it in my back pocket, so I searched my other pockets. I stopped the car and searched everywhere hoping it slid behind the back of the seat. Well, there was no wallet to be found. I asked my parents if they had any money but the response was negative. What was I to do? I drove to the toll booth and said that I lost my wallet and had no money. The toll people asked me to drive forward to the side and go to the office to see what they could do for me.

As I walked into the office, they were waiting for me. I explained to the bridge officer that I must have lost my wallet in the Polish Club in San Francisco while visiting there and now I don't have any money to pay my fare. After some questioning, the officer reached in his pocket and give it to me, along with an envelope saying that on the way back to the city to place my twenty-five cents in it so I could repay his kindness. He said the money was his own and if he gave everyone a quarter he would go broke. As he handed me the envelope, I noticed his name was on it and I thanked him for his favor and left. As we drove home, I had to tell my parents about the whole episode in the office. My father was amazed that I was helped by the police and that one gave me the money. I could not blame anybody for not having any other money in my pockets, but I expected that mother would have some. Her explanation was simple; while changing her purse she must have misplaced her change-purse, and that was that, she was not at fault.

As we talked about the Polish Club, mother mentioned that some lady had a granddaughter and it would be nice if she and I meet—well, maybe the next trip. This trip was a great disappointment for me because how could I lose my wallet? I felt very irresponsible. When we got home, Dad asked me if I had the Polish Club phone number. I said that I had it in my wallet, but I would find it in the morning since it must be listed in the phonebook and indeed I was right. I went to the public phone booth and called them. The keeper of the club said that he had found my wallet with the ID's and money in it so I could come and get it.

What a relief to get this wallet off my mind. When I returned home I informed my parents that I had to go back to San Francisco to pick up my wallet. Tato offered to go with me to keep me company. The round trip took us about two and a half hours, including stopping and giving my twenty-five cents back to the bridge officer. All in all I changed my mind and now decided that our trip to San Francisco was worthwhile.

The next trip to the Club, when we arrived there, as we walked inside, the Proprietor said I should button my back pocket because you know why and thus we had a good laugh. A little while later, two older people walked in along with this lovely looking young girl. Wow, what a beautiful girl! Tall, with long auburn curly hair, clean looking and with a pretty smile and all the other lovely qualities. I was overtaken with her presence. I wondered if that was the girl that mother mentioned on our last trip. Well, it turned out the grandmother spotted my mother and started the conversation. As I watched mother and the other lady, I was sure that the girl was the one in question. After a while mother came to me and suggested that I meet this young lady. It didn't take much arm twisting because she caught my eye as she walked into the Club.

As I approached her, I introduced myself and said my name was Frank. She responded that her name was Dorothy, but her friends called her "Dot". So I asked if I could call her Dot and she said it was fine with her. I paid her a compliment about how nicely she was dressed and looked so nice and she asked me why I had such broken English. As we sat down, I didn't want to tell her all about me for the fear that she might not be interested. After some small talk I learned that she was in her junior year in high school. I didn't know what "junior year" meant, so she was eager to explain it to me—that she was in her third year of high school. I said something to the effect that it couldn't be so because she looked so young. She just smiled with her big eyes and beautiful smile.

I was overcome and wondered what kind of impression I made on her. The time came again to leave the Club and this lovely girl, but it had to happen. Before we left, I asked if it was possible that we could meet again. Her answer was, "yes" with a smile. She then introduced me to her grandmother and grandfather. We exchanged a few words, and I mentioned that I asked Dot if I could see her again and that she accepted my invitation. On the way home we talked about new friends and I said to my mother that I never had a real girlfriend before and I had some difficulties accepting this new relationship. My mother said, "Franek, you mean to tell me that until now you never went out with girls?"

Since we were driving, there was some time to kill so we had an occasion to talk about it. As I was recalling the events of my teenage life to them, I gave a short biography of those years. "Remember when I joined the Polish Army in Kermine, then I landed in Teheran (Persia), there were no girls there—then came Palestine (Israel), and Egypt, and there were no girls there either. It was all boys and teachers. Then I went to England and there were no girls in the resettlement camps; and since I couldn't speak English, it was difficult to find young girls. Where? On the street? Besides I had no funds to entertain a girlfriend and I was more involved in finding work and lodging for myself. And now you know me for what I am, and not what you make me to be. I suppose it was all my fault for being cheated out of my youth. Please don't think I am weird or something, but that's the way it is." As we arrived home we didn't talk about me for a while, but father in his wisdom said, "Franek, all that you told us I believe is true. But don't forget that other young boys and girls lost not only their youth but their lives, so don't be bitter about it. God took you under His wings and preserved your life for His purpose, so don't be bitter."

A very short time after I met Dorothy (Dot), I made arrangements to go visit her grandparents in San Francisco. One Sunday morning after coming back from church, we made the trip to visit them. When we arrived, the grandparents greeted us very warmly. As we were served some pastries and coffee, grandma said that Dorothy was babysitting but she would call her and she would come right over, for she was expecting us. Not long afterwards Dot came in cheerful and full of life and pretty as a flower and I was very excited to see her again. As we greeted each other and talked a little, one of us, I believe it was I, suggested that she should escort me and show me some highlights of San Francisco, to which she agreed. I very much enjoyed her company. I loved the way she spoke to me and her grandparents spoke limited English so she learned to communicate with them in simple English.

We enjoyed such sights as Twin Peaks, San Francisco Pacific Ocean Belt, the Cliff House, Sutro Baths and Museum and the Golden Gate Bridge. I had never heard about the Golden Gate Bridge and that the assistant bridge designer was of Polish origin. Dot was eager to tell me all about the history of all that we had come to see, and I was very appreciative of all of it, but most of her company. The weather that day was very nice and the ride was that much more enjoyable. We went down to the Marina District and she said that this part of town was mostly occupied by Italians, and that was fine with me. The street which intrigued me the most was the snakelike street called Lombard. Wow, I was afraid to go down it as it was very steep and very curvy and studded with lovely flowers on either side. It all happened very quickly and I was overwhelmed with seeing this beautiful city with my beautiful companion. Then Dot said that we'd better head back home.

When we returned, they were happy to see us and that nothing had happened to us. After some talk we had something to eat and the time came to head back to San Leandro. As we were saying our goodbyes, I asked Dot if I could come and see her again. She said I could come, but I would have to bring this beautiful sunshine with me. I promised I would do so. I believe we exchanged hugs, maybe not, but we said our goodbyes to Dot's grandparents, Mr. and Mrs. Zycinski. On the way home mother wanted to know how we spent our first afternoon together, and of course I told them step by step and that I enjoyed her company very much. I didn't know much about her, but I was sure that time would permit us to know each other quite well. Was I getting serious about this girl? I don't know but I was serious about having a friend, a girlfriend, to whom I could talk and enjoy her company. That's what I was interested in. Anything beyond that would be a bonus. I had yet to meet her parents or her brother, Jerry, but in time if all goes well, it would fall into place.

While working at my job, my mind was wondering about this girl who was coming into my life. I wondered what kind of impression I made on her and what we should go to see when we saw each other again. My work didn't give me much chance to think about my private life. I had to learn and produce and innovate the progress of our production of the big trucks, which cost so much money; the smallest truck cost about $221,000 so we had to do an excellent job because of the high purchase price. I think that I was very dedicated to my job and did it to the best of my ability.

One day I was called to the office of Mr. George Brombach. He seated me down and said that the owner's yacht had some electrical problem. Would I go there to see what might be wrong with it? He suggested that one of the drivers take me there and stay with me so that if I needed some parts or his help, he would be there. The next morning as we got to the Oakland Harbor, I stepped on the deck and was overcome with the beauty of the yacht. She was built out of beautiful oak, adorned with polished brass hardware. It was nice to be on such a beautiful yacht. To tell you the truth I have never seen anything close to this in all my life. But it was not my purpose of being there on the deck. There was a man on board and he pointed out the problems with the lights that would not turn on at some points and some plugs were not working in general. There were also some other small problems.

I checked and traced the troubles with my volt meter and it was quite a small task to correct. In a few hours, the driver and I got back to the plant. I gave a full report to George on what I had done to correct the problems and complaints. He thanked me for work well done and said that his judgment about my ability was correct. "Keep on doing a good job Frank." That night when I got home, I was very excited to tell my father about this beautiful yacht and what I had done to it. He said to me, "Franek, where did you learn all that you do?" I simply said that the good God endowed me with this talent and it is not all me but its God's will, for which I am very thankful.

Living at home became more complicated since we now had Stefania's two boys, but they were wonderful boys. Little Randy was getting stronger and brighter, and Eddie was now about four years old so after work, I could go out for walks with him. He loved to hold my hand and boy, could he talk! He wouldn't stay quiet for any length of time. My father and I would take care of the boys in the evenings while mother worked; then during the day my mother and father, after some rest, would help. Although life was somewhat complicated, it went quite smoothly. Father, with Eddie's help, tended to the roses in the front yard.

From time to time, Dad would ask me to go to the store to get some liquid detergent so he could mix it with water and spray the rosebushes to kill the aphids and this would make him happy. As time went on, I would go to San Francisco to visit this lovely girl Dorothy (Dot). When I would see her, it would make my heart beat faster. I would come up the stairs, ring the door bell and wonder how I would react when I would see her.

When the door opened, she would smile with those big brown eyes and oh what a beautiful smile. She would greet me with a hug, and that was enough for me. It was worth the long trip and even the bridge tolls. We would almost always go for a ride, mostly to the beach where there was a big amusement park. We would go on the rides where you could ride bumper cars and do those silly things, such as taking pictures in the little photo booths or go on the slides where you would walk up about two stories and then slide down the chutes on gunny sacks all the way to the main floor. It was a very exciting evening for us.

We got along quite well and even though I was a little older than she was, it made no difference. Dorothy was just a junior in high school, and I was a mature twenty-two years old, without much experience on how to charm this beautiful girl. There was not much time for me in the past to get involved with girls, so I cherished the moments when we were together. She, on the other hand, was too young and involved with school work. Attending an all-girl Catholic high school didn't leave much time to go out, besides she had a different upbringing. Her Polish-born grandparents demanded much of her attention. Dorothy's parents worked, so she was left alone with her younger brother Jerry. Her grandmother would come over sometimes and help her prepare meals for her parents.

So Dorothy's life was somewhat complicated, and she didn't have much time for herself. As the years went by, I would drive to San Francisco to visit and while I was with her she would teach me some fine points of English. I needed all the help with English that I could get, and I enjoyed her company very much and I became accustomed to having this lovely girl as a friend. On some occasions, we would go see the movies, hold hands and chat about things which at that time made a lot of sense. Were we getting serious about each other? I don't know about her, but I was getting very serious and I would tell her so.

Going back to San Leandro, I had a lot of time to reflect on things that were unfolding for me. At some point, I would say to myself or I would ask myself where all this would lead. Am I ready to settle down in this country with this beautiful girl? If so, how would it all unfold to our benefit? By the time I could gather all my thoughts about what was happening, I would be home and the thinking was gone. I had to get back to my life at hand—the boys, my parents and my poor sister Stefania. It came to me that I was destined to some different sort of life. Why me? Do other people have this sort of complicated life?

On some occasions I would discuss these questions with my parents and more often than not I would get answers like, "Who knows what directions your life will take? It is most likely God's providence." As mother would say to me, "Franek, things always work themselves out so don't worry as worrying will not change a thing, so why worry?" So that was that . . . . next subject. Then she would give me a big hug and say, "You are the only one I have in my life and I count on you to do the right things with your life. It was so good to be held in her arms. I missed my mother's touch since I was a little boy. Life went on, and we were getting ahead financially as we purchased more and more furniture and began to have a more relaxed living and the boys kept us very busy. I became more and more accustomed to having the two nephews around me day after day, and they wanted to be with me. I would take them for nice rides in my still-new car.

During summertime, there was a lot of time to spend with them. We would stop to get an ice cream at Frostie's, that was a lot of fun for all of us. The cost of driving around was quite reasonable; gasoline at that time cost only about twenty-eight to thirty cents a gallon, so I could afford to have the boys enjoy themselves. As for me and my love life towards Dorothy, it was growing stronger. When I would visit her, we would touch on the subject of our friendship and a possible long lasting relationship. She was attending high school and she had to graduate before we could plan anything binding. Things would work out, as my mother would say.

Dorothy's parents tolerated my presence at their home, but was I welcome? I think so, but there were always some problems. I would hardly be in the door before I would knock something over or break a thing or two. I was quite nervous, and frankly, I wasn't polished to be at ease in someone else's home and especially in places where I needed to impress the occupants. I would reflect on my behavior and came to the conclusion that I didn't have an appropriate upbringing. Were could I have learned to behave properly? In the Army tents? Who gave me examples to follow? I was living on my own since I was fifteen years of age, and now I have to learn from scratch how to become a young gentleman in courtship of this beautiful girl. Was it difficult? You bet your life it was, but I had no options. In my opinion, it was necessary to conform to the norm; people accept you for who you are and how you behave, and I realized I had to polish my behavior.

Things went pretty well as I became more civil. My parents noticed some changes in my behavior and maturity, and they told me so. However, I was overburdened with too many responsibilities. My parents wanted to visit Stefania in the hospital as often as they could. We would take her two wonderful boys and drive to visit her, but Stefania was very sick. She was hardly aware of where she was or who the two boys were. It was sad to see her, especially for my parents and my heart went out to her. I had been longing for so many years to come to know her and become friends with her. Now this was my older, beautiful sister. What can I say? It made me sick to see her in that condition.

In addition to visiting her, after some introductions, I went to see her doctors in the hospital. I inquired about her status and the prognosis of her sickness. I was told that she was very ill, and that it would take some time for her to get better, if ever. On the way home, I tried to tell my parents what the doctor said and what we should expect about her health. My mother was a very strong lady and wasn't about to give up as she was a fighter and had a lot of determination. Her opinion was that doctors were only human and only God could hold plans for her daughter—and only He! She added that we would do whatever was needed. Our lives had to go on and they did. Little Randy was growing and running around. He was a very happy boy and it was fun to have him around. The two brothers were getting along quite fine.

My work was progressing well, and I received a few recognitions for my progress and leadership and this also brought monetary rewards. I was very happy and proud of myself. With more and more financial stability, I was beginning to plan for my future. After all, I was going on my twenty-third year and needed to make a life for myself. I was longing to establish some closer relationship with Dorothy and she was on my mind constantly. Not only was she nice and beautiful, but was of Polish heritage. We had a lot in common and we could understand each other and I believed she cared somewhat for me as well. All I had to do was be civil and patient and the rest would work itself out.

I decided to see her every week on Friday, Saturday or Sunday and maybe go to shows or something like that and really get to know each other. As much as I admired her I was never very aggressive. I let Dorothy be herself as the friendship had to develop itself before I could get romantic. I believe I behaved as I should have and I treated her as my best friend and I think she liked that. Besides, she had to finish her senior year in high school and graduate. So the time for romance was ahead of us. School work and graduation were on her mind more than romance, and we were getting to know each other more and more.

I was under the impression that people in America were free of big problems in their lives. Well, I learned that they had the same troubles as people in Poland and elsewhere. I learned that Dorothy's parents divorced when she was only a small child and that her brother was only her half brother. People in America had problems in their lives, and the people were not all as I perceived them to be. Did I feel good about it? No, I did not and I was disillusioned. This was supposed to be a perfect nation. I suppose that I was quite a naïve young man. I was maturing rapidly because I realized that I was not worse off than anyone around me, maybe even better than most. After all, I proved to my parents and my boss that I was somebody—a trustworthy somebody.

I had a new car, a home and I was pretty independent as far as I could judge for myself in comparison with my colleagues at work. Even when I visited our Polish Club in San Francisco, I was aware that some of the young people there were worse off than I was so I didn't have to take a back seat to most of them. I prided myself as being resourceful and stubborn as I worked hard to get ahead in life. After all, it had been only two years since we arrived in America, and look where we were after this short time. No doubt things will only get better as I learn more and more English, and thus make it easier to accomplish things.

My father's roses, under the watchful eye of Eddie and Randy, were doing well. We had flowers everywhere. The house smelled like the rose garden and Dad was in his glory. Being in our house, little Randy learned to speak Polish as did his brother Eddie. We all spoke Polish inside the house. It was funny to come home from work to hear all the Polish-speaking people inside. The boys called me Wujek in Polish, which translates in English to "Uncle". (they still call me wujek). We were one happy family. We would go on long rides, have ice cream cones and sodas, and all was well. The boys were too small to realize what was happening, and it wasn't the time to tell them the truth. It was best to leave them be and let time smooth it out. Time will come to tell them what happened to their lives.

Each time I'd visit Dorothy things were getting more serious. Wow! I kissed her, was I in love? I was in love with her from the first time I met her. I waited for this moment and it was worth it, and I think she respected me for it. She was a very respectful young girl, and her ambitions were very respectful; she had a good upbringing so I was very proud of her and wanted her to never lose her self respect. If it was in God's hands that we would eventually come to a conclusion, why rush things? Life will unravel itself as it did before and will again. In the following weeks we would talk about our lives and do some planning of what we should do in our future. Each time we'd see each other we would get more and more serious about each other. Needless to say we would kiss a little more often, but that was as far as we would go for she and I had too much respect for each other and didn't want to spoil our love. This time would come for intimate love.

When I would visit Dorothy, my mother couldn't wait to ask me what my intentions were. I said I was very serious about her. So she said, "Franek, you should be an honorable young man. If your intentions are as you say, why not get engaged and not keep her guessing?" I didn't know how to go about it, so I said that I would see what I could do.

As I was going to San Francisco, I was thinking about how I could tell her of my intentions. What if she should say "no"? How could I take that? I have fantasized all sorts of things. Well, whatever will come, will come. I will ask her and she would have to make her decision. I will deal with it when it comes. Anyway we went to see some show, but I wasn't paying much attention to it, although we did hold hands and sat close to each other. After the show we drove to where she lived and parked there for awhile. She asked me if there was anything wrong. I said that I was nervous and wanted to talk to her. I began that we were seeing each other for some time now to which she agreed that we had done so, so what's the problem? I said that I was in love with her and that I had great aspirations to get serious about us, but wasn't sure if she felt the same way about me. If it was alright with her, I was proposing to ask her for her hand, and that I would like to become engaged to marry if it was okay with her.

My God, I did say all those words to her, and she got closer to me and kissed me and said that she would marry me but not before she graduated. I explained that graduating was most important not only to her but to me as well. I suggested she come with me to chose a nice engagement ring. She said that I should surprise her and choose it by myself, and that would be okay with her. I suggested that I would give her the ring next weekend in the presence of her parents. It would be appropriate if she wanted it so.

Her answer was positive and we sat there for a while now talking big time business and planned our future and wedding dates, etc. It was getting late, past 1:00 a.m., so I had to get home. After some goodbyes, I took her to the front door, and as she disappeared safe inside I went home. When I arrived in San Leandro, I sat there in front of our house for awhile reflecting on what happened that evening. I was sure I made the right decision and that my parents would be proud of me.

There was a small shopping center across the street from the Peterbilt plant, so I went there to scout around for a jewelry store and I found one. Looking around the store and its displays, it was quite fascinating seeing all the shiny rings and bracelets and other things. I was approached by a saleslady who asked if she could be of help. I said that I was looking for an engagement and wedding ring set. She showed me a few sets, but the prices were quite high. I figured out that I would have to spend some money anyway so why not get something nice. This would be the statement of my love! So I selected a set of rings made of white gold, studded with diamonds and hoped my future wife would approve of my selection. I was assured by the saleslady that the purchase could be exchanged if we were not 100% satisfied with the rings.

Well, I was prepared and I had with me a string which was looped to fit my sweetheart's finger. The saleslady was quite impressed. The rings would be ready in a few days so I could pick them up before my next trip to San Francisco when I could show them to my Dorothy. This would be no small matter for I had to ask her parents permission for Dorothy's hand in marriage. I was scared to death for I didn't know what they thought of me. I am sure Dorothy would have told them all about me, but still the fear was there. As the days went by, I went out on my lunch break to the jewelry store to view my newly purchased treasures. I was amazed at the brilliance and shining stones as well as the box which contained those precious treasures.

On day after work, I picked up the rings on the way home. Oh yes and I paid for them with cash and I spent about a month's salary. At that time it represented a lot of money. When I showed the rings to my parents, they were quite pleased with my selection. Were my parents pleased and happy for me that I was getting married? Well, yes and no. No, because they just got to know me since we were apart for so many years, and especially my mother would like to have me longer for herself as her own treasure. That is what she said to me. It sort of broke my heart to hear what she had to tell me. It made me realize that I was very loved by my mother. This was one of the very few times since we parted way back in Russia in 1942, and now that we started to know each other after eight long years, she believed that I would abandon them again. I promised my parents that I would never abandon them again, and I would always be close by and take care of them. This put them somewhat at ease and they understood that I had my life to lead.

Saturday would never come soon enough for me. I was eager to show my rings to Dorothy, but still scared to ask her parents for her hand in marriage. I got myself all dressed up for the occasion and decided to go forth for better or for worse, to go and propose and see what will happen. I came to the apartment where Dorothy lived with her younger brother, Jerry, and her parents. Jerry was a very nice young boy. He liked me very much and I also liked him, so that was a big plus for me because it must have made a good impression on Dorothy's parents. Dorothy met me at the door and after her greeting, I went in and said "hello". I was offered tea and there was some small talk. I didn't know when and how to start my announcement. As my hand started getting all wet and sweaty, I sat there mesmerized. As Dorothy looked at me, I knew I was to take charge and do what I came to accomplish.

I stood up and praised Dorothy and addressed her parents that I came here tonight to propose and to ask for their permission to marry Dorothy if it was okay with them. I also added that I was capable of this task, and I loved her and would take care of her always. I suppose that I was convincing about my intentions or maybe that's how it was supposed to be. I was given hugs and handshakes and "yes" I was given parental permission for the marriage. I was relieved to have this episode behind me. The next task was to arrange the time, date and place for the marriage, but since Dorothy was still in high school we had plenty of time to make these decisions. To celebrate this important event we decided to go to a movie, hold hands and with plenty of talking stayed out quite late that evening. But all good things must come to an end, so we returned to her house. At the same time, since it was late, I had to go home.

The next morning I recited the evening's events to my parents. My mother made only one comment. She said, "Frank you are a brave boy and you will do okay. Don't forget that the decision you made last night will be binding for the rest of your life. Not only you promised it to Dorothy, but you have to promise it to your father and to me." Which I did and wondered if she and my father were happy for me. I detected some other feelings, but then perhaps it was because I was taking on my own family and their expressed concern that I might abandon them.

As Dorothy and I went ahead with plans for our wedding, we did discuss the arrangements with my parents. How could I or my future wife abandon my parents? My life is only beginning, lots of new doors are opening for me and I have to decide which ones I should choose.

Planning ahead what course to take to lead me and my love to our future was a daunting task. I never had much happiness in my past and always stood at the edge of disaster. How can I avoid going through it again? I remembered my own promise to myself when I entered this promised land that I will not fail. I came here to make a success of my life and that of my future family. The beginning of which my mother and I made a great success; we already owned a new car, had purchased a house and only owed about $3,000. Wow, that's not so much. Now I just got engaged to this beautiful young girl, have some money in the bank but most of all have this great job and the company likes me a lot. It looks like I can climb the ladder and get ahead in my position. My goal had to be to get ahead and become somebody. Would it be hard? This was not a question, but it was a commitment.

In the meantime my father, frail as he was, had to do something. His profession was a farmer in Poland, and he once told me, "Franek, once you get dirt under your fingernails you will never get away from it." He enjoyed his rose garden in the front of our house and the admiration of the neighbors, but said that Americans were funny people and had a different way of life. My father was deprived of his homeland, his identity and his family who were left in Poland. He would ask mother and me to go for rides just to see if we could find some Polish people by looking at Polish names on their mailboxes.

There weren't many Polish people in California in those days. But some we found couldn't speak Polish. That angered him very much and he would say, "What kind of Polish people are these who can't speak Polish?" My father never recovered from that kind of anger. He missed his homeland, his farm and his Polish language. On the other hand, my mother became involved with America while working nights and shopping and other fun things. She, like me, was very hungry to get ahead in her new homeland.

Going through my mind about my future as well as Dorothy's, it occurred to me that there may be many problems! I have all kinds of responsibilities with my sister and her sons and now I am undertaking a marriage to this innocent girl and why should she be involved in all this mess?? So I tried to tell Dorothy that she should drop me and find someone without the burdens of my nephews and my past struggles. Her answer was simple, "I've had a lot of problems in life but I survived and we will survive your problems too." True, we became one team and together we will succeed. As long as we were true to each other and above all, open, then we will have no problems. What a girl I found—for the rest of our lives! Dorothy would graduate mid-year 1953 and then we would get married. I loved her for what she stood for. She believed in me and I in her. We understood each other to the fullest and had faith that all would come out well.

As the months passed, Dorothy and I were getting to know each other, and it was good for both of us. In the meantime, I was working on my house to prepare for our occupancy. The house was suited for a single family, but since my parents lived upstairs and had their own bathroom, we would have to share the bathroom with them. There was a kitchen, bedroom, living room and one small room (closet) and I wondered if we had enough space for an extra bathroom. I was quite handy to do all sorts of things, but I had no experience with plumbing to dispose of waste. Dorothy's grandfather, Mike, had some knowledge in that field and since he took a liking to me said he would be happy to give a hand in transforming the small room into a moderate sized bathroom.

As we started work on this project, it was promising that all would come out just fine. Before I knew it, I had to purchase a tub, toilet and lavatory, plus an electric wall heater to keep the room warm during the cold weather. In about six weeks the job was completed to the satisfaction of Dorothy and her grandfather, my parents and myself. What a great addition to the whole house, not only for ourselves but it increased the real estate value. Dorothy and I were constantly exploring the possibility of improving the lower portion of the house, such as paint and floor coverings.

All through the time of our engagement we would go to the movies, sightseeing such as rides to Twin Peaks, especially in the evening, and watch the San Francisco lights and trains of moving tail lights in one direction and headlights in the other. It was a lot of fun to see this phenomena, especially when there was no fog in the air (cold evening nights). We could enjoy watching and dreaming as well as planning our future. We talked about Dorothy's school progress and I assured her that the grades were more than satisfactory, and all was going as planned.

After careful and long discussions, we decided to inform our parents that after Dorothy graduated from Presentation High School about the middle of June, we could get married about four or five weeks later, and Dorothy chose St. Anne's day which fell on July 26th. We announced our decision on Christmas day, 1952. They were pleased on one hand and surprised that the time would come so soon. At Peterbilt, I told my colleagues about my future marriage. As I had known, one of my co-workers had a working band which performed at several night clubs and bar establishments, so I asked Larry if he could arrange to play at our wedding. After a few days he agreed and said he had in mind to have a five-man band, including himself, and a female singer for the price we discussed.

When I told Dorothy about it, she was quite pleased, so when I went to work I told Larry to go ahead and secure that date. We were quite happy about the progress toward the goal of matrimony. Christmas Day, 1952 came and went. The New Year celebration was at the Polish Club and the party was excellent with live music and good Polish food. But the most fun was dancing, and dancing we did. Both of us loved to dance, especially polkas, tangos and waltzes. What a wonderful way to spend the New Year's celebration with my Dorothy.

Life couldn't be any better. By the time we closed the club and I took her home, it must have been about four a.m. We said our goodbyes and I arrived back in San Leandro at about 5:00 a.m. Lucky it was New Year's day and not a work day so I could sleep a little late before going to church to celebrate New Year's Mass with my parents. My parents enjoyed hearing about the Polish Club festivities the night before. They said they liked to listen to my experiences because it was truly the first time in our lives that the joy of my life was celebrated with the three of us.

Early in the afternoon, mother wanted to go to the hospital to see our Stefania to celebrate the New Year, but the visit was quite disappointing. Stefania was not getting any better even after getting some shock treatments. She didn't seem to be happy to see her two sons or the rest of us and hardly spoke. What a disappointing day for my parents and her two little boys whom she loved so much just a few months earlier. The boys didn't realize what was happening but I am sure they knew that there was something very wrong with their mother. After the visit we started back home. Mother could not control her emotions, reflecting on her life in America where she was supposed to experience the love of her daughter and grandchildren.

Instead sorrow fell on her life again. After consoling mother and father for some time, we finally got back home.

After a fast dinner, which mother could make in the shortest time, we finally settled down to have some fun with the boys. As young as I was, I was portrayed as the father of these two wonderful boys. They called me "Unc" and I loved it because I could take care of them and pour out my love for them. Our life was getting more complicated each day. People from the Veterans' Administration were constantly coming to our home to check up on the boys and their welfare—how their care was going. They gave us all the paperwork to submit and I had to install a phone in the house for the first time in my life to communicate mostly with the VA, either answering their questions or asking how I could properly fill out papers to satisfy their requirements. It was more difficult to do the paperwork than to take care of the two little boys. Then some other people were coming to check on us from Children's Protection Agency, as well as many others.

But now I could call Dorothy quite often and life went on and was getting easier each day. Each time I would go to San Francisco to visit, or better yet, to see my sweetheart and I would go quite fast through the streets of Oakland and over the Bay Bridge to see her and then I'd be in seventh heaven. The worries of the past days would go away, and the new dawn would appear. The days and weeks were shrinking and the school days were coming to an end, and the culmination of waiting for the big day was on the horizon. The only thing that was bothering me was why Dorothy was willing to go along with the program. But then, what do I know about life? I would only guess that she was in love with me as I was with her. We had one thing in common and that was a lonely life. To dwell on this subject would be counterproductive so I would try not to think about it.

The fact was that we were involved with each other and that was fine with us. My work at Peterbilt was progressing just fine, and I was getting promotions and better pay and could afford more luxuries for my parents, especially my father. I could go to the store once in a while and purchase a carton of cigarettes—he was looking for them in order to give up rolling his own. He enjoyed these little things to the fullest and he would often say, "Franek, this is the kind of life that could only happen in America." But then on the other hand he would long for his native Poland. He would talk about his brother, Michal or sister, Clarkia. How we lived with them, that the life was good and he was happy when he was a young man. He would reminisce about the time when he was in the Polish Army during World War I. But now he was applying those times to my time and he was my hero from the past. I got to know my father better in the last few months than ever before. But, then, we never had the chance to talk about our lives because we were separated for so many years. There was so much to catch up on, so many subjects and yes, time was not on our side.

My work was getting more and more complicated. I had to keep my nose closer to the research of our new product and version of the trucks. I would even bring some difficult schematic prints home to study in order to be able to implement them in reality, and in the end I did. My mother would only watch me and admire my ability. Occasionally, Dorothy would come in and we would make plans as to what color paint to use and how to decorate our future home. It took a lot of effort to coordinate all these things. Not having a lot of help in my work except for Dorothy's grandfather, I had to do it all myself. Was I happy about that . . . . a big yes!

The time was getting close so Dorothy started to take some measures to proceed with our wedding plans. She was also very busy conducting her own affairs by keeping her attention on finishing her high school and receiving her diploma. Soon after that, we would marry. At first, we had plans for a small wedding, but by the time we added musicians and so on, it was getting out of hand. But still it was our wedding and with God's grace why not go all out and cherish our union? My parents were very happy with our planning and so were Dorothy's parents, her grandparents and the rest of the family.

Were all things about our wedding in perfect order? I would definitely say they were NOT! All my life I had some sort of problems and this time, my most happy time of life when I could devote all my time to my happiness, but I had to devote time to my parents and others. Yes, my Dorothy, my wonderful girl of my life. Yes I had to devote part of my young life to my sick sister Stefania and her two little sons. There were no other choices but to do what needed to be done as we were all family. Stefania was the one who sponsored us to come to America, so how could my parents or me abandon her and her boys? My Dorothy, how sweet to have her give me and my family this complete support. Have I ever thanked her for all she did for Stefania? Well, yes and no. She knows that without her help, I could not do it by myself. Thank you Dorothy my love!

Our wedding day, July 26, 1953

When the wedding day came, my father, mother, and I got dressed up for the occasion. July 26th, Saint Anne's feast day, we set out from San Leandro to San Francisco, but my mother said she left her white gloves on the living room table. Since we just started from the house, I stopped at the corner and ran back to the house to pick them up. As I ran back to the car with mother's gloves in my hand, there at the car was a San Leandro Police Officer writing out a citation for leaving the car at a cross intersection, obstructing the right of way for passersby, for leaving the car door open with the engine running and for leaving passengers unattended, as well as giving me a lecture on how careless I was for doing all this. Well, I could not talk myself out of this ticket even though I explained to the officer that it was my wedding day. All he said to me was that I would never forget this infraction and he was right! I still remember it clearly to this day. I had to pay about $30 for the ticket, but it was worth it. I learned a great lesson.

The wedding that day was splendid. Dorothy had six bridesmaids, all decked out. I had six friends standing up for me. The priest who married us said this was his third wedding celebration so when I cried with emotion, he cried with me. After the picture-taking was over in the church, we went to the Polish Club to celebrate the festivities. All the food was prepared by relatives or friends, and there was a lot of it. Of course the wedding cake was store bought. We had a six person live band together with a female singer. The band was my friend, Larry, from Peterbilt. Needles to say we all had a wonderful time. Our going away car was my still-new 1951 Chevrolet. I purposely parked it some distance from the Polish Club to avoid all sorts of writing on it, as was customarily done to newlyweds' cars. As the wedding party was coming to a close, after changing to our regular clothes and taking the customary getaway pictures, we headed away on our honeymoon.

My best man, Bob drove us to our car for our getaway honeymoon. After hauling suitcases and some goodies that the family packed in a cardboard box for our journey, we just sat there for awhile. We kissed and held hands and just talked about everything that had just happened to us. We again promised each other that this was just the beginning of our happy life together. As we left San Francisco for Sacramento—this was my first trip to Sacramento since I never traveled past the Bay Area before. My bride was quite a traveler together with her grandparents, but she was too nervous to navigate to our destination, so I had to depend on road maps. This was okay with me because I crossed the world and don't remember ever being lost.

Sunday afternoon, the roads are congested, and old Highway 40 was no different. We finally arrived at the Capital of California but guess what! The bridge over the Sacramento River was up because some big boats had to pass, so we had to wait. It was probably a good omen since we had some time to plan were we would stay that night, the honeymoon night. As we entered the city, we started to look for a motel. Old Highway 40 went through Old Sacramento; and as we passed the Capital Building, we spotted a nice quiet motel. Since it was getting dark and our destination was Lake Tahoe, and I wasn't familiar with the road there, we decided to spend the night. As I got out to go to the office, I noticed that my car was rolling backward. I ran to it and managed to get inside, restart the engine and drive forward to my original parking spot. Then I parked the car the way it should have been in the first place. We sat there for awhile and laughed about the whole incident. My bride said that I was in too much of a hurry. "Slow down," she said, "It will be alright."

I registered us as Mr. and Mrs. Frank Jasinski. That was great, but scary, as I realized that began my new life devoted to my new wife as I walked out of the motel office. I must have matured having this beautiful young girl as my wife. How do I go about living with this young lady? We have no experience or idea of what it is all about. My gut told me that we would do alright. We had something to eat before we turned in. The next morning we had breakfast and continued on our way to Lake Tahoe. The road in those days was narrow and forever curving, but Old Highway 40 was the only way to get there. It took us most of four hours to arrive. As we neared the lake, we stopped to admire the view—the beautiful, big, blue lake was waiting for us and it was saying, "come enjoy and be happy as I will give you much joy." We finally go to the shore and again spotted a nice looking motel. It looked quite new so we decided to spend the night there.

This time as I parked the car I made sure the gearshift was in the "park" position. I even increased my parking lever to the utmost position and went to the office to register. When I returned, Dorothy said that she would be okay as I was a fast learner. It was still early in the day so we went out to the beach for a little swim and adoration of the beautiful blue water. It was truly clear and as you looked at it you could see the rocks and small creatures swimming in it. Oh, what a paradise! How can I cope with all this? Here I am from poverty in the Siberian concentration camp, naked and hungry, and now I am standing on the shore of this beautiful lake, with my bride at my side, in my new car and with money in my pocket. Am I dreaming? Is this what I deserve? How could this all happen to me? Life in America is easy when one is eager to have it; hard, honest work is the only requirement. No other choices are there. Look at my world; I am a perfect example. On the other side of the coin, only in America you can achieve your goal this fast, for this is the land of opportunity.

That evening we discovered that across the California boarder there was a building all lit up at night where people participated in all sots of games and gambling. I recalled that while riding on the train coming to California (two and a half years earlier), while stopping in Reno, Nevada, I was looking to purchase some milk and bread. Instead I found gambling casinos in "The Biggest Little City in the World". So we changed $5 for some nickels and watching how other people played, we started to play ourselves. At one point, we got some nickels back, but of course, we played some more. At one point, the machine started to ring. We didn't know why, so we dropped another nickel in and the machine stopped ringing. The person next to us said that we just lost about $7 because we didn't wait for the attendant to pay us off. Oh well, now you tell me that we just lost that money!

The moral to our latest adventure was obvious, if you don't know what you're doing, then don't do it. With this we went out for the evening sightseeing. The next day we went off to learn the whereabouts of Las Vegas. After leaving Reno we finally headed south across the desert toward Nevada's capital city for gambling. The first clue we got in the service station was to fill our gas tank and that all motorists were filling cans with water. But so what? People do some strange things so I made sure my radiator was full and also my cooling device which was mounted on the right door window; while driving the hot air coming through this device came into the car much cooler than the outside. It made the ride in the summer months much more comfortable.

The terrain looked very innocent but as we drove some hours, it became hilly and the heat more intense. We didn't pay much attention to the road conditions. We were in love and dreaming about our future and not things like road conditions. While on a long uphill drive, I noticed that my heat gauge was rising rapidly. It went to the top of the scale and the engine stopped on us. Now what? As I slowly backed the car to the side of the road, I opened the hood to inspect the condition of the radiator. It was obvious that all the water evaporated due to the heat outside and the hard work the engine had to do going uphill for such a long distance.

Now what do I do? We were stranded in the desert with no water and even if I had some, how would I fill this radiator? My dear bride had no idea. She offered to sacrifice a coupe of bottles of champagne to partially fill our radiator, but I added my own idea to empty our cooler from the window and fill up the radiator. The champagne was easy to empty, but how do I empty the cooler? There were no rocks to break the bottom of the champagne bottle, but my tire wrench was in the trunk and this did the job for me. After we filled the stupid radiator and got quite dirty in the process, the engine started up just fine and we were on our way at last. Wonders never cease to amaze me. After driving for about 500 yards on the other side of the crest of the hill we saw a big sign, "water available 500 feet ahead". We just looked at each other and began to laugh. Dorothy said, "Isn't it funny? They should have placed that sign a half mile ahead, not here." I refilled our cooler and drove on.

A few hours later we saw another sign. This one said, "You are invited to see Scotty's Castle". We agreed we had enough excitement for one day and didn't need to risk another episode like the one we just went through. So we proceeded to Vegas (that's how the locals call their city). The closer we got the darker it became, so by the time we found our motel and a place to eat, it was quite late.

The next morning when we decided to have breakfast, we discovered that we were in quite an isolated place, and the place to eat was about a mile away. But all this color lighting at night looked so fascinating and inviting. Oh well, this is Vegas. After breakfast we rode around sightseeing the city's new hotels and the many people coming and going. While the temperature in the morning was still quite cool we managed to stroll around the city. On our way back to our motel Dorothy said she would like to see Hoover Dam, but she didn't remember where it was located. After looking at the map, we found it was only a short distance away, so why not go there while we're so close? One should never miss the opportunity to visit Hoover Dam, since it's huge and very impressive. We read the statistics and how many tons of cement it contains, how many tons of steel rebar and how many man hours it took to build such a dam. It was certainly a fabulous sight to see this unbelievable manmade structure.

We then made our way to Los Angeles to see Beverly Hills, downtown Los Angeles, and the other places of interest. I wasn't much interested in this because of its enormity. It was too big for me to appreciate its beauty. We had fourteen days to our honeymoon and a limited amount of money to spend, so we decided to see more cities. Dorothy told me that her girlfriend lives in San Diego so why not go and visit her. "She was my schoolmate and it would be fun to see her again." So we drove south to San Diego. What a wonderful visit and reception we received. It was great to see such friendly people and they treated us to a wonderful barbeque dinner. It was nice to be in such a giving environment.

I learned that this schoolmate of Dorothy's used to live with her for some time so they were sort of like sisters. They advised us to visit their famous San Diego Zoo. We took their advice and indeed it was a great attraction to see. We spent one whole day there and still didn't see the entire zoo. The vast area was just too much to see in one day, so we decided to spend another day there before leaving. They offered their home for us to stay overnight and we could not resist. The next day we visited the coastline and the waterfront plus the city itself. It really opened my mind and eyes as to how large this country was and its splendor, beauty and wealth; how it is adorned with good roads and railroads and how the whole nation is employed and its people prospered. This land is now my land and Dorothy and I will prosper, and we will live in its finest environment now and into its future.

We could not leave San Diego without driving along the seashore and looking at the enormous might of the US Naval assortment of vessels and the whole armada. Something to remember, but it was time to head for home. We departed San Diego, hoping to reach San Luis Obispo by nightfall, but it was a long ride. The weather was hot, going by Los Angeles it was quite humid, and that made our travel that much more tiring. Before we knew it, we were at our destination. Motels in this town were scarce, but we finally found one with a vacancy sign on. We got out of our car and went in to check out the accommodations and the cost per night. The price was reasonable, but boy, this was a dump. Since we didn't know where to find another motel, we decided to stay for one night. Big mistake! The first problem was the shower. The half door to the shower was wooden & it was a mess. As we cleaned ourselves we went out to have something to eat, then afterward we retired for the night. The bed must have been at least twenty years old because as soon as we got into bed, we found ourselves in the middle of it, sinking almost to the floor.

Oh well, it's something to remember and we still talk about that night. The next morning after bailing out of our motel, we decided to go and maybe have some breakfast on the road. We didn't realize what we were doing. There weren't any towns nearby so we drove for quite some time and never spotted any places to eat. We had plenty of gasoline in the tank so sooner or later we will find something and yes, we finally got to Monterey and we were starving. As we drove into a drive-in we were really hungry so we feasted on some good food and took our time to enjoy the meal.

Since coastal Highway 1 is not a very fast way to travel, we spent another night in Monterey because I didn't think I could make it all the way back to San Leandro by nightfall. Driving home to San Leandro the next morning on beautiful coastal Highway 1 is a wonderful route, winding back and forth along the Pacific Ocean with gorgeous scenery to stay with you for a lifetime.

But all good things come to pass, when we got home new things awaited us, as we started our married life together. It's like entering the old pyramid, you never know what awaits you around the next corner. We were warmly greeting by my parents and the two boys. They were all ears, wanting to know about each day that we were away, what we did, the places we visited and the highlights which we talked about. With the aid of a map, which helped us during our travels, I could show my father the overall trip. Needless to say, we came home tired, dirty, hungry and almost broke, because I didn't realize that traveling was so expensive. On top of that, there was a letter from the San Leandro City Hall citing me for an infraction and fine and I'd better take care of it or I could lose my driver's license and in addition have to go to court. I didn't need this problem, so I purchased a money order and mailed it to City Hall. So much for leaving my car unattended with the engine running and the door wide open. A lesson was learned for sure. The reality was setting in because now I had a wife to take care of, and life changed.

Back at work, I had to add Dorothy to my insurance coverage as well as all other legal papers. With Dorothy's help I could do all these things much more proficiently and with ease. Now we had our own bills and furniture to purchase, together with pots and pans and utensils and so on. Dorothy suggested we open a checking account to pay our bills plus food and other commodities. Marriage is something else! It requires your full-time attention. It was all new to me of course, because I'd left my parents back in the Soviet Union. I grew up on my own and never had the opportunity to witness any kind of family structure such as paying bills and being cared for by the family. It's strange that it all ended and the new life just began and I would stay awake at nights thinking how I would support my lovely wife. But I put it in God's hands.

I knew I was able to be a productive person, had a very good job and that I would be successful, so help me God. No use dwelling on the future because, as my mother always said, "Franek, if you make your bed well, you will sleep well in it". So I more or less laid out plans in my head that there was nothing in my way to make me fail to reach my goals. My new bride and I got along very nice with no big disagreements or fights. After awhile, Dot, as I called her, found a nice job working for Montgomery Wards as a clerk of some kind in Oakland. It was nice to have two paychecks coming in as it would ease our burden if it all works itself out.

Dot would ask me to go to San Francisco to visit her parents and Grandparents as well as her aunt, whom she called "Ciocia" in Polish. She was lonesome and would ask me to visit them often. She would light up when we crossed the Bay Bridge. Sure, the city would glitter at night whenever it was clear of fog. That by itself is another story. Fog in San Francisco is like bread and butter. It's cold in the summer and cold in the winter whenever the good old fog rolls in. But then it rewards you with warm air and clear nights at other times. As Dot told me a while back when I would come to see her, I would bring a nice day to bask in the sunshine. Our marriage was blossoming each day and I was deeply touched by how good I had it living in America. How free I was to make decisions as how I would live my life . . . and then our life.

I often wondered how long my new bride would take this heavy burden with me and tolerate this marriage that she didn't ask for. She was always very compassionate toward Stefania, and she sympathized with my predicament, as I had no way out. If it weren't for Stefania, I would be somewhere else and not in America—maybe in Argentina or Australia, so I was sort of obligated to save my sister's life and that of her two sons whom

I loved so very much. So it became my other family and Dot's as well. How lucky I was to find such a wonderful human being for a wife and we got along so well.

My mother was teaching Dot to speak Polish, although Dot did speak some American Polish. But she took it quite well and did learn some good Polish. Eddie, the older boy, was getting old enough to start school, so we looked for some schools in the neighborhood, but there weren't any close by. The problem was that there was no one in our household who could take him to school, so we worried how we would cope with this new problem. We still had time, so we postponed this subject until later.

One day at Peterbilt, as I bent down to pick up some wires, I could not straighten myself upright. I had a severe pain in my back and finally lay down on the floor quietly hoping it would go away. After some time and being questioned by some of my co-workers, it was obvious that there was something wrong with me since I was a healthy young man just a few minutes before. Lucky for me, our company doctor was next door. With some help my co-workers got me to his office where after a few minutes he said without hesitation that I had a problem with my appendix, and that it was an emergency situation and that I should be hospitalized at once.

After calling my dear wife, she promptly arrived to take me to the hospital, but the ride was very uncomfortable. Every bump in the road was hurting me inside my stomach. I pleaded with her to drive more carefully and avoid rough pavement. At about eleven o'clock at night, I was wheeled into the operating room for surgery. The next morning, awakening in my room, there was my whole family, including my mother-in-law. What a surprise to see all of them waiting to see me! To see their caring faces was beyond description. What a tender love they displayed toward me. After three days in the hospital, my dear wife drove me home. I was so happy to be back home for I was worried about the whole family and how they were getting along without me. I sort of made myself the head of the family. Was I wrong to think of myself in that position? Well, at home they took excellent care of me, changing bandages, making sure I was not suffering any discomfort. Yes, this made me realize that we could always stand some help. After recovering from the surgery, on about the fifth day I decided that I was well enough to do some work around the house.

There was this one thing that needed some attention. There was a narrow strip behind the house where Mother and Dot hung wet clothes to dry. So I decided to frame this strip with 2x4's to make a form for pouring concrete so the ladies could stand on it to hang wet clothes in style. Well, all the ruckus broke loose. “Franek, you can't do all this because you just had surgery, and you can injure yourself and then what?” As far as I was concerned, this was play work and it didn't take hard work to accomplish the task. The only thing missing was a wheelbarrow so I went to my neighbor to borrow one. The only thing he asked was that I not fill it too full so I could manage the weight. He also suggested that I wrap myself with some kind of cloth to support my stomach muscles. I thanked him for his advice and brought the wheelbarrow to my house. The next morning the big cement truck arrived with the cement to help me finish the job. Little by little I filled the frame in the back of the house and finished troweling it so it would be nice and smooth. Dot and my mother could go in the back of the house now and hang their wet clothes on the newly erected lines without stepping in the dirt or mud when it was wet. The house was getting to look much better than when we first purchased it.

The time came to go back to the hospital for a visit to remove the stitches and the visit was very short. The doctor (Sureda) was very surprised that I healed so fast and that the stitches came out so easily. He said that I must come from a very healthy family. I wondered what he would say if I had told him about my cement fiasco? He probably would have killed me. It was nice to go back to work and be greeted by my co-workers who were happy to have me back. Life was good, and my family was happy to have this wonderful country to live in. As any other newlywed, my dear wife announced one fine morning that I was going to become a father. What a scary feeling came over me as well as great joy. My own childhood is coming into work and to me life. The whole situation of our life changed within a few minutes. I was pleased to inform my parents that they were going to be grandparents again from my family. The occasion called for celebration, and mother said I should take Dot to the store for some supplies. My mother could prepare a meal in no time at all so we had a few schnapps of Polish Vodka to celebrate. With the freshly prepared food consumed, we were all quite happy about the forthcoming event.

After finding a pediatrician in San Francisco, whom Dorothy's mother recommended, Dorothy took the bus to visit the doctor, whom she didn't know, to see if she would like him. When she got back home and told me that he was nice, “and treats me very nicely”, she decided to stay with him. It was important to both of us to be comfortable with one's doctor. The most fun for Dot was the walk from the bus station across Van Ness. She said to me many times, that while being a San Franciscan, she could learn so much more walking and learn more about her native

San Francisco. Her visits to San Francisco were fun for awhile, but soon the fun became a burden and it was quite expensive, so we talked about moving to the city.

By making this drastic decision to return to San Francisco, we had to establish a concerted plan of action—selling our home, find a replacement in the City, quitting my fine job and finding a new one, finding a place to live for my parents and the boys. Of course, this new place had to be within walking distance to schools, shops and transportation since my parents could not afford an automobile nor knew how to operate one. So the location was most important. The relocation task was astronomical because of the lack of good English on my part as well as to determine which district to live in, but it was achievable. So Dorothy, my parents and I decided that such a move was the best for our family.

The home in San Leandro was inconvenient to schools, transportation and shopping as well as the church. Our finances were better now and our sights were a little more sophisticated. It made more and more sense to make the change. To begin with, Dorothy's Aunt Harriet was a Real Estate Agent, so I asked her to find us a starter home. I described our wants and needs and the price we could afford. She agreed to find something for us. Besides, she was Dot's mother's sister as well as Dot's Godmother, and the move would bring us closer to her. In the meantime, I inquired at the Real Estate office where I purchased the home in San Leandro. It turned out that I could sell the house for approximately $8,000 to $9,000.

What a deal! I would wind up with a large profit which I was assured would come in very handy in a very short time. My parents were very surprised that I could make such a profit within such a short time. Well, I guess that luck was on my side. Here I have a beautiful wife who is with my child, some money in the bank, and a bigger home in sight. What more could I ask for? But what about my future job? I was not concerned since I was pretty sure that I would find one. Remember that luck was on my side so why worry? One day we received a phone call from Aunt Harriet (Ciocia in Polish). She had found something in which we would be interested. The house had two bedrooms, about 1200 square feet, was close to schools, shopping and transportation and the price was right. She said if we were interested we should come to the City and see if it was something we liked. The house was in a good location, as Ciocia described it before and we liked it a lot. The asking price was $11,000 but we could offer a little less. We decided to go for it and offered them $9,000 subject to the sale of our home in San Leandro. I wrote a goodwill down payment of $500 and

Ciocia took our offer to the seller. My parents also approved because of the nice location and the appearance of the house.

Our trip to the City was very successful. On the way home we had a very serious conversation because the house we were looking at had only one story with a large basement, but there was no room for my parents and the boys. We came to the conclusion that they would have to rent a house or apartment for awhile, and then we would see how things turned out. Anyway, we listed our house on the market for sale at $11,000 or best offer. The man in the same Real Estate Office who sold us the house came to see it and couldn't believe the improvements that I made. He then assured us that it would sell within a month at the longest.

In the meantime, we found an apartment for my parents where the rent was very affordable; two small bedrooms was only $60 per month plus utilities and it would be ready in about two or three weeks, which was fine with all of us. The offer on the Rivera Street home we wanted to purchase was rejected but there was a counter-offer of $10,500. We finally purchased it for $10,000. My in-laws could not believe that we were so successful to purchase it for that price. The final sale was in "as is" condition. Dot's uncle, who was a general contractor, inspected the house and proclaimed it to be a sound building. He was Dorothy's mother's half brother, so we relied on his judgment. In the meantime, on our San Leandro house, after a couple of open house's we got an offer for $8,750. We counter-offered for $1,000 more, which was accepted. So now we were in a good position. How lucky for us that it all turned out in our favor and we could come out ahead on this transaction! It would cause some difficulties but in the end we would be better off.

With the help of Dot's Uncle Ben and his truck, we were able to move to our new house in two trips, as well as move my parents and the boys. Of course we had to get approval from the VA for such a move. The transition to the City was very well done. The commuting went very well for awhile until one day when I got home just in time, for my dear wife after dinner said she had a stomach ache. I said she probably had too much to eat.

It turned out that she was going into labor. She called her mother for expert advice and her mother advised us to call the doctor and see what he would suggest. He advised us to go to the hospital and register and that he would see us there. After awhile, they wheeled her to the delivery room where my dear wife, after a period of time, presented me with a beautiful baby daughter—dark haired and closed eyes—but a beautiful girl. Was I proud or what? I went out and got her a beautiful bouquet of roses. To come home with this beautiful child was a treat in itself. I learned that with a new baby we needed drying lines in the back yard.

Yes, we had a lot of diapers to wash and dry, so our work had just begun. The work at Peterbilt was going just fine since the commute traffic was going in the opposite direction than I was. In the morning all the traffic was going into the City and I was going in the opposite direction. But it was hard and expensive to commute that far every day. I asked my union representative if it was possible to transfer to work in the city. He looked at me somewhat puzzled and said, "Frank if you find a job in the City, I will help you transfer, so go ahead."

One afternoon when I came home from work, Dot asked me to go to the store and get some milk. I was happy to help, so without hesitation got out of the house and into my car, but the car was not in the driveway where I parked it. I looked around for it for a while, then I looked in the garage and not finding it there I went upstairs and announced that our car was stolen. Now what were we going to do? We called the Police to report the incident. They took all the necessary information and said that they would look for it and would let us know when they find it.

Going by bus to San Leandro was no small job to say the least. It took the Police twenty-nine days to find our car, and when I finally got the address where the car was located, there were about twelve parking tickets under my windshield wiper.

That really got my goat; didn't the office that issued all the parking tickets realize that the car was stolen? I didn't have to pay all the fines since I had reported it being stolen but, still, what an inconvenience it created not to mention the headache. The incident made me go and find a job in the City. I decided to take time off and go the Machinist Union to look for a job. The Union Representative advised me to go to McAllister Buick because they were looking for help so I was very happy to receive this information. As I entered the huge dealership, I was awed by the large workshop they had. Finally, I found the top man, Mr. Taylorson, the Manager. I explained that I was looking for work and that the Union sent me to see him about it. After the interview, he said that he would give me the chance to work for him, and he would pay union scale, including health insurance for me and my family. I told him I would have to give my employer notice, and I could start the coming Monday if that was okay with him. He was pleased that I was doing it right.

The next day at Peterbilt, I was very nervous waiting to see old George Brombaugh to announce to him that I was resigning and explain the reasons why I was making this move. I thanked him from the bottom of my heart for the privilege of working for him this past three and a half years and said I would never forget who gave me my start here in America. He then wished me well in my endeavors. I've never had an opportunity to see him again but have often talked about him on different occasions. What a great break he gave me to start my life in America! I'll be forever grateful for his big heart.

My new job at McAllister Buick was going well, and I was well liked by my co-workers. Since I was still rusty in English, they were more than willing to help me along. It was pretty hard at first, but as the time went along it was getting easier day by day. In the meantime, my parents and the boys were doing quite well; my mother found a job as a cleaning lady at different homes while my father watched the boys so life was going alone fine. But Stefania was still confined to the State Hospital. My parents were receiving the veteran's pension to provide the upkeep for the boys, plus they received a back pay lump sum. All the money they received was never spent; it was saved for the future purchase of the home. Dot and I and our beautiful daughter often visited my parents. We named our daughter, Dianna, but for some reason I nicknamed her Nina and it has stuck with her to this day.

My mother mentioned that we should look for a house instead of renting and just throwing money away on rent. She mentioned that there was around $5,000 under the mattress. I got in touch with the VA Social Worker assigned to our case and tried to get permission in this matter. After a long battle they agreed it was time to purchase a home. Driving around on Saturday and Sunday to visit open houses became our new pastime. We finally spotted a house close to shopping, school, St. Anne's Catholic Church as well as to the streetcar and bus line. It was the ideal place for their needs and the price was right at $12,000 firm.

My mother fell in love with the house. It had three bedrooms and the rest of the house was quite large. We accepted the price and signed some preliminary papers with the proviso that the VA needed to approve the purchase. The VA did give us the "go ahead", I suppose, because it was a good value and good for the children. There was enough money for the down payment. Upon the death of Stefania's husband Robert, aside from getting very little money, which the death insurance called for, because of Stefania's condition, the benefits were apportioned in monthly installments. Mother saved most of the monthly installments and placed it in the bank. By working herself, she supported the boys and my father and since they lived rent free, she was able to save this money. Before we all knew what was happening, everything fell into place nicely and my parents and the boys moved into their own home. What a good feeling came over all of us. With some of the furniture in position, the rest had to come from used furniture stores and so on.

It was wonderful for me to have my parents and the boys close to me because we lived only a few blocks from each other. As a result, we could jump in a car to visit Stefania in the hospital. My God, each time we would go, Stefania's condition did not meet our expectations. What a heartbreak we all suffered each time! Here I was looking for a great life and love toward her because she was the only survivor among my siblings, and here it didn't work as I had envisioned it. I was heartbroken, but then life had to go on.

Soon Dot informed me that she was pregnant with our second child and again this overshadowed some of the tragedy in my life. We were very happy because of this news and soon began making plans for the upcoming even. Dot again began visits with our Pediatrician, Dr. Buckley and I suppose he was happy to see us again.

Dot really liked her doctor and I was happy for her too. My parents were very happy for us because we wanted a bigger family than just one child. We had a house with two bedrooms and we wanted to fill it with children. As a healthy couple I didn't think there would be much of a problem accomplishing our dreams. The house we purchased was getting dirty and needed a coat of paint in the worst way so we decided to paint it. As we started this project, I discovered that the front entrance steps needed some attention. It looked to me that the wood on the inside of the stairs was crumbling.

Not knowing what happened or the cause, Dorothy informed me that her uncle Ben would know what caused this problem. After she called him, he promised her that he would come over and see what happened, so after a few days he came over. When he inspected the problem, he simply stated that we had dry rot under the stairs. "How could that happen," I asked? I've never heard this term before. He explained that we live close to the ocean and that this created constant moisture so the wood never has a chance to totally stay dry and therefore it rots. The only way to repair such a problem is to replace it with dry wood and then restucco the entire staircase, which will be quite costly. After he left, we started to discuss our new problem and we didn't quite know what to do about it.

A few days later, the baby started to develop a red rash. Well for me I never had contact with little children and their sicknesses so I was not aware of the cause of this rash. We called Dr. Buckley about this matter and all he could say was why don't you bring the baby in so I could look at her. Upon examination he advised us not to give her cow's milk, but to try some Goat's milk for she might be allergic to the cow's milk. Dorothy had very low output of her breast milk to sustain good development of our growing child. Well, I found one grocery store who could supply us with fresh goat's milk. Dr. Buckley was very serious about our baby's health and he said he didn't care where we could get this goat's milk, but under no circumstances should we feed her cow's milk.

In the meantime, Dorothy's parents moved to Reno, Nevada with her brother, Jerry, as well as her Aunt Harriett (Chocia in Polish). Some weekends we would pack up our 1957 Chevrolet Nomad station wagon and go for a visit. The drive to Reno took about six or seven hours on the old Highway 40. It was fun to see this vast country of California and part of Nevada. I recognized some buildings when I was running around looking for bread and milk when I first arrived in February of 1951. Quite a bit had changed in this "Biggest Little City in the World" Reno. I could reminisce on my first visit to the USA. The children were happy to see their grandparents and to be in the hot climate and go to the swimming pools with warm water. I, too, had lots of fun visiting the town around Reno but my biggest discovery was Virginia City.

Dorothy and the children loved to visit the old cemeteries, abandoned mines and the old buildings and churches. This was truly a place to visit and see the old mining town where silver was mined. The gambling aspect of this was not very interesting because I could not afford to lose our hard-earned money on gambling, nor did I have time for it. Because our youngest daughter, Debbie, was allergic to cows' milk, we had to find goats' milk, which was quite difficult to find. I finally got a lead where there was a farmer, quite far away, but the milk was available at a modest cost. So when that hurdle was crossed, everything was fine.

The goat's milk was about two to three times as expensive as the regular cow's milk. Well we could easily afford this expenditure, but the problem was this: if we were to go to Reno, Nevada to visit Dorothy's parents, we would have to scour the region for goat's milk as it was not readily available at the stores. Some stores would direct us to go to such and such a home where they had goats. So I could find some and could obtain a quart or two for my new baby.

For some time to come, Dorothy noticed that Debbie, our daughter, would switch her goat's milk with Nina's cow's milk. Well, this was something to watch, and Dorothy detected that this was happening quite often, so she called Dr. Buckley and explained what she had observed. He suggested that we first give the baby half and half and watch what happens. If everything is okay well, then try to give her just the cow's milk.

Our weekend drives were around San Francisco, mostly seeing open houses and, boy there were plenty of them to see. Number one, most homes were old structures, and some were old designs and were interesting to look at. It was fun to look at them and get a lot of different ideas on how to furnish and decorate and sort of mimic different lifestyles.

Most Sundays we would return from church, pack a lunch and go to Golden Gate park which was close by and have mini-picnics and play with the girls. On a lot of occasions, we would pick up Stefania's boys and let them enjoy the picnic with us. We had a lot of fun on these little outings. It didn't cost too much to spend time in the fresh air and get together and play together. On one such occasion, we spotted an open house at the entrance to the park, so I said to Dot that I would go and see what they had to offer. The house was a newer version and had a lot of possibilities. It was a two bedroom with separate dining room, plus as a bonus it had a one bedroom apartment, and it was occupied by the owner. I loved the whole place, especially the idea that the apartment would help with house payments and that means we could lead a somewhat different lifestyle.

After visiting so many homes, it made sense for me to talk to Dot about making an offer and maybe purchase this house because it was close to stores, schools, church, and of course Golden Gate Park. God knows we spend a lot of time there! We took the boys back to their home and I told my mother about this house which was open for inspection. She wanted to see it too so we went shopping for the house (this is what we called our outings). To my surprise we all liked the house, especially mother. It was close to her, only four blocks away.

The asking price was negotiable but still the owner wanted $18,000 and at that time it was a lot of money. We decided that we would offer much less, and if they didn't accept our offer, well nothing ventured, nothing gained. We offered $15,000 providing we could get the proper loan and all the other amenities. Guess what? The lady who owned the house liked our little family, and I suppose she wanted us to live with her so she accepted the offer. Well, it was one thing to look at open houses, but to go and purchase one was a different story. Now I was scared to death. What in the world were we thinking by doing such a stupid thing by buying another house? Dorothy, bless her heart said, "It's just buyer's remorse. You'll get over it and it will all work out just fine." Of course, as she said, after a day or two I did come to the reality that we had done the right thing. With the sale proposal, the owner expressed that she wanted to stay in the apartment and that she would pay $95 per month if that was okay with us. Well, this made even more sense to purchase this property. I made out like a bandit, a landlord with income to boot.

We placed our home up for sale for the same price as the one we just purchased and just waited to see what would come of it. Life just seemed to keep getting better and better with a great job, good co-workers, a beautiful wife, two beautiful daughters and now two homes. My parents adjusted their lives with their two grandsons and sort of got used to the idea that Stefania is better off in the hospital under doctors' care than she would be at home. She was still stick, and it would take some time before she could come home. It was hard for all of us to go visit her, but there was no other way. The boys got used to living with their grandparents and of course, they spoke Polish quite well, but spoke English outside when playing with friends.

One morning while going to work, I was close to my parents' home so I decided, for some unknown reason, to stop by and pay them a short visit. Mother was up and was preparing breakfast for the boys while father was still in bed just resting. Mother was at a lost wondering what happened when I came over because I'd never done that before. I said I was early and just wanted to stop by, that's all. Father was happy to see me and we exchanged a few words; I kissed them all and went on my way to work. It was good for me to pay my parents a visit and see the boys. I thought I should do this more often.

After 2:00 p.m. the Foreman called me into his office because there was an emergency telephone call for me. What kind of emergency could it be? Dorothy was on the line. She very calmly said that my father had fallen down and needed my help, so could I go there and see what I could do. I asked the foreman if I could be excused because something had happened to my father. My wife said it was an emergency so I have to go and see how I can help. While driving there I wondered what possible problem had arisen that Dot would call me at work, as she never did that before. Besides, I was at my parents' home six or seven hours before, so now what?

As I drove into their driveway and got out of my car, the front door opened and mother greeted me with tears in her eyes. I asked, "Why are you crying Mama?" She said, "Your father had a heart attack and is dead." As I ran up the steps, I saw my father lying on the kitchen floor and everyone was waiting for the coroner to take him away to perform an autopsy. Composing myself to the point where I could take charge and calm everyone down took some time. I asked mother if she called the police station and she had not. So I called and gave them the story. It seemed to me that no sooner had I hung up, the Sergeant and his staff arrived. After questioning us, they removed my father's body. We learned from the neighbor that she heard my father fall down and heard a hard thump. Since she knew no one was in the house, she got my phone number from the telephone book. "My God," I said, "I just saw Dad in your bedroom a few hours ago and now this? When will all this misery end?' Mother told me that the school called her because Grandpa wasn't there to pick up the children. The school called my mother's employer. She was a cleaning lady for a gentleman who was a New York Insurance Company boss, and that's how the school notified her. By the time we got home, the boys were still waiting on the front steps because the door was locked.

What next could I expect to happen in my life? Good for Mary Brilliant—she used her head and we thank you, Mary! The next day when I got to work everyone wanted to know what happened to my father. I said we were not sure, but it looked like he had a massive heart attack. He was gone when I arrived home. They were all very sympathetic toward me and I thanked them for their sympathy. I had no experience in these matters so I just let it be. Just before we buried my father, our Shop Foreman came to me and handed me an envelope with a card in it which was signed by my co-workers. He said, "Go ahead and look inside." As I took the envelope from his hand, I saw paper money inside. I asked what the money was for, because I'd never seen this kind before. He said something to the effect that we do this instead of giving flowers when loved ones are buried. "Oh my God," I said to myself, "What kind of country am I in? Look, I have all this money to help me with the burial." When I got home, I showed the envelope to Dorothy. We counted some $173 dollars. We were in awe with this gift. This money will almost pay for father's funeral.

I never knew what kind of loss I would have to bear. I am feeling like I have been abandoned again. The loss of my father was more than I could endure. But life had to go on and my little family needed me more than I needed my sympathy. I had to learn to go forth with my life. The reality was that I had to concern myself with the possible purchase of our dream house on which I had just placed a deposit with the intent to purchase and I also had to negotiate the sale of our present house. It was turning out to be a big mess and I wondered how I could handle it.

My mother was very supportive about purchasing the new house. She said it will give me a new opportunity to provide more space for my growing family. First of all, better transportation to work, better shopping and, most of all it would be closer to her in case she needed any help. This kind of encouragement was all that I needed to go ahead with the purchase. After getting all the necessary contract papers as well as the loan, we closed escrow, and, before we knew it, we were moving in. We sold the old house in no time at all. We made a nice profit so the improvements on the old house paid off quite handsomely.

My work at McAlister Buick progressed quite well. My English was getting much better and I was quite relaxed around my friends at work. On one occasion, the Superintendent of the Service Department came to me and wanted to talk. As I was finishing servicing brakes on a particular car, I didn't immediately get up to see what he needed me for. I was finished important safety work. When I finished, which took me about a minute, I walked toward him. He asked why I didn't come to him immediately. I explained that I was at the end of a safety task and didn't want to forget where I was at that time. He said he wanted to see me after working hours and I said that I would stop in his office to see him. As I walked into his office, he asked me to sit down. It crossed my mind that this was probably my last day on the job because why would he bring me to his office?

After a short pause, he said, "Frank, I had some doubt about your ability to work for me, but you have proved me wrong. Your Foreman gave you excellent marks, and I also was impressed with what you did this morning—that you made me wait because of your level of concern for our customers. I am also aware that you lost your father, have a new baby, and other events in your life. To make sure you stay with our company I will increase your salary by 10%." I was astonished and relieved that I still had my job plus more money! I thanked him.

The next day my co-workers asked me why Mr. Taylorson wanted to talk to me after hours. I said he wanted me to know that he was sorry about the loss of my father. That's about all. Of course, Dorothy was very proud of me because of all that was happening to us. The new house which we just purchased needed some work and some improvements. If you could envision an apartment downstairs which caused the loss of the use of our backyard. That meant that the children could not play or use the backyard. I figured that since we had three windows facing the backyard in our master bedroom, I could make a door opening and erect a deck to connect the bedroom to the backyard. This would solve our problem. In about two weekends, by purchasing the necessary lumber, door and door casing and other necessary things, it was done. What a good feeling to have the ready use of our backyard and a valuable improvement to the property.

I don't know how the news traveled, but we received a phone call from a man named John Luezynski. He said he was Dorothy's uncle and wanted to see her, the children and me. I said I would talk to Dorothy. I called him back a few days later and invited him to our home. It was a very cold visit so we just exchanged small talk. He mentioned that he was one of the Pioneers of the Polish Club in San Francisco and was one of the recruiters for the Saint Stanislaus Society and that if we wanted to do so, we could join that associated. I declined his invitation. After he was gone, we were wondering whether he came to visit his niece or to sell us insurance, for he hadn't seen Dorothy for a very long time and it didn't look to us like the visit was family oriented.

Stefania was still not getting any better, but we continued to visit her often. The boys were growing and attended the local school. They were very bright boys and brought home very good report cards. My mother and I were very proud of them. In the meantime, my mother was constantly making packages for her sisters and brother in Poland. Her family was very poor and needed almost everything, especially clothing. Now and then she would plead with me to come over to her house and address a few packages. There I would see a dozen or more packages waiting for me to address. Each package would be wrapped in white linen and sewn very tightly so they would survive the long journey to Poland. Addressing the packages would take a very long time, time I didn't have to spare, but it was for my mother so I did it to please her. When I would come, she would say nareszcie (it's about time). It was so funny to hear her say that.

Life was getting easier and there was a light at the end of the tunnel. My dear wife informed me one day that she was pregnant again. I was very happy with the news because we wanted another child and were hoping for a son, but we would welcome another daughter as well. Things were looking good. I often remember my past and what it was like in my youth with my brother and sisters and how I was robbed of my youth and family ties. Now I have all this and how lucky I was to be here in America with this home and my little family, and above all, a good job. Now having another child—how wonderful life can get. My mother would say, "Franek, you are so gifted by God. He gave you golden hands and you use them well and you are smart enough to make something of yourself." She often said how proud she was of me. It was very nice to hear her praising me once in awhile. That gave me more motivation to show her that I was about to do even better, for I was somebody, and was self-motivated from the time I came to America.

I will do whatever and work as hard as I can to become independent and be somebody. My friends around me were somewhat pleased that I surpassed them financially without any help, and that they couldn't catch up with me. One day I came back from work to find two police cars, one in my driveway and the other parked by the curb. I was shocked to see these cars at my home. "My God, what happened? Why are the police at my home?" As I walked in the door, the children and my dear wife started to tell me all these things but none of it made any sense. I was informed that Mrs. Burns (our former owner who rented the apartment) committed suicide. I went downstairs where I found some police officers as well as city sheriffs. I introduced myself and got some information.

Apparently, Mrs. Burns was very disturbed about something, so she simply jumped in a small city lake and drowned. In the meantime, the city authorities sealed off the entry to the apartment for further investigation. As I walked upstairs, Dorothy informed me that indeed Mrs. Burns walked out in the morning. Before leaving, she gave her a check for the rent because this was the last day of the month. The check looked okay to us, but the next day when I went to deposit it, the check was not accepted because it was predated and, secondly, the account was closed. The bank would not reveal the reason. Since I was not accustomed to such dealings, I asked the Police Department about this matter. I was told that I would be contacted by proper authorities and that I would be paid for the delayed rents and other expenses which were due me. Although that made me feel good, as I had counted on this income, there was nothing I could do about it.

I could not complain about the progress in our lives. We were getting ahead monetarily and I could tell that in time all would be okay. I began to speak better English. I could afford to purchase some tools to repair cars at home in my spare time. Before I knew it, I was making quite a bit of money on these repairs. I would repair two, three or more cars per week. This would bring us a nice income in addition to my wages. Before we knew it, it was time to go to the hospital because Dorothy was in labor with our third child. My mother (God bless her heart) came over to take care of the two girls while we awaited the delivery. Not going into theatrics, but I was scared that it would be another girl, but it turned out to be a healthy, big boy! You would think I reached the top of Mt. McKinley or something like that.

We were a very happy couple, but bringing Floyd home was not easy. This little fellow would eat us out of house and home. He would hum and hum and then hum again when he would suck on his bottle or eat his cereal or whatever. It seemed that he was growing as we looked at him. After about six months, Dorothy would carry him in her arms and his legs would dangle because he was such a big boy, but there wasn't any hair on his head. We all loved him to pieces. The time came to make arrangements to christen our son. As always we made a big deal about it because we had quite a bit more money since I began repairing cars at home. We didn't know how good our decision was to break through the bedroom window to make the backyard accessible for everyday use. For the Christening event, it was heaven's gift, for we could accommodate the entire family.

On this particular Sunday, the whole family gathered at St. Anne's Catholic Church for the christening of our son, Floyd. After the ceremony we all gathered in our home. The food was splendid. My mother prepared all Polish food, such as ravioli (pierogi), stuffed cabbage (Golabki) rolls, and other Polish delicacies. Dorothy made all kinds of salads, pasta and other goodies. Some guests even brought their favorites and I supplied the beer and wine. This truly was a gala christening. We ate inside and out, one of the good times in being in the USA. The only thing I regretted was that I couldn't show my father that I indeed carried our Jasinski family name into the future, for I was the last male in our generation. Although he was gone for some time, I knew that he would have been proud of me.

No matter how well things went for me, I ached inside for my sister Stefania and her two sons. My lovely, beautiful sister was stuck in the hospital and could not see the progress or her sons progressing in age and scholastics—they were plenty smart and brought home very nice report cards each quarter. I believe my mother was very instrumental in having them do their homework. I was still very much involved with the VA about Stefania and her two sons' welfare. I became so involved with the Governmental procedures that I felt like a family lawyer. My English was getting quite good and that gave me more freedom on my job and conducting our lives in America.

One day Dorothy got a phone call from her biological father named Bernard L. Lewis (formerly Luczynski) saying that he was her real father, and he said his brother John visited her and spoke very highly of her. He wondered if he could come over for a visit for he wanted to see his daughter and her family. Her response was very reluctant because she hadn't seen him for some eighteen years. It was very difficult to say anything about this matter. Since I was at work, she asked him to call back in a few days because she wanted to talk with me about this matter. At this time, I had no opinion about divorce and the problems it creates when it comes to raising children and how it affects them. In my native Poland, divorces didn't exist or if they did they were done quietly.

So for me, it was difficult to guide Dorothy in this matter. One thing I would admit was that I wanted to meet this man just to be able to see what he was all about. He finally showed up one day, and we sat down and talked awhile, but it was a very cold meeting and didn't last long. We met on other occasions, and at one point he mentioned that he owned a farm of four hundred acres somewhere in the City of Orland. Seeing that I was somewhat talented, and coming from a farmer's family, he suggested that it would be a great opportunity for me to try my hand in leasing this land and moving my family to his place to see what would happen. The land already was producing a crop known as Ladino Clover for seed. We discussed our future and possibilities which would come if we would accept his proposal.

One day we decided to go and visit him where he lived in Willows, CA, about eighty-five miles north of Sacramento. Upon arriving at his home, we met him and his wife and, strangely enough, we somehow tolerated each other. We then went out to visit his farm about five miles from his home. The farm was huge. I didn't visualize how big four hundred acres was. It was in a sort of disastrous condition for he was leasing it to some people who didn't care about anything. The buildings and machinery were in sad condition. He promised us that he would guide us and help me repair the equipment that needed attention. The possibilities were there to make a lot of money. After the visit with him we drove back to San Francisco.

We had lots of time to discuss the matter to which we were introduced. The decision would be made in the near future; the move to the farm would be very difficult and drastic; we needed to talk with my mother and Dorothy's parents to see how it would turn out. Years before, my father gave me one piece of advice; he said, "Son, a farmer's life is very risky; one year you win and some years you lose. If you can stand the risks, then go for it, but remember that you can't control the weather. It's up to God and God will not speak out to you." We were told by Ben (Dorothy's father) that there was a good possibility to make big money if everything turned out good. In the past years things turned out okay. The big problem was that we didn't have too much money to go into this endeavor, but he promised that he would co-sign loan papers if we would invest some of our own money. This would mean that we had to sell our beautiful home and gamble our future on the elements. We could make a lot of money in a short time or we could go broke in a short time.

My dear wife said that whatever happens, she would support me and that I had to make the decision. We will survive whatever happens. It took some time to sleep on the decision. There was more to it than it seemed on the surface. The children were small, not yet out of preschool, my mother and my sister Stefania and her two lovely sons—was it right to leave everything behind and chance it all, or to stay put and earn things the old-fashioned way. On the other hand, one gets the chance once in a lifetime, so what now? To make such a decision was very difficult, and frankly, I was scared of it. There was no use procrastinating so we put it aside for awhile.

My friend, Eugene Regent, whom we sponsored to come from England, had served with me in the Polish Army and married a Scottish gal, wanted to emigrate to America and settle in California. One day I approached him. We talked about the proposition from Dorothy's father. It seemed that Gene was ready to go with me to try our luck at farming. His wife Betty was a lovely lady about the same age as Dorothy. Gene and Betty had two children so we had a lot in common. We had quite a difficult decision to make. The decision was strictly ours and we had a lot of thinking to do. My Mother was skeptical about the whole matter, but mostly because she wanted us to be close to her. This was a normal, mutual feeling. Finally we made the big decision to sell our beautiful home, give up my job as an automobile mechanic and all the local functions in which I was participating, contracted papers with Ben to move on to the new adventure.

We sold our home for around $40,000 so we had a pretty good start. The move to Orland was pretty smooth and the relocation wasn't too difficult with one exception: moving from a city like San Francisco to the countryside, to a farm in the middle of nowhere was a stark reality. It was 1957, late September, so it was still quite hot. The children had lots of fun running around in the open spaces around the duplex which we moved into. I surveyed the grounds and the house and a big workshop with all the equipment which looked old and in need of lots of work. But it was only the beginning of the new adventure, so I looked at this in a positive way and as a challenge to make this a success. Lucky for me that I owned all the mechanics' tools, was a good thinker and had good skills in repairing things. There was not time to dwell about how much work was ahead of me, but to roll up my sleeves and do whatever there was to do. Oh, there were tractors, movers, combines, thrashers, wagons and so forth and they all needed attention, plus I had to help Dorothy establish a home and help her with the children. It was work from morning 'til night.

Ben was very helpful with the introduction of the role of being a Ladino Clover farmer and very helpful in explaining what it was all about. It was a difficult time adjusting to this kind of environment in comparison to working from 8 a.m. to 5 p.m. five days a week. But this was farming and I remember from my childhood watching my parents farming days. The only time off was on Sunday to go to church. The other days it was work from sun up to sun down. Now it was my experience following in their footsteps. As the weeks went by the repairs on the equipment were progressing just fine. God must have been with me because I had never seen some of these tractors, so I had to learn to repair them, but I suppose it took some common sense to do what is right. One day a wealthy sheep owner came to me with the proposition to leave the whole 400 acres to graze his sheep. He offered me $1 per day per sheep. I contacted Ben, and he said that was the going price and that I should so it. It was a lot of money and it would defray some of our expenses.

We spent the Christmas holidays in San Francisco at my mother's house. It was fun to be with both families again. The children had a lot of fun playing with cousins Eddie and Randy, my sister's boys. My mother would say to me, "Franek, you have to save your energy because you work too hard and you have lost some weight." She said she worried about me and my little family. On the way home, our kids thanks us for going back to the City and see Grandma and had a lot to talk about.

Our future at the farm looked better each day. Spring was coming and the grounds were getting greener, and the fields were looking for some attention such as repairing levies and the like. One day we were visited by a gentleman who introduced himself as the US Government Advisor for farmers. This was fine, buy why did he pay us a visit? I was very apprehensive about this visit. He reminded me of our experience in Siberia.

I asked him who sent him to our home to snoop around. He apologetically explained that this was a free service sponsored by the Government to assist us in knowing how to succeed in growing crops that would yield the most and earn the most for the owner. He also said that he would visit me weekly to assist me and there would be no charge. As he departed, Dorothy and I could not believe that such services were available to us. After awhile, I came to remember that my Uncle Andrew (my mother's brother) was also an advisor in Poland and Czechoslovakia. He was instrumental in my parent's successful farming in Poland. I paid a visit to Ben who lived in the neighboring town of Willows. I told him about the visit from the Government. He said that this is what the Government does all the time and that I should adhere to their suggestions for they know the business to the fullest. I was glad that I talked to him about this matter. We did well growing this wonderful-looking crop. It permeated the air with a wonderful aroma every time it blossomed.

There were down times on the farm because as the weather warmed up, the critters such as spider mites would infect the area with spider webs which would suffocate the blossoms. When this happened, we would have to hire an airplane to spray the whole farm. Such sprayings would cost two to three thousand dollars, so it was not cheap. Besides, we would have to evacuate our home because the spray was poisonous to humans as well. The biggest problem was irrigating. To irrigate four hundred acres of land I had big underground pumps pumping twenty-four hours per day, changing each lever so none would stop working. Thanks to Gene's help, we did a good job. The Advisor would come at a time when you least expected. Each time he was amazed how things evolved for being such a rookie farmer. He said more than once that I was gifted, and should do okay. Between spraying for one creature or another and fertilizing and watering, I had no life for myself, but then that's what I chose. It was too much work for Gene and me, so I hired a wonderful local man to help.

As summer approached, the weather was getting hot and reached 100 degrees F. so the children were hot and cranky. When we would go to San Francisco to visit my mother, I stopped at the Army Surplus Store and I found an Army canvas pool about twelve feet in diameter. It was reasonably priced so we purchased it for a few dollars. When I set it up and filled it with water, our three kids and Gene's two had a wonderful time. Hot days and cool water equaled relief. With Gene's wife Betty and Dorothy watching them play in the big pool it was just a pleasure to see them so happy. Life on the farm is never easy, but we made it as casual as we could for our children and all of us.

The nearest suppliers for the tools I needed to repair all the machinery was in the City of Chico. Chico is a university town in Northern California, so every time I had to go there I reminisced about seeing students with their books attending to their schooling. In short, I was learning a lot about my life as a farmer. About the end of June my Advisor came with a wooden square to measure the count of clover flower pods. He explained that the count of flower pods per square foot multiplied per acre would determine the yield in pounds of seeds. At 50 cents/pound/acre it would yield "x" number of dollars.

He said that it looked good for the future harvest. He suggested that I should wait for about two more bloomings to have a full harvest. It takes about ten to twelve blooming cycles to get a good harvest of seeds. The seed has to be very pure and without much infection, such as grass or other seed-producing plants. Because it costs much more to separate poor clover seed from the impurities, I had to hire an airplane to spray chemicals to kill the grass and to speed this up. The eradication is called IPC to kill grass growth and thistle growth. It was cheaper to spray and kill the unwanted growth than to separate the end product.

My initial investment when I started this farming endeavor was about $50,000, plus the advance from the Association on the outcome, about $200,000. I was in the hole for about $250,000 plus nine months of my time working like a slave. But all this time my Advisor assured me that it looks wonderful and his assessment was right on target. My next door neighbor, Mr. King, also mentioned to me that the growth and the look of the blossoms was great. That made me feel much better for he didn't have any hidden agenda to say something he didn't mean.

The plan was that the harvest would begin the first week of July. I started final preparation of my equipment to make sure that when the time came I wouldn't encounter any setbacks. One day before July my friend Gene came to me with a sheepish look and said he wanted to talk. I sensed something was wrong so I asked him what it was as we often talked about many things and had no secrets since we were friends from "way back". He stated that the crop looked good and that I was on the way to make a lot of money. He said he wanted some part of the proceeds because he, too, worked hard. I was stunned to hear him complain in such a manner. I said, "Gene, we made the agreement. You are being paid every week and you have the apartment free with all utilities except telephone. You even get gasoline from my tank free of charge and we talked about a hefty bonus if we have a good year and it is looking good so far, so be patient." I also added that I had invested about $50,000 of my own money plus the amount I borrowed from the Association, and so far I have never received any compensation. I asked that he stick with me, and we will see what happens in the end.

At that point, I walked toward him to ask what he was doing. With a few words from him he indicated that in short if there was no splitting of gains he was not willing to work with me. After packing his trailer, without any goodbyes from either his wife Betty or his children, he simply got in his car and drove away. This was my good friend whom I sponsored to come to America, with whom I shared meals all the way back to our days in the Polish Army. He had no consideration, but abandoned me at the very time I needed him most. I have never heard from or seen him or his family since.

What can I say about this grave incident. My dear wife Dorothy, lost her best friend and they were like sisters, and their kids were like brothers and sisters to our kids. But in the end, I had to accept things as they were and had to move forward. I called Ben to inform him of what happened. He said that he had talked to Gene but couldn't change his mind about leaving. He also told Gene that the prospect of having a successful harvest was there but it was not done yet. A Farmers' life is unpredictable for it is seen as a success only when the harvest is over. He said he would find me some helping hands and that all will work out, but at the time Dorothy and I could not believe what had just happened to us for we had such a good friendship and got along just fine. What could cause such a division all of a sudden? She said she had noticed some cooling of the friendship but she put it aside thinking that the swing in mood was temporary and will come back to normal. Besides, what happened is beyond reparation and life will go on and we will find some other worthy people who could share our lives.

The first week of July was upon us and the harvest must go on with Gene on board or not. Both Ben and I had to find people with some experience to help out with the harvest. It turned out that there was more help available than I could use. Besides, they were all able bodied and experienced. The harvest morning came, and a couple of guys showed up to start cutting the beautiful clover. It was a hot time to start cutting, for hot days dry out cut clover for thrashing. It was an easy task cutting this stuff because the shears on the side of the tractor were five feet in length. An experienced operator could cut a lot of clover in one day. The harder work came in thrashing and extracting the seed and collecting it in its own container. When the container for this beautiful golden seed was full to about a cubic yard, it was transferred to the truck with similar cubic container capacity. The truck contained eight such containers.

When they were all full, we took them to our Association to be cleaned and processed. It all looked like a miracle was happening. It was the proudest moment of my life. What an achievement! As I was advised by the Government Advisor, I was to harvest about two hundred acres and to dry up the remaining two hundred acres to start at the end of the first one. I was looking forward to it because my expectation inspired me to work as hard as I could to prove to all of us that this venture was going to be a big success. One more bloom while the fields were drying up would be a success. My regular Government Advisor was beaming with pride that all was a "go" the following Monday.

Knowing the ropes is what it takes to harvest. I, too, was quite prepared for this task. Two or three days before I was to start harvesting, I got up in the morning and went outside and it was raining. I called Ben and talked to him and asked how often it rains in July. He said, "It rarely ever rains in July so this won't last too long". Well it rained for ten days and water filled all the levies and saturated all the dried up clover lying on the ground. It looked disastrous to me. Is this a disaster, and am I doomed? The advisor came and looked. He wasn't pleased with what he saw and consoled me and said, "It won't be as bad as it looks. The hot weather will dry up the field in a couple of days and then you will salvage what you can and he added that no one controls the weather."

As time went on, the second half of the farm gave me almost half of what the first half gave me. After all accounts, gains and losses, I was in the hole about $60,000, which included the $40,000 from the sale of our house. What option did we have? Stay on the farm and undertake a new adventure or quit and go back to San Francisco and start a new life all over again? My dear wife was so sympathetic towards me. She knew how hard I tried to advance our family finances and how eager I was to show the world that I would succeed, and now I was a complete failure!

Was I defeated or was I just a big talker that could not be counted on or was I able to provide for my family? All my dreams went away with this episode. I came to America to achieve something that I could not achieve in my native Poland. After the bad news from the Association, I sat down with my dear wife and asked her what should we do now? She simply said that the decision is up to me. She said that she is willing to go with me to the end of the earth. No sooner than we finished this disastrous talk, Ben, her father, called and wanted to talk to me. With the small talk he finally asked me if I could call the Association to ask if they would advance me $5,000 because he needed the money to pay for something or other. I advised him that I would let him know after discussing it first with Dorothy. After hanging up, Dot asked me what it was all about because I acted very scared. After explaining what the conversation was about, she asked me what I was going to do.

I was quite mad because this man knew what position I was in. I lost $50,000 from the sale of our home and I lost the salary I could have had if I worked at my profession, besides I lost all that labor repairing his equipment and then I lost self respect because the whole episode had failed, regardless of why it happened. And now he wants me to go out on a limb and borrow another $5,000 to appease him and at the same time to enslave my dear family to his wishes. It didn't make any sense to stay on this farm any longer because we didn't have any finances to do so and it would be counter productive if we stayed.

To compound the disaster, he came to me for an advance of money that he needs. He knew that I am flat broke and that I can't go in the hole anymore than I am in now. So why would he ask me to do what is not viable? I told him, "I have bad news for you." I was extremely disappointed that I had met a dead end. But I was not defeated and believed that something would come up. But my dear Dorothy said it had only been a couple of days since we returned to San Francisco, and were living with my mother and Stefania's boys, rent free, so I should be more patient for I will find some work, "in the meantime, relax and be more patient". I went to see the dispatcher in my Union Hall, but the answer was the same, "We will call you at the first opening." So that was my day accomplishing nothing. It was very disappointing to go home and tell your wife that you could not find any work.

When my mother got back from her job, she said that she had some good news for me. She said that Mr. Buchanan asked if I could come see him for he had some work to be done around his house. My mother had told him some time back that I was returning to San Francisco because I received a big misfortune due to the rains. The next day I went to see Mr. Buchanan. He was happy to see me because we had met before. He asked if I could work on the backyard patio, maybe lay some tiles in his entrance hallway, hang some pictures, paint some walls and on and on. It looked to me like I could work for him six months or more. How lucky I was to meet him again and be able to do some work for him. What about pay I asked him. He said he would pay me what I was making at my old job with no benefits, and I would work eight hours a day, if that is okay with me. So we agreed with a handshake.

We then sat down to plan what work needed to be done. When I returned home and informed my family about my new adventure everybody was happy for me, and naturally we had to have a drink to celebrate such a big occasion. I liked what I was doing, and the pay was good. I was beginning to save some money. All we had were food and personal expenses, so we were getting ahead. After about three months, we got pretty tired of living like newly arrived immigrants so Dorothy and I decided to maybe find something to rent.

One Saturday, my day off, I went to the Andrews Real Estate office in San Francisco. A very nice man greeted me by introducing himself as Andrew Garibaldi and he asked if he could help me. I explained my situation and told him I wanted to rent something for my family. He didn't say anything for awhile and then looked at me and said, "Frank, I have something. I don't know why but I would like to help you. Instead of renting a house, I will sell you a six unit apartment building with a small down payment and it will be my help to you. I will do so because you deserve it." Wow, I could purchase an apartment house, but how? The owner wanted to sell it in the worst way and we can offer him a price he will not refuse. How much will it cost and how much down payment was needed? After shuffling some papers, he said I would need a minimum of about $3,000 plus closing costs. "We will offer him $25,000 for that place 'as is'. This will put our foot in the door." Then he said, "Let's go and see the building and the one apartment which is empty then we can talk some more."

I had to sit down for awhile and think, concentrating on what I was doing. Thoughts went through my mind like lightening from the loss of my job to living with my mother and the boys, finding a temporary job and now this. Am I dreaming or is this a reality? I agreed to go and see the place. It was located on Lincoln Way across the street from the famous Golden Gate Park. I must have passed it a thousand times going to work each day. I said to Andy (that's what he wanted to be called), "I have never been inside of this building but I remember it from the past, so let's get in and see what it looks like inside." We entered on the ground floor, going through the hallway to see apartment #2, which was empty. On entering we found a large kitchen, one small bedroom or a small sunroom, one large living room and a good sized bedroom with a good sized bathroom equaling about 800 square feet. I was impressed at what I saw and I also knew my Dorothy would like it as well for it was located close to a Catholic School as well as shopping and the park, but most of all it was close to my mother.

So I said to Andy, "There's a lot of work here as it is in poor condition, but I will bring my wife and mother and if they like what we have here, we will get back to you." He agreed with what I said and gave me the keys to the place. "Go look at it and bring me some money as I am sure we have a deal." When I arrived home, Dorothy and my mother looked at me and asked if I was alright because I had a big grin on my face from ear to ear. After hearing the whole story of what I had done all this time, they did not believe one word of what I told them. While I was out, Dorothy's grandfather came to visit. He lived nearby and visited us quite often. I said, "I have these keys in my hand so why don't all of us go out there and see it for ourselves?"

They all liked the building and the apartment. They agreed it was on the small side, but the children were small as well and we could live there for awhile and get ahead while improving the place to our liking. Besides we would have five rents coming in every month so we'd be in good shape. After seeing the place, we had a discussion of what we should do. I liked the place very much and so did my whole family. The only question was where do we get the down payment? Because everybody liked the place, my mother offered to give us $1,000, then, to my surprise, Dorothy's grandfather Mike, offered another thousand dollars. Now we had $3,500 which was maybe enough for the down payment.

Dorothy and I decided to go see Andy and have a talk about this. As we entered, he sat us down and said, "where is the money?" It wasn't funny. We were sort of scared, but we were sure that we wanted to start all over again, and this was a golden opportunity to do so. The angels were with us, and maybe God was helping us along. Good old Andy Garibaldi, our guardian angel, had done all he promised to Dot. We finalized the purchase in a short time. We rejoiced for the opportunity to be able to have our own place and to live and to cherish our lives. One day Mother called to say some person called and wanted to see me, so she gave me his phone number. It was Mr. Taylorson from McAllister Buick. When I talked with him he offered me my old job back. I thanked him and said I would start work on Monday. I was almost finished with the work Mr. Buchanan needed, such as installing a water softener and a dumb waiter to the next door restaurant so he could get food sent to him without going there to eat, and various other jobs. I was paid well and thus was able to save some money. This was 1959 and things were inexpensive in those days.

I thank God for looking after me as there was new prosperity was on the horizon. He let me purchase this property, get my job back—what more could I ask for? The job went fine. Mr. Buchanan had some more work to be done so I promised that I would do it on weekends which was okay with him. In my mind, it would allow me to make some extra money. As it turned out, with the purchase of the apartment building, the rent I was collecting was more than my monthly payment. Some time later I visited Andrews Real Estate and talking with Andy, I asked him why the former owner sold his building for such a low price. He simply answered that it was God's will.

Our oldest daughter soon started kindergarten at St. Anne's school. It was walking distance so we were happy about that. One day when Grandpa Zycinski came to visit, my dear wife needed to go to the store for some groceries. She asked Grandpa if he'd watch the children and he was happy to do so, so she turned on the TV and switched it to some cowboy program which he liked. When she returned home she found him dead, sitting in the armchair as she left him. What a tragedy! Otherwise, out lives were going smoothly and we were prospering. My job at McAllister Buick was getting easier because of my experience on the farm.

Life seemed to go along just fine even after all the problems. Mr. Andrew Garibaldi called me about a year later inquiring about our lives and what he could do for us because he felt he was our "godfather". We had just started to get our feet on the ground and this time we wanted to establish ourselves. Of course, there were family problems to contend with. First of all, Dorothy's Uncle Ben was a real estate agent, as was her aunt. Since they perceived that this Frank, their niece's husband, was a green immigrant, he needed some help. I was and am now self-sufficient. I have made some mistakes, like moving my family to the farm, but that was a calculated endeavor which I lost. But now I have learned a different lesson and I would not allow myself to be taken advantage of by anyone for their benefit.

I explained to Mr. Garibaldi that for the present time I was happy to stay put. As the children grew and our Siamese cat had kittens in our bedroom dresser drawer, we became more cramped than ever, so we decided to look for a larger home for the family. We did succeed in finding one not too far from my mother's home. I contacted Mr. Garibaldi telling him I was interested in that home. It turned out that it was for sale for $20,000. After selling our apartment house, we were just a few thousand dollars short for our new home. It was much closer to school for our children and for my mother to come and visit. My poor sister, Stefania, was still in the hospital for the mentally ill and her two sons were under my mother's and my supervision. My life, overall, was getting easier, but never without grief for my lovely sister Stefania. The house needed a lot of work to encompass our needs but we had a lot of time to work on it.

I was called into the manager's office at my job at McAllister Buick. The manager must have liked me because he said, "Frank I have some good news for you. This business has been sold to British Motors so if you'd like to stay here you are welcome, but if not I will pay you for the rest of the day. I figured on going to my Union Hall and find out if there were any openings at other dealerships. I was referred to Geary Ford, which was much closer to my home. When I arrived at the dealership, I found I could get a job there. The Service Manager asked me a few questions and said, "Frank, if you bring your tools today I will pay you for a whole day." I said I'd be right back. I was back about two hours later and was assigned to my workstation. I didn't know anyone but was introduced to my co-workers. I was very happy to find this new job because it was a smaller place and offered possibly more opportunity for advancement.

Dorothy was very pleased with my new job because it was very close to home. As time went on I was promoted to Service Advisor, which gave me a 10% over scale salary and I worked with a pencil instead of tools. It also gave me more prestige and ability to consult with customers. About a year later, Mr. Balatti called me to his office. Since he was the owner of the dealership, it crossed my mind that this was my last day on the job. Instead, he praised my work and said that a lot of customers offered praises on my conduct with them, and said I had a "good work ethic". He then offered me a job as the Service Manager, and with happiness I accepted the position.

He explained that I would be placed on a managerial salary plus commission on the operation of the Service Department, plus, if the Service Department prospered, I would get some credit in the parts department. I answered that I was pleasantly honored and accepted the offer. He proposed that I should dress properly for the job, and he would announce the change the next day. Well, I worked at this dealership for twenty some years. I made lots of money, and supported my family and children through Catholic grammar and high schools. Most of all, my family and my mother were proud of me as well. This foreigner coming to a great country, not speaking English, applied himself, worked hard, kept his nose to the grindstone, out of police troubles, and was making strides to better himself.

In the meantime, after working hours I devoted my time to renovating our house to better serve our needs. I added one additional bedroom downstairs, along with a bathroom. We lived like a family which was native to San Francisco with some good family backing. Any backlash from the past? Well, yes, one day the doorbell rang. When I answered it, I was asked if I was the person he was looking for. I discovered it was a subpoena and court order to appear in Superior Court. Dorothy's father served the papers because we owed him $7,000 from the farm episode. He had never mentioned this matter to us and instead he filed a lawsuit. There was nothing I could do but get some funds together and pay the debt, instead of going through the court proceedings. In the back of my mind I expected this could happen, but after such a long time, I believed it might have been forgotten. After all, we lost $50,000 and one year of my wages if I had been working somewhere else. The good God never let me know and I believe that he will not do so in the future.

Since Dorothy's parents had moved to Reno, Nevada some years earlier, we would go visit them from time to time on vacation. This served us well because the summers in San Francisco were quite foggy and cold so the wife and children enjoyed the hot weather in Reno. This time I suggested that she and the children go there and I would come back and remodel our kitchen because it was the last room in the house which needed remodeling. Dorothy agreed, so I drove them to Reno and returned to finish the remodel. As I was working and making the kitchen cabinets, everything was going fine with no interruptions and quiet around the house, so I was making great strides. I got a phone call from Dorothy for me to come back to Reno.

She was sick and might have to go to the hospital. "Please come right away because it's an emergency." Naturally I jumped into our family car, a 1963 Lincoln Continental and drove back to Reno in about four hours plus. I found my dear wife in bed all listless and under blankets. She asked me not to ask any questions but gather our three children, and we would get going right now back home to San Francisco.

I did as she asked, and said goodbye to her parents. It was still early morning, so we got to Sacramento before noon. The children were getting hot inside the car and asked me to turn the air conditioning on. When I did, Dorothy asked for a blanket because she was cold and shivering, so I stopped the car. Inside the trunk I always carried blankets and other things to use at the beach and other places. When I covered her with the blanket she was alright for awhile, but soon asked to turn off the AC because she was extremely cold. When I turned it off, the children complained that it was too hot for them. It was difficult coping with this situation and I was puzzled knowing what to do, so I started to speed up to get to San Francisco as fast as I could.

Well, you don't speed on the highway because a highway patrolman might stop you and sure enough a red light behind me made me pull over and stop the car. When he came to my door, he asked if I was going to a fire. I said that my wife was very sick, and I was taking her to the hospital in San Francisco, that this was an emergency, and would he escort me to get there before she got worse. He noticed the children were sweating and my wife was shivering under a blanket. He was very kind and said that he would escort us as far as he could and then he would call for help to get further assistance. We finally arrived at San Francisco's St. Mary's Hospital.

Dorothy was taken to the Emergency Room and soon after she was taken to the isolation room for further evaluation. I was told to take the children home and make them as well as myself comfortable and call or come back tomorrow. When I returned to the hospital to learn what was the matter, they said that the diagnoses was not completed, but they believed it was an outbreak of lupus and, if so, it is a very dangerous sickness. They told me to go home and take care of my children and come back later. As I returned later that afternoon to hear the diagnosis, they said she indeed had this rare disease called lupus and I should make arrangements for her to stay in the hospital for some time. They were not sure how long, but estimated possibly up to three months.

When I got back home, I explained to the children that their mother was very sick; she was placed in an isolation room and we could not see her until the crisis was over. I then went to see my mother who was taking care of her two grandsons, and now she is asked to take care of our three children. I was very sorry for her that she is asked to help me as well. Dorothy's sickness hit us very hard and our children were sort of abandoned. Luckily I had a few days left of my vacation so I could take charge, but what will happen down the road? Oh well, God will help us and we will survive and go on with our lives. Going back to visit Dorothy at the hospital wasn't easy and the surprises were killing me. The battery of doctors didn't have a clear diagnosis. They said that paralysis of her whole body was setting in so they started to administer some cortisone into her bloodstream to slow down the process. The news was all bad that the doctors gave me as they hadn't seen this kind of case in the past.

The recovery will take a long time. I had to go to work, also had to tell the owner of the company that my wife was in the hospital with an illness called lupus. He said, "Frank, we will help you all we can, so don't worry." So I would visit her in the early morning before work. Some days I would go there after work, and I spent a lot of time on weekends visiting her. The children were forbidden to visit because they were worried that it could be contagious to young ones. I was sort of abandoned by her family. They would occasionally come and visit, but at the same time I was alone to carry the burden. God bless my mother. She helped with the children, cooked for them, sent them to school and brought them back home and all the other details that had to be done around the house. This seemed to go on forever, but luckily only lasted for about six weeks.

In the meantime, as always, more problems came to me. My dear mother had been ailing for some time, but all she could tell me was that it was nothing to worry about, she was alright except she needed some rest and the doctor advised her to slow down and rest awhile and all should be okay. I agreed with the doctor's opinion for what else could I do? I asked her not to worry, that our daughters are getting older and they could help me take care of Dorothy. Mother did stay at home, but she couldn't relax. She took care of her grandsons and Stefania. Stefania was doing much better now and was home, but mother could not stay away. She would come to my house each week and she sometimes just appeared. She would help us keep the house clean or prepare food for the next meal, or even do the laundry.

When I came home, my children would welcome me warmly with hugs and kisses or at times would not look at me showing their anger for not having their mother at home to take care of them. After awhile, Dorothy was finally brought home in our car, but to get upstairs was another problem. I finally had to carry her upstairs with the help of our daughters. It was very hard but we made it all together. In the meantime, Mother was getting weaker and she was now under the doctor's care, and he suggested that she should admit herself to the hospital for further diagnosis.

Mother was informed that the prognosis wasn't good and that her parathyroid was cancerous. She would have to have more tests and evaluation and that she should come back to the hospital as soon as possible. After I got her back home, the grandchildren and Stefania were happy just to have her home again. Since Mother wasn't well, she would struggle to come to visit Dorothy and see if she could help her. She would wait for me to come home so I could give her a ride home, but she was getting weaker and weaker. I wondered what was happening to my family. Poor Stefania with her mental illness, her two sons Eddie & Randy and the home had to be taken care of . . . what about me? I could not take more weight on my shoulders!

Being a Ford dealership Repair Department Service Manager was not an easy job! The worry about the whole stress was getting to me. I suppose the owner of our dealership, Mr. Ed Ballatti noticed that my behavior had changed and my usual smile had disappeared. He summoned me to his office and asked me to sit down and asked me what is going on at home? After listening to my whole story, he was very sympathetic and told me to go home early once in a while and take a deep breath and relax and he would help me all he could and don't worry. I needed some reassurance that somebody would support me. That afternoon I went home somehow regenerated. Things seemed to stabilize. The girls were headed to high school, Stefania's boys Eddie and Randy were at the University of San Francisco, a Catholic University and they were doing just fine.

My job was secure and I even received a raise because Mr. Ballatti was feeling sorry for me, but it made me somewhat very happy for his support. For awhile, what could I say? I have endured a tremendous weight on my shoulders at the young age of only 38. I have lived through the tragedies of two or three people many years older! I wondered "is this over now or will it unravel any more?"

A few days passed when Dorothy called my work saying that the hospital had called advising that Mrs. Jasinski was unconscious and someone had to come to the hospital to help out as she is going to pass away. I was at her side within 45 minutes and that's the fastest I could get there. I found her lying on her bed with the towel rolled under her chin. She was still alive, but breathing very slowly with her eyes closed. I talked to her and touched her but she didn't respond and watching and praying for her and her soul and for God to spare her agony in her death. The resident nurse came into the room seeing tears running down my cheeks, she gently embraced me but didn't say a thing. She then said that mother will have a little while left and that she is not suffering anymore and then left us alone. As I held mother's hand, after awhile her hand felt limp and she was gone to her maker. God Bless my mother. We buried her remains alongside my father.

One day the doctor called me at work, telling me that Dorothy, after a visit to his office, was getting better but due to some paralysis she would have to have surgery on her left eye muscle to straighten her eye to correct a cross eye. They asked me to come to give permission for such surgery. Dorothy and I discussed the problem, and we agreed that the surgery was necessary and indeed it was successful. After a few days I went to the hospital to bring her home and I believe it was late Friday. First thing Saturday morning I had to go to work to do some warranty work so I had to have quiet time for this kind of work.

Before I left home Dorothy asked for some orange juice as she was still in bed. So I did as she asked me and left for work. I was only there for about ten minutes when I got a phone call from my eldest daughter Nina. She was in tears and frantically asked me to come home because Dorothy could not breathe. I told her to call 911 and tell them the same things she told me. Lucky for me my home was only about ten minutes away. When I arrived home, I heard the siren blowing and got there a couple of minutes later. Dorothy was in the living room almost unconscious. The attendants got her into the ambulance, and we were off to the hospital. I asked them if they knew she had just been released from the hospital just two days earlier from St. Mary's Hospital, but they wanted to take her to San Francisco General. I would not allow them to take her there so when we got close to St. Mary's, I began to scuffle with the driver and made him turn into their ER driveway. His partner said I could be arrested for my action, but I made the decision to take her back to St. Mary's.

My daughter Nina notified the hospital that her mother was on the way, and they should be waiting for her. I was so proud of my big girl who was only 10 years old. Here we go again, back to the previous situation, so two weeks later we got Dorothy back home again, but this time my mother wouldn't be in my home before 7 a.m. to take care of Dorothy, since she'd just passed away. Things went pretty well this time, and I was more relaxed during my working hours. Mr. Ballati was inquiring about Dorothy's condition and I quite often gave him progress reports. He repeatedly assured me that if I ever needed anything, that he would help me. That meant a lot to me because it gave me encouragement that this sickness of my dear wife will go away some day. After all, even the owner of this dealership is pulling for me as well as my co-workers but also my family.

Following a two month stay in the hospital, Dorothy finally came home, but she wasn't very healthy. I had to teach and help show her how to stand up and walk again. The children were the most instrumental in their mother's recovery. How wonderful it was seeing her when she was well enough to send me out to work, and then send our children to school. I was the happiest man around as my wife was getting well again.

Exploring the good fortunes of life, we became involved in our lifestyle. After the prolonged fate of Dorothy's sickness and disastrous affects on our children, we became a close and open family as we should have been to begin with. The children had really grown and matured at this point, and our daughter Debbie and Tom's romance became very serious as there was no mistake about it as they announced to us that they wanted to get married, so with our blessing we agreed and the date was settled. Surprise! Surprise! After adding up all the expenses it came out to a lot of money and over a year of my wages!! Wow! You could purchase a house (old one) for the same price. Jokingly I said to Debbie, "Why don't you just elope to Reno, Nevada and take all that money and buy yourself a house?"

The answer I got was not what I wanted to hear. She simply said, "And did you go to Reno, or did you get married with both families witnessing and celebrating your marriage?" I said that she was perfectly correct, and that we will give her away as our prize daughter as is our tradition. The money was not an object. The Italian Club in old San Francisco was a very elegant place and the church ceremony and reception was also very elegant. All our friends in attendance were sort of surprised that this immigrant fellow with all his problems could afford such a gala reception. My oldest daughter, Nina (Diane) was sort of envious about the whole thing, but she soon got over it in fine fashion.

Things at my job were sort of crumbling and business was getting difficult, maybe because the Vice President of the dealership passed away at a very young age due to some liver disorder. So then there were questions about my expense account and other things, and it made me very uncomfortable. I questioned my friend who had become the second Vice President. He simply said that things were changing and the company was doing business in a different way. I accumulated some vacation time from the past and current year, so I could afford a change. When I got home, I discussed what had happened at work, and we decided that I should do what would be best for all of us.

In the meantime, back when I worked at McAllister Buick, my Polish friend with whom I worked and have maintained contact with for all these years was a manager for a Buick dealership. So I called him, and after some small talk, I asked him if he had an opening and needed some help. After having lunch with him, he offered me a job as his assistant. This was good news to me because it was just a mile from my house. We agreed on the compensation and that I would start in about two weeks because we wanted to take a vacation before starting my new job. Dorothy's parents, who now lived in Palm Springs, were very happy to have us visit for a couple of weeks.

The new job was very pleasant and I was very happy with the decision. Soon after getting accustomed to my new job, I got a visit from Mike. Mike was the boyfriend to our oldest daughter Nina (Diane), and a nice gentleman and a Police Officer with the San Francisco Police Department. Coincidentally, both Tom and Mike were born on the Island of Hawaii and in the same hospital. I wondered if something was wrong or maybe one of my children had committed some crime! But in this case I was wrong.

This was a family matter and it was all about my beautiful daughter Nina. He proceeded to squirm a little, not knowing where to start, so

I asked him if all was okay with him and he finally came out with the question. Would I object if he could ask not only me but also my wife for our daughter's hand in marriage. I gave him a big hug and said that I would be honored to see them share their life together. As always my watery eyes tell it all. I was happy for my daughter to have such a nice gentleman for her future husband. As I arrived home from work I repeated the whole story to Dorothy. She asked if I was so blind that I didn't recognize that this was happening. At dinnertime, we had some laughs and wondered what the future would bring.

So here comes more wedding expenses, but we had some time to save some more money to pay for the wedding. As time went on my sweet Nina announced that the plans for the wedding were to have a Mass and wedding at St. Anne's in San Francisco, and the reception was to be at the Marina Yacht Club in San Francisco by the Golden Gate Bridge. I said, "Well, honey, this will cost us a fortune!" "Oh no, Daddy, it's not as much as you think. At the most it will only be for all the trimmings, reception and live band, and oh, maybe thirty thousand." "Thirty thousand pesos or zlotys? (that's Polish currency). No, no that's dollars! Oh my God!" With that I said, "Take the money and go to Reno, Nevada and for ten bucks get the same things, plus put the rest as a down payment on a house." Well, she said that I offered the same thing to Debbie, and she declined, and now she also wanted a church wedding.

So here I go again. (I was proud that she was getting what she wanted.) I had to explain to my friend Mike Pawlowski that a private meeting with a San Francisco Police Officer was all about permission to marry my daughter. We had some good laughs and reminisced about our own proposals of marriage. A few months later, we had a big wedding with both families and all the friends. The wedding went well, and two bands performed quite well. My pockets were empty, but it was all worth it to see these young kids starting their lives together in such big style and happiness.

Meantime our son, Floyd, was accepted by Chico State University to study Engineering, where he was quite successful getting good grades and was progressing to all our expectations. During summer break he would work in a parking garage making and saving all his money to have some to spend during the semester. We were very proud of his achievement and his maturing while he was away from home during his college days.

All was wonderful in the family and happiness was the word. One day my dear wife, as happy as we were, said that there was some pain in her leg and she didn't know what was happening. "How long ago did this start,"

I asked. "Oh not too long, but I didn't want to worry you, but now it is getting worse." The doctor said that circulation to her leg was not sufficient, and that was the reason for her pain. After exhaustive manipulation, the gangrene set in her right foot, and to my regret, we had to amputate her foot and leg below the knee.

What a sorrow to my heart and my life. Here we thought we had conquered all these problems, and now this. I got her home in a wheelchair and carried her up the stairs. Oh my God, be kind to me and my family. The whole recovery and getting used to being without her leg was unbearable. We will overcome this illness with the grace of God and we will survive, we will be strong and we will endure. The kids and I will see to it that all will be okay and we will function again as a whole family.

She had to wait for all the healing process and for the swelling to come down before she could be fitted for a prosthetic leg. Well, we walked out of the office with the help of a cane. It was a great feeling for her to be able to walk again to our car and ride home. It was a different story to climb a set of stairs. But slowly, with help, we made it home and what a joy it was getting up those stairs.

About this same time, my widowed sister Stefania, was diagnosed with breast cancer. Since I lived just a few blocks from her and worked close by as well, I took it upon myself to help in her care, taking her to the UC San Francisco hospital for visits, radiation and all the things she required. It was pretty hard to devote my time between my work, taking care of my wife, my sister, paying attention to our married daughters and make sure that my son wasn't side stepped or forgotten in all this process.

By helping my sister with her illness, I felt that I was paying my dues because she was instrumental for my being here in the US. What would have happened to my parents and me if it was not for my sister? And besides we are a family and it was my obligation to help. Some of my friends looked at me sort of weird. They even asked me why her two grown sons couldn't help their mother. They, too, were struggling, and having just gotten married and struggling to make ends meet. Besides, they knew that Uncle Frank will take care of everything. Hasn't he always managed to do it all? Let me ask . . . . you're probably wondering where were Dorothy's parents all this time, during their daughter's illness, operations, rehabilitation, and need for support and comfort? Well, here in America people do not always have time and everyone is so busy doing what they think is important. For them, living quite a long distance away in Reno, Nevada and then Palm Springs, California, it was pretty hard to help us or their daughter in all her sorrows. After all, she had me, her three children and mother-in-law which should be enough.

We got used to being alone and being self sufficient, and it didn't matter any longer. Since I was brought up in Poland, our family lifestyle was very different. We would do anything and everything to support our family. As the saying goes, we would give our shirt to the needy or someone in our family. This I found out is not so here in the US.

Finally the time came for our son Floyd to graduate from Chico State College in Mechanical Engineering. (Funny that he was studying the same things as I, but I never got the privilege to graduate because World War II ended and school disbanded back in Cairo, Egypt.) We all had to load up and off to Chico to witness the first Jasinski to get a degree from a university. Is anyone surprised this event was such a big miracle?

I did not write to my relatives in Poland because I did not want to boast that our son was graduating from a major university with a degree in Engineering and that we are very proud.

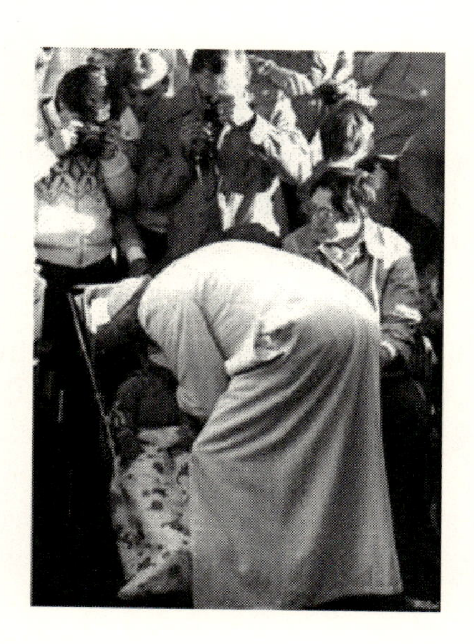

Our visit with Pope John Paul II in Alberta, Canada in 1984

Living in our home with a flight of stairs was becoming unbearable, so we decided to find a house with no stairs. This created a big problem because most homes in San Francisco are on small lots of ground with the home built above the garage. So it is guaranteed that the living quarters would be above the garage. Thus, you have thirteen to fourteen stairs to get up to your living quarters. Well, we were fortunate to find a house on one level, and guess what? We purchased this house and sold ours and made some profit, as we did on all of our sales.

Joy of joys, we moved to our new home. But as happy as one can get our fate was short lived as we discovered that Dorothy had a relapse, and her other leg was in identical catastrophic condition as the other. So we had to amputate her other leg due to gangrene and she was fitted with another prosthesis. She progressed quite well and was able to be independent.

Our son, Floyd and his fiancé Toni, had announced that they wanted to marry, and we gave them our blessings. With all new expenses, it was a relief that the bride had to suffer all the consequences of the wedding, reception and all other expenses. The wedding was at the Catholic Cathedral in Auburn, California on a hill and was an appropriate place to have this wonderful event, and the reception place had plenty of space for a sit down meal and celebration. We and our married children were there along with all our friends and everyone enjoyed themselves. The newlywed couple settled down in Roseville, California. Well, this time we had some experience in this matter plus my Dorothy was in pretty good health now.

Toni, our new daughter-in-law is a school teacher in Roseville and Floyd got a good job with the Roseville Telephone Company. They were a lucky couple, for they were able to purchase their home after renting one for a short time. Dorothy and I couldn't be happier the way our children settled down, and after a short time they were able to purchase their own homes with a little help from us.

It was back to life as we knew it. We were wondering what is next because it never seems to end. It was one thing after another and where will it all end? I was still employed by my friend, Nelson at Marathon Company, which was after I had retired from the automotive business. But I kept busy most of the time and was still involved in the Polish community in San Francisco, being its President of the Board of Directors and other functions. That alone took a lot of my time. After the wedding, the children were scattered here and there, which took about one to two hours driving to visit them. So we decided that our stay in San Francisco would end in the near future. We started to explore all our options on what place would be a logical place to settle.

Years ago we had purchased a mountain estate at Donner Lake (that's where the Donner party almost perished). Since I am on the subject of Donner Lake, let me explain how we came to find such a beautiful place.

Well, we always like to go for rides and explore new places. But Donner Lake is a hidden gem and is hidden away from the Interstate 80 freeway where people are flying by at over 70 mph, so people ignore or don't notice it. Well, we fell in love with it and after finding a realtor, found a brand new cabin that had just been completed. This nice salesman suggested that if we really liked the place we should make an offer, which we did for $110,000. After some negotiations, we settled on $124,000. What a wonderful experience it is to have a brand new place for us and our children and grandchildren. Only in America do nice things like this happen to those who work hard, save their money and lead a good clean and happy life.

Since we would go through Roseville on our way to Donner Lake, we thought Roseville would be a nice place to retire. After a year or so we came upon a new development with the help of our son, called Springfield at Whitney Oaks, and we fell in love with the lot on the crest of the hill above this lovely golf course. After reviewing many options and places, we decided that Rocklin had our attention. We told our salesman that we were interested. He said that this lot has had a lot of people's attention, so if we were interested, we should put a deposit with subject to obtaining financing and so on. Going through the model homes, we liked this particular home plan and he quoted a price on the entire purchase.

The purchase of the lot plus a view and building the new home, plus this and that, it all came to well over three hundred thousand dollars. Nothing ever is cheap anymore. The whole lifestyle dictated that we could afford the move, so we decided to go ahead with our decision. I didn't realize that it takes a lot of time for all the permits and other works to build a house from start to finish. We were excited to move to the brand new home as were all of our children. The time came to put our home in San Francisco up for sale and it didn't take too much time to consummate the sale.

What happens when you sell your residence? Dorothy and I are well aware that boxes are needed and a lot of them to pack all our possessions. Thank God that I was working where boxes were available to access so I would bring them home daily. I don't remember how many times we moved from one house to another, and this move was the ultimate one, for we had lived in it for about eighteen years. Can you imagine what accumulates in one's home during that time? Well our home in Rocklin was finally finished and it was time to move. My friend Nelson, who I worked for, offered his delivery truck and a couple of his workers to help in moving our belongings to our new home. How lucky was I, that this Polish immigrant who came to America with nothing in his pocket and with no command of the English language, along with bringing his parents and all, and now he and his own family are moving to a brand new community where he built his brand new big home with a spectacular view and paid cash for it? Yes, I was proud of myself and what I accomplished here since coming to this blessed United States of America. Where else could I accomplish this in our big world?

It took us three trips to complete the move, and oh what a job, and then to unpack and to arrange all our furniture. Keep in mind that this new home was a third larger than the one in San Francisco so all of our possessions were lost in it. But that problem was easily solved by Dorothy who filled it in no time at all. Well our new possessions were on this lovely street and all the homes were arranged with brand new trees and new lawns and adorned with a variety of shrubs and flowers. Oh how lucky we are to find this jewel of a place and all these new, wonderful neighbors.

In addition, we were pleased to see our beautiful Club House with all their lovely furnishings plus all these additional rooms to host different activities and events for future occasions. Not to outdo ourselves, how about two swimming pools, Jacuzzi hot tub, that's heated to 103 degrees. What a heavenly place to go when you're unpacking your belongings in this hot climate. Is heaven this nice? Why would you not want to go there?

Our 50th Wedding Anniversary celebration on July 26, 2003

Frank's extended family portrait taken in front of his Rocklin, CA home, May, 2009

Back row, from left to right: Danny, Stephen & Brian (Kelly grandsons), Randy Fry (nephew), Michael, daughter-in-law Toni, Anne, son Floyd Jasinski, Elizabeth Carey, Kathleen & husband Jared Martin.

Front row, left to right: Mike Kelly & daughter Nina, Eddie & his wife Rita Fry, Frank & Dorothy Jasinski, daughter Debbie, Joanna, Jeanine & husband Tom Carey.

When I came here from my native Poland, I don't think there were only a handful of people that lived in such comfort. Our children and grandchildren were and still are very proud that their parents are very well established in their new environment. Life is good and comfortable, playing golf when time permits and playing pool on the brand new pool table is a lot of fun. We joined the Springtones Singing Choir, so we practice singing everywhere in our free hours, and give concerts not only for our community but also at old people's convalescent homes. What fun to live in this wonderful community. We still go to our mountain home, but not as much as before, for we are too preoccupied with all the activities here in our community.

I came to believe that God wanted to reward me with much of his love and possibly, possibly reward my whole family with his love. A few weeks ago, I received a letter from the Polish Consulate in Los Angeles, requesting my presence at the USC Campus in Los Angeles for a presentation which was given to me by Polish President Lech Kaczynski dated April 23, 2007. My God what an honor to be bestowed on this son of the peasant family. With humble acknowledgment, I am forever grateful as well as my family, colleagues and friends for this honor.

I was very proud to be one of the delegates to welcome the President of Poland, Lech Walesa to the San Francisco Airport. Mr. L. Walesa was invited by the Polish World War Two Veterans to be our main speaker at the celebration of the Polish Constitution as well as the Speaker of the Year at the Commonwealth of San Francisco.

RZECZPOSPOLITA POLSKA

LEGITYMACJA

Nr 47-2007-5

Warszawa

dnia 23 kwietnia 2007 r.

POSTANOWIENIEM

z dnia 23 kwietnia 2007 r.

Pan Franciszek Jan

JASIŃSKI

odznaczony został

KRZYŻEM OFICERSKIM
ORDERU ODRODZENIA POLSKI

PREZYDENT
RZECZYPOSPOLITEJ POLSKIEJ

Lech Kaczyński

GRAND CROSS OF THE ORDER OF POLONIA RESTITUTA FOR FRANK JASINSKI

One of Poland's highest and most prestigious awards, the Grand Cross of the Order of Polonia Restituta (the Order of Poland Reborn) has been conferred upon our fellow club member, Frank Jasinski. Frank was summoned to the Polish Consulate in Los Angeles. In a reverent ceremony there, the Consulate General presented him with the medal and a written certificate signed by the President of Poland, Lech Kaczynski.

This honor is given in recognition for outstanding achievements in the fields of education, science, sport, culture, art, economics, defense of the country, social work, civil service or for furthering good relations between countries. Among civilian awards the order is second only to the rarely awarded Order of the White Eagle.

Frank was chose as deserving because of his life-long commitment to the Polish nation and his dedication in multiple areas to the advancement of Polish culture and understanding. He has been a central figure in the Bay Area as well as the Sacramento Clubs by serving in various officer positions and giving of his talents to the many projects in upgrading the club structures. He is known for his long-standing participation in the Polish American Veterans of WWII and the Polish American Congress. Recognition is also made due to him joining the Polish Army at the age of 15 and serving as a soldier under the command of General Anders upon release from exile in Siberia. Frank is presently writing a gripping memoir about his life and World War II experiences.

Typical of Frank and his humility, he did not let us know of his honor. Fortunately for us, we found out about it and were able to give him the deserved acknowledgement at our May Family Dinner. Some notable recipients of this award include: Wladyslaw Anders (1892-1970), Polish General and member of the Polish government-in-exile in London. Andrzej Butkiewicz (1955-2008), Polish political activist and co-founder of the Student Solidarity Committee.

Wladyslaw Szspilman, Polish pianist and composer. Wilm Hosenfeld, German Army Officer who saved Poles from death, including Szspilman. Janusz Korczak (1878-1942), Polish children's author, pediatrician and Martyr in the Holocaust. Douglas MacArthur, American military commander. Jadwiga Pilsudska, Polish aviatrix, daughter of Jozef Pilsudski.

THE UNITED STATES OF AMERICA

ORIGINAL
TO BE GIVEN TO
THE PERSON NATURALIZED

No. 7546804

Petition No 124213

Personal description of holder as of date of naturalization: Date of birth May 19, 1928 sex male; complexion medium color of eyes brown color of hair brown height 5 feet 10 inches; weight 155 pounds; visible distinctive marks cut, left index finger
Marital status married former nationality Polish
I certify that the description above given is true, and that the photograph affixed hereto is a likeness of me.

(Complete and true signature of holder)

UNITED STATES OF AMERICA
NORTHERN DIST. OF CALIFORNIA } ss:

Be it known, that at a term of the District Court of The United States held pursuant to law at San Francisco on May 22nd, 1956 the Court having found that FRANCIS JAN JASINSKI then residing at 1215 25th Ave., San Francisco, California intends to reside permanently in the United States (when so required by the Naturalization Laws of the United States), had in all other respects complied with the applicable provisions of such naturalization laws, and was entitled to be admitted to citizenship, thereupon ordered that such person be and (s)he was admitted as a citizen of the United States of America.

In testimony whereof the seal of the court is hereunto affixed this 22nd day of May in the year of our Lord nineteen hundred and fifty-six and of our Independence the one hundred and eightieth

Seal

C. W. CALBREATH,
Clerk of the U. S. District Court.
Deputy Clerk.

It is a violation of the U.S. Code (and punishable as such) to copy, print, photograph or otherwise illegally use this certificate.

DEPARTMENT OF JUSTICE

Congratulations Frank! We are very proud of you. "Sto Lat" in health and prosperity!